English in Use

ENGLISH in use

G M SPANKIE

NELSON

Thomas Nelson and Sons Ltd
Nelson House   Mayfield Road
Walton-on-Thames
Surrey KT12 5PL   UK

51 York Place
Edinburgh EH1 3JD   UK

Thomas Nelson (Hong Kong) Ltd
Toppan Building 10/F
22A Westlands Road
Quarry Bay   Hong Kong

Distributed in Australia by

Thomas Nelson Australia
480 La Trobe Street
Melbourne   Victoria 3000

and in Sydney, Brisbane
  Adelaide and Perth

First published by Thomas
  Nelson & Sons Ltd in this
  edition 1975
Reprinted 1976, 1978, 1979
  (twice)
First printed in this revised
  edition 1982
Reprinted 1983, 1984 (twice),
  1985 (twice), 1986 (twice)
ISBN 0-17-555362-9
NCN 73-ELP-8955-06

Printed in Hong Kong

Foreword

This new edition of *English in Use* has been prepared with clarity and ease of reference in mind. None of the original material has been omitted from this edition although some of it has been slightly revised. The expanded index included in this edition will also be useful for reference to specific points. Solutions to the exercises, previously supplied separately, appear within the covers of the new edition to provide a means of instant checking.

The revision of *English in Use* has not altered the intention of the work in any way. It is designed for students of English as a foreign language at any post-elementary stage up to post-intermediate level i.e. somewhat beyond Cambridge First Certificate.

The items have not been set out in order, as a course, but have been arranged and indexed in a way that allows teachers to select particular items as and when they need them, either for initial teaching or further practice, and in accordance with the requirements of their own teaching and learning situations. *English in Use* can be helpfully and usefully co-ordinated with textbooks, class readers and other learning materials, as occasion demands or permits. The book can also be used profitably by anyone studying on his own.

Cordially, I thank all those colleagues past and present, in many lands, who have tested all the material in *English in Use* and whose recommendations have contributed greatly to my own experience, gained over a good many years of teaching English as a foreign language in Britain and abroad.

G. M. *Spankie*
October 1981

Indefinite article:
a, an

- Nouns are either countable (one horse, six horses, three girls, two boys) or uncountable (sugar, coal, butter, petrol). Countable nouns take *a*, or before vowels, *an*, to show that the noun is singular and that we do not refer to any particular specimen. *A boy* is any undefined boy.

- When we form the plural of countable nouns we drop *a* and *an*. *A boy* in the singular becomes *boys* in the plural. Uncountable nouns do not generally take the plural form.

exercise 1

Look at the following sentences. Make a list of the countable nouns and another list of the uncountable nouns. Write down the plural form of the countable nouns.

1 A potato is a vegetable.
2 A dog dislikes a cat.
3 A horse often has a long tail.
4 A boy likes to play a game.
5 A diamond is a beautiful stone.
6 A girl likes chocolate.
7 We put sugar in a cup of coffee.
8 A slice of bread and a piece of cheese make a sandwich.
9 We make an omelette with an egg.
10 A book is made of paper.
11 Paper is made from wood.
12 We write a letter on a sheet of paper.
13 A cowboy lives in America.
14 We get milk from a cow.
15 A cow lives on a farm and eats grass.
16 A soldier salutes an officer.
17 You can draw a straight line with a ruler.
18 People drink tea from a cup.
19 A dog is a good friend to man.
20 An Englishman often has bacon and an egg for breakfast.

● When we refer to a person's occupation or profession we always use *a* or *an*:

He is a student.
His father is a doctor.
My brother is a captain in the army.
Van Gogh was a great artist.

● NOTE: *One* is a specific, definite singular number:

One swallow doesn't make a summer.
We have two daughters and one son.
Please put only one lump of sugar in my coffee.

exercise 2

Put in *a* or *an* before singular countable nouns.

1 ... sick child needs ... doctor.
2 Mr Brown is ... bus driver.
3 His son is ... pupil at ... school near here.
4 He wants to be ... engineer when he is ... man.
5 ... author is ... person who writes books.
6 My father is ... author.
7 Her brother is ... teacher in ... college.
8 Peter is studying to be ... architect.
9 ... little boy sometimes plays at being ... fireman.
10 George is ... mechanic in ... garage.
11 Mr Black works as ... printer on ... newspaper.
12 On ... bus we have ... driver and ... conductor.
13 His brother is ... musician in ... orchestra.
14 ... man who runs ... shop is ... shopkeeper.
15 ... little boy often wants to be ... policeman.
16 Mr Chop is ... butcher in ... shop in town.
17 ... jockey is ... man who rides ... racehorse.
18 ... girl sometimes goes to work as ... shop assistant.
19 Miss Brown is ... secretary in ... large firm.
20 ... tailor can make ... suit or ... pair of trousers.

exercise 3

Turn the plural countable nouns into singular countable nouns. Remember to put in *a* or *an* and change the verb from plural to singular when necessary.

1 I have apples and oranges in my bag.
2 Policemen are sometimes very tall fellows.
3 Mothers look after little children.
4 Houses often have pretty gardens.
5 Schoolboys like holidays.
6 We write with pens and pencils.
7 Rivers run into the sea.
8 We need pens and ink to write letters.
9 Tables are articles of furniture.
10 Children are sons or daughters.
11 Weeks are periods of seven days.
12 Cats catch mice.
13 Dogs chase cats.
14 Apples grow on trees.
15 Men in white coats are doctors.
16 We can go to America on ships or aeroplanes.
17 Boys and girls go to the same school.
18 Horses and donkeys both work hard.
19 Onions and potatoes make a good salad.
20 Cherry trees and plum trees are beautiful in spring.

Definite article:
the

- *Countable nouns* in the singular form take *a* or *an* before them to show they are

    (a) singular, and
    (b) undefined.

- Plural countable nouns drop the *a* or *an*, also to show that they are undefined.

- When nouns, either countable or uncountable, singular or plural, are defined as particular specimens or groups of their kind, we put *the* before them. Students must be careful not to put *the* before uncountable and abstract nouns particularly, except when they are clearly defined in the sentence. Consider:

    Health is wealth.
    Silence is golden.
    Time is money.

  but

    The health of the nation is good.
    The silence in the forest is very restful.
    The time we spend on our exercise isn't wasted.

- We often begin a conversation by talking of an undefined thing or person:

    There is an old man in our garden.

  We then continue, talking of *the* old man, who is now defined as the same old man as the one we spoke about in out first sentence:

    Look! The old man is coming to the front door.

- NOTE: Works of art and historical regions often take *the*:

    the Acropolis
    the Eiffel Tower
    the Louvre
    the Mona Lisa
    the Fifth Symphony
    the Houses of Parliament

exercise 4

Put *the* in the blanks, only where necessary.

1   . . . horses have four legs and . . . long tails.
2   Write your name at . . . top of . . . paper.
3   . . . sugar is sweet and . . . coffee is bitter.
4   . . . health is more important than . . . gold.
5   . . . little girl in blue is Mary.
6   Bakers use . . . flour for making . . . bread.
7   . . . second letter of the alphabet is B.
8   . . . apples grow on . . . apple trees and . . . pears grow on
    . . . pear trees.
9   I remember . . . day we went to . . . seaside.
10 . . . water was cold but . . . sand was warm.
11 . . . sun was in . . . sky nearly all . . . time.
12 People make omelettes with . . . eggs.
13 . . . wealth is not always . . . happiness.
14 . . . man on the left of . . . picture is Mr Green.
15 I shall always remember . . . kindness of those people.
16 . . . money makes . . . money, people say.
17 Where do horses sleep at . . . night?
18 . . . horses sleep in stables at night.
19 . . . hunger is the best sauce.
20 . . . food and . . . drink are necessary to life.

- All geographical names for natural waters and canals take *the*. Only the names of lakes do not take *the* before them:

    the Red Sea, the Pacific Ocean, the English Channel, the Suez Canal, the Dardanelles.
  but
    Lake Como, Lake Superior, Lake Windermere.

- Chains of hills and mountains take *the* before them. Individual hills and mountains usually do not take the defining adjective:

    the Andes, the Vosges, the Himalayas.
  but
    Mt. Everest, Mt. Blanc, Mt. Kilimanjaro.
  There are a few exceptions to this:

    the Jungfrau, the Matterhorn, the Mount of Olives.
  are the most common.

- Single islands do not take *the* but groups do.

    Trinidad, the Hebrides.

- The geographical names of countries do not take the defining adjective, nor do the names of towns and continents. Exceptions are:

    the Hague, the Netherlands, the Congo, the Sudan, the Crimea, the Ukraine.

- The political titles of countries always take the definite article. Thus we have:

    France (geographical), *the Republic of France* (political),
    America (geographical),
    the United States of America (political),
    Russia (geographical), *the U.S.S.R.* (political),
    Great Britain (geographical),
    the United Kingdom (political).

exercise 5

Put in *the* only where it is necessary.

1 ... English Channel lies between ... France and ...
England.
2 ... Suez Canal joins ... Mediterranean Sea and ... Red
Sea.
3 ... Danube is the longest river in ... Europe.
4 ... Mt. Blanc is in ... Swiss Alps.
5 ... London is on ... Thames.
6 ...Hague is ... capital of ... Holland.
7 ... Netherlands is another name for ... Holland.
8 Ships can go from ... Atlantic to ... Pacific through ...
Panama Canal.
9 ... Canada and ... Alaska are in ... North America.
10 Which is the capital of ... United States, ... Washington or
... New York?
11 ... Andes are high mountains in ... South America.
12 ... Elbe is one of ... Germany's most important rivers.
13 The highest mountain in the world is ... Mt. Everest in ...
Himalayas.
14 ... India and ... Pakistan are both in Asia.
15 ... Cyprus is a large island in ... Mediterranean.
16 We love boating on ... Lake Geneva in ... Switzerland.
17 ... Scotland is the northern part of ... Great Britain.
18 The languages of ... France, ... Italy and ... Spain are like
one another.
19 Tea comes from ... India, ... Pakistan, ... Ceylon and ...
China.
20 ... Barbados is one of ... Windward islands.

● Cinemas, hotels, theatres, restaurants, clubs, taverns and public places all take the defining *the* except when their titles are proper personal names in the possessive case:

> *the Alhambra Cinema*
> *the Royal Theatre*
> *the Blue Danube Restaurant*
> *the Astoria Hotel*
> *the Conservative Club*

but

> *Smith's Hotel*
> *White's Club*
> *Luigi's*
> *Romano's*
> *His Majesty's Theatre*

● The names of ships always take *the* before them as do the names of special trains and aeroplanes:

> *the Queen Elizabeth*
> *the Flying Scotsman*
> *the Dutchman*
> *the Blue Train*
> *the Acropolis Express*

● Directions (north, south, northeast, etc.,) take *the* when they are used as nouns.

● NOTE:

> *the sun, the moon, the earth, the sky, the stars, the winds, the south wind, the northeast wind.*

● Groups of stars and planets usually take *the*:

> *the Great Bear*
> *the Milky Way*
> *the Southern Cross*

but

> *Orion's Belt*

● Named stars and planets do not usually take *the*:

> *Betelguese*
> *Mars*
> *Venus*
> *Jupiter*

● Very few streets take *the* before them although roads often do when their names show where the road goes to or comes from:

> *Oxford Street* is in London.
> *The Oxford road* leads from London to Oxford.

● We do not usually put *the* before our ordinary meals:

> *breakfast*
> *lunch*
> *tea*
> *dinner*

The dinner is an organised event of an association or committee for a particular purpose:

> *We all went to the dinner organised by the Ladies' Club Committee.*

● Note that when we write the date (22 January, 10 May, etc.) we say:

> *the twenty-second of January*
> *the tenth of May*

● There are a few instances when the omission of *the* makes a difference to the meaning of the sentence:

> *Jack goes to school* (as a pupil).   but   *His father goes to the school* (to see the headmaster or for some other purpose).
> *My brother is in church* (at a service).   but   *My brother is in the Church* (a priest or a minister, he is a clergyman).
> *We have a friend in hospital* (as a patient).   but   *We have a friend in the hospital* (doctor, nurse, secretary).

exercise 6

Put in *the* only where it is necessary.

1 On 19th March I left . . . King George Hotel to cross . . . Atlantic on . . . Queen Mary.
2 Peter is having . . . lunch at . . . Red Rose, with John, to-day.
3 To-day . . . sun is very hot but . . . northeast wind cools the air.
4 . . . Sea Lion flew across the water with . . . southwest wind behind her.
5 I shall meet you at . . . Rialto Cinema in . . . Prince Road.
6 We are having . . . dinner at . . . Claridge's before going to . . . Adelphi theatre.
7 . . . moon and . . . stars are shining brightly tonight.
8 Shall we go to . . . Embassy Cinema or to . . . Green's Theatre?
9 My husband usually has . . . lunch at . . . Blue Pig.
10 . . . sky is red and . . . sun is just setting.
11 Peter is staying at . . . Smith's Hotel in . . . Greentree Avenue.
12 . . . S.S. Ocean Princess leaves . . . New York on 14th June.
13 . . . Sky Rocket flies from . . . London to . . . Rome in three hours.
14 The ten o'clock train for . . . north is . . . Flying Scotsman.
15 North of . . . equator we can see . . . Great Bear.
16 South of . . . equator we see . . . Southern Cross. (*north* and *south* are not nouns in these sentences).
17 We saw a good film at . . . Capitol and went back to our rooms at . . . Astoria.
18 John's Hotel is opposite . . . Royal Theatre in . . . Red Lion Street.
19 Shall we have coffee at . . . Brown Cow or beer at . . . Kellerman's?
20 . . . moon goes round . . .earth and it goes round . . . sun.

Summing up

● The indefinite article, *a* or *an*, is used before singular countable nouns when no particular person or thing is indicated.

● Plural countable nouns and uncountable nouns do not take *a* or *an*.

● The definite article, *the*, is used for singular and plural, countable and uncountable when nouns are defined.

● The following three groups of nouns may help you

   (a) to remember that many nouns have several forms
   (b) to understand their meanings.

singular countable nouns (undefined)	singular and plural countable nouns (defined)	abstract and uncountable nouns (undefined)
a man	the man, the men	man *mankind*
a youth	the youth, the youths	youth *it goes away*
an age	the age, the ages	age *and age comes*
a lemon	the lemon, the lemons	lemon *in your soup*
a fortune	the fortune, the fortunes	fortune *luck*
a work (of art)	the work, the works *factory*	work *labour, toil*
an onion	the onion, the onions	onion *not a whole one! a taste of onion, perhaps.*

● NOTE:

The Queen Mary is a ship.   Queen Mary is a queen.
He went to prison for stealing.
  He went to the prison to visit someone.
We live at home with our parents.
Mr Brown lives at the home for Old Soldiers.

Demonstratives:
this, these, that, those

- *This* and *that* are singular, *these* and *those* are plural.
  This and *these* refer to things which are near to the speaker,
  perhaps even in his hand, while *that* and *those* refer to
  things at some distance from the speaker.
  When we ask *what's this?* or *what's that?* the answer is
  usually *it's a . . .* When we ask *what are these?* or *what are
  those?* the answer is usually *they're . . .*

- *This* and *these* refer generally to things which are here, near
  the speaker or present in time. *This* and *these* refer to
  things, persons and times here and now.

- *That* and *those* refer to things, persons and times there and
  then.

one, ones

- An adjective cannot stand alone in English in place of a
  countable noun. It must be followed by a noun or a
  pronoun, either singular or plural. Generally *one* (singular)
  or *ones* (plural) stand for countable nouns. Consider:
  > *Give me two large potatoes, or three small ones, please.*
  > *The small carrots are a penny each, and the large ones are
  > twopence each.*
  > *Mary bought a green hat and Joan bought a blue one.*

- Adjectives, of course, are often used predicatively:
  > *The sky is blue.*
  > *This milk smells sour.*

exercise 7

Put in *this, these, that, those,* as appropriate.

1 What's . . . ?
2 Who are . . . boys?
3 What's . . . over there?
4 What are . . . things called?
5 Whose is . . . ?
6 What's . . . on your desk?
7 Who is . . . sitting at the back?
8 Who is . . . in the picture?
9 Whose book is . . . ?
10 What's . . . for?
11 Are . . . new books? Yes, they are.
12 Is . . . a red book? No, it's pink.
13 Are . . . good sweets? Yes, they are.
14 Is . . . chair taken? No, it's free.
15 What's . . . book about?
16 What's the name of . . . film you want to see?
17 Can you tell me what . . . are?
18 Is . . . your classroom? Yes, it is.
19 Have you read . . . article?
20 Is . . . your new car?

DEMONSTRATIVES:
THIS, THESE, THAT, THOSE

exercise 8

Put in *this, these, that,* and *those* as you think best.

1 . . . is my home town and . . . building over there is my old school.
2 In . . . modern times everybody goes to school.
3 . . . is Peter's first visit to England.
4 . . . little girls on the other side of the street live near our house.
5 . . . books you see in my hand are for . . . students at the back of the room.
6 The weather isn't very warm . . . summer but it was . . . year we went to Spain.
7 Please give me six of . . . small oranges and six of . . . in the other box.
8 We have our English lesson in . . . room and mathematics in . . . one.
9 . . . chair isn't very comfortable so I'm sitting on . . . one.
10 His mother makes . . . nice cakes we had at . . . party.
11 Do you remember . . . people we met at . . . café in Rome?
12 Yes; . . . was the evening we bought . . . souvenirs on the sideboard.
13 Good evening . . . is my brother John and . . . is his motorbike outside the gate.
14 May I pick some of . . . flowers in . . . part of the garden, please?
15 Please, conductor, does . . . bus go to the Palace or must I take one of . . . green ones?
16 Not one of . . . new buildings was here ten years ago. In . . . days, there were farms here.
17 Hand me . . . two boxes on the top shelf please and . . . one on the next shelf.
18 . . . is my desk and . . . is yours.
19 At . . . time last year . . . trees in the next garden were full of birds' nests.
20 Take . . . papers to the headmaster and fetch . . . other ones back again.

exercise 9

In place of the nouns in *italic* put in either *one* or *ones*.

1   Look at the elephant! Isn't it a big *elephant!*
2   These are excellent apples. May I have a small *apple*, please?
3   Of course, help yourself to a large *apple*. There are some riper *apples* in the kitchen.
4   Are these cherries sweet *cherries?* Yes, madam, try a ripe *cherry* and buy some.
5   Thank you, give me a pound of the red *cherries*, please. I like those *cherries* best.
6   Two red pens, three blue *pens* and a black *pen*, please.
7   John doesn't wear his new slippers. He says his old *slippers* are more confortable than the new *slippers*.
8   Have you a large house in the country? No, just a small *house*, we don't like very big *houses*.
9   Large *houses* need servants and good *servants* are hard to find.
10 Give me a large loaf, please. I'm sorry, madam, I have no large *loaves*, will two small *loaves* do?
11 Thank you, I'll take one small *loaf* and come back tomorrow for a large *loaf*.
12 This train is a very long *train*, isn't it? It's the longest *train* I've ever been on.
13 I like fast *trains*, don't you? A slow *train* is so boring.
14 Have a sweet! Thank you, may I take a pink *sweet?* I don't like the red *sweets* very much.
15 Good! Take all the pink *sweets* and I'll keep the red *sweets*.
16 John likes mathematics except when the problems are hard *problems*. He prefers an easy *problem*.
17 These large oranges are cheap but the little *oranges* are sweeter. I'll have six small *oranges*.
18 Although the fish he caught were rather small *fish*, the *fish* that got away was a very large *fish*.
19 Peter had twenty marbles; ten green *marbles*, nine blue *marbles* and one red *marble*.
20 The church in the square is a very old *church*. Another old *church* stands on the hill.

some, any

- *Some* and *any* are both used with either countable or uncountable nouns to indicate an *indefinite* number or an *indefinite* quantity.

    There are some books on the table (a number of books; three, four, seven, eight?)
    There is some butter in the dish (a little butter, a small piece, a lot).

- *Some*, and the compound forms *something, somebody, someone, somewhere* are used in affirmative contexts. *Any*, and the compounds *anything, anybody, anyone, anywhere* are used in negative and interrogative contexts.

- NOTE: *Sometimes* does not follow this pattern, but takes: *never, hardly ever, rarely, scarcely ever*, etc., as its opposites in a negative sense.

exercise 10

Put in *some* or *any* to complete the meaning of the following sentences. (Note that *never, hardly ever, rarely, hardly* are negative in sense).

1   I haven't . . . lemonade but I can give you . . . cold milk.
2   There are . . . good apple trees in the garden but we haven't . . . cherry trees.
3   Grandma can't find her glasses . . . where. They must be . . . where in the house.
4   Is there . . . body in the house? Yes, there's always . . . body at home.
5   That man never does . . . work. He's always trying to get . . . thing for nothing.
6   Have you . . . money on you? No, but I have . . . at home.
7   Do . . . of these boys speak English? Yes, . . . of them speak it quite well.

exercise 10 (contd.)

8 There aren't . . . dangerous wild animals in England. There are . . . tigers in the zoo.

9 Peter will lend you . . . books to read. Mary hasn't . . . new ones.

10 Father received . . . good news yesterday but he won't tell . . . body what it was.

11 The boys ate . . . sandwiches but didn't drink . . . milk at all.

12 One can still see . . . horses in London streets although there aren't . . . trams now.

13 Do you take . . . milk in your tea? Yes, but I drink it without . . . sugar.

14 Do you need . . . help? No, thank you, I haven't found . . . difficulty with this exercise.

15 We did . . . exercises yesterday without making . . . mistakes.

16 When I was a boy there weren't . . . houses here, except for . . . old cottages, of course.

17 Please, give me . . . thing to eat. I haven't had . . . thing since early morning.

18 I'm not going . . . where this evening because I have . . . work to do.

19 Do you put . . . thing in the bank each month? Yes, I try to save . . . thing for a rainy day.

20 John often brings . . . friends home to tea, but to-day we haven't . . . guests.

21 Does . . . body want a cup of coffee? Yes, we should all like . . . .

22 Have you seen my newspaper . . . where? No, perhaps . . . one has borrowed it.

23 There is . . . body on the phone for you. That's funny, I'm not expecting . . . body to ring up.

24 Our firm does . . . business with Germany. We haven't . . . trade with Ireland.

25 I can hardly see . . . thing without my glasses. I must get . . . new ones soon.

- With countable nouns, singular and plural, and uncountable nouns, *some* and *any* are often heard in a rather different sense.

- *Any* often indicates that we do not specify colour, size, description, quality, identity, or limitation. Consider:
  - (a) *Come for dinner any evening next week.*
  - (b) *His mother gives him anything he wants.*
  - (c) *I will do anything I can to help.*

In these sentences *any* = *no matter what*.

  - (a) *Come to dinner* on any evening in the week, your choice of evening is unrestricted.
  - (b) *His mother gives him no matter what he asks for.*
  - (c) *I will do whatever I can* (no matter what it is) *to help.*

- *Some* is often vague, and intentionally indefinite especially when the speaker does not wish to be precise, concerning a date, a name, and so on. Consider:
  - (a) *Come and see me some day next week.*
  - (b) *She works in some little shop in town.*
  - (c) *I shall be old some day.*

In these three examples *some* refers to some vague, very indefinite time or place. In (a) there is a rather lukewarm invitation, at best indefinite, while in (b) the shop is of such little interest that the speaker emphasises its anonymity by using *some*, and in (c) *some day* is still far enough off to be very vague and indefinite. *Some* refers to singular and plural countable nouns as well as uncountables, in this sense.

- *Some* is often used in interrogative sentences when the speaker feels that the answer is almost certainly affirmative:

    Shall I give you some tea? – Yes, please.

Compare the following pairs of sentences:

  ·   *May I give you some more wine?* (you've had one glass.)
      Do you want any more wine? (you've had enough.)

- *Any* is generally better in an open question i.e. when the answer may be either yes or no.

exercise 11, exercise 12

Put in *some* and *any*, taking care to notice where *some* may be used in questions.

1 We never have . . . bacon for breakfast.
2 Would you like . . . fresh tea, madam?
3 We hardly ever go . . . where at weekends.
4 Promise that you won't tell our secret to . . . body.
5 Have you read . . . good books lately?
6 No, I scarcely ever read . . . thing but the newspapers.
7 Shall we visit . . . of our friends this evening?
8 Let's do that, we rarely see . . . of them these days.
9 I should like . . . milk if you have . . . to spare, please.
10 Do you still hear from John . . . times?

Put in *some* or *any* and notice where either may be used with a possible change in tone and meaning.

1 Good-bye, I'll see you . . . day soon.
2 Of course, . . . day next week will suit me.
3 Is there . . . news from Peter yet?
4 We hope to have . . . information tomorrow.
5 He saw . . . body at the Ministry.
6 Can you give me . . . information, please.
7 Yes, madam, I'm here to help . . . body who asks.
8 Are you going . . . where on Sunday, John?
9 Come in and have a game of cards . . . evening.
10 I'm afraid I haven't . . . time this week.
11 They live in . . . little village in the country.
12 Was it you who told me . . . thing about Mr Tucker?
13 No, I don't know . . . body of that name.
14 That silly fellow says . . . thing that comes into his head.
15 I hope to live in the country again, . . . day.
16 . . . one knows the difference between a clock and a watch.
17 Who was at the door? Just . . . poor old beggar.
18 Do you want . . . thing to eat? Yes, . . . thing you have.
19 Peter works for . . . small firm in town.
20 Can't he find . . . thing better to do?

nobody, no-one, nowhere, none, nothing

- These words are all emphatically negative in sense and are used as the negative subjects of verbs and as negative objects of verbs and prepositions.

    Nobody and *no-one* stand for *not anybody*.
    Nowhere is *not anywhere*.
    None is *not any* and refers to a negative quantity or number, that is to say, it is both countable and uncountable in sense and usage.
    Nothing = not anything.

- *Nothing* is often the very short answer to a question regarding a person's activities or doings:

    What did you say? – Nothing.
    What are you doing? – Nothing – or I'm not doing anything.

- *Nobody* answers *Who . . . ?*

- *Nowhere* answers *Where . . . ?*

- *None* is the brief answer to *How much?* and *How many?*

- *Nothing* answers *What . . . ?*

- NOTE: When . . . ? is answered by *Never*.

- *None* is nearly always used in place of *nobody* as a partitive in the negative sense of countable nouns and is usually followed by *of*.

    (a) *None of the boys come(s) to school on a bicycle.*
    (b) *None of them was (were) ready to begin the lesson.*

Notice that the singular verb is grammatically correct but since the speaker is thinking in the plural

    (a) *a group of boys* and
    (b) *of them*

the plural verb seems natural and is tolerable in ordinary conversation and everyday writing.

exercise 13

Answer the following questions emphatically

(a) with one negative word (e.g. *Nobody*) and
(b) with a complete phrase (e.g. *I saw nobody* or *I didn't*
      ***see anybody*.)**

1   Whom did you meet in the park?
2   Where are you going next Saturday?
3   How many eggs did you have for breakfast?
4   What's in that box?
5   What are you reading at present?
6   Who gave you permission to come in here?
7   Where can I find a good, cheap house?
8   How many exercises have you written today?
9   What will you give me for this old car?
10 How much money have you spent this morning?
11 Where can I get a good cup of tea outside England?
12 Who told you John was here?
13 How many of you are over sixty years of age?
14 Who was that on the telephone?
15 Where are you going for the Christmas holidays?
16 How much milk shall I put in your tea?
17 What do you expect to happen?
18 Where did you put my pipe?
19 How many times a week do you shave?
20 How much salt have you put in the soup?

exercise 14

Put in the most suitable negative words to complete these sentences.

1 . . . knows you better than your mother.
2 . . . is more beautiful to me than my old home town.
3 . . . of them knows what really happened that day.
4 . . . cures a headache faster than aspirin.
5 Go away! I want . . . to do with you.
6 . . . wants to work unnecessarily.
7 We've lost our dog. He's . . . to be found.
8 Peter has two pencils but John has . . .
9 . . . of us can remember what happened, exactly.
10 There is . . . in this house who knows where my money is.
11 Say . . . and speak to . . . about this, at present.
12 . . . of these children has ever seen the sea.
13 There is . . . like a good cup of tea to cheer one up.
14 This kind of apple grows . . . else in the world.
15 Will . . . help this poor old lady to cross the street?
16 Is there . . . in the class who has done his homework?
17 We can't ask you to stay the night as we have . . . to put you up.
18 . . . pleases him more than a quiet day in the country.
19 John has three brothers but Mary has . . .
20 . . . understands this artist's pictures very well.
21 We have . . . to play football now as the farmer sold the field.
22 . . . of these shops does very much business.
23 Well, I'm sure they don't stay open for . . .
24 I'm sure . . . found this exercise difficult.
25 There's . . . to it.

● Notice that when the negative word is used as a subject its verb does not take the negative form.

much, many

See also countable/uncountable nouns, p2.

- *Much* and *many* are respectively singular and plural in sense. *Much* refers to quantity and *many* to number.

- In current English *much* is used in negative and interrogative sentences, but we avoid it in affirmative sentences. Instead, we use expressions such as:

    a lot of, a great deal of, a large amount of, plenty of.

- NOTE: *a lot of,* is good in conversation and informal writing but is not yet generally accepted in all contexts. *Too much* and *very much* are good in affirmative phrases. *Many* is used in affirmative, negative and interrogative constructions, although we often hear such expressions as *a large number, a fair number,* which provide a little variety.

exercise 15

Put in *much, many, a great deal of*, etc.

1 Our government spends . . . money on schools.
2 Do you know . . . about mathematics?
3 We don't have very . . . friends in this town.
4 I don't carry . . . money in my pockets.
5 My brother eats . . . fruit. I don't eat . . .
6 Do you remember how . . . coal I ordered?
7 Yes, it was really too . . . this time.
8 . . . people dislike mustard.
9 Give me one potato and . . . meat, please.
10 The girl in the shop gave me too . . . change.

little, few

- *Little* and *few* are used to qualify uncountable and countable nouns respectively:

  > *a little sugar*
  > *a little milk*
  > *a few potatoes*
  > *a few people*
  > *a little butter* is a small quantity of butter
  > *a few apples* make up a small number of apples.

- Extreme smallness, almost non-existence, of the quantity or number is emphasized by dropping *a*;

  > *Few families have triplets.*
  > *We have little money for luxuries.*

- *Little* and *a little* often go with adjectives and adverbs:

  > *It is a little warmer to-day.*
  > *Although he's seventy he looks little more than fifty.*

no, not

- *Not* is used to construct the negative form of a verb while *no* is used to show a negative quantity or number in a noun:

  > *We do not (don't) go to the zoo very often.* (negative verb)
  > *There's no sugar in my tea.* (negative noun).
  > *We have seen no good films this year.* (negative plural noun).

- Remember to use the correct auxiliary verbs when making negative verbs:

  > *We do not (don't) like football.*
  > *John doesn't read newspapers.*

- *No* + noun is often emphatically negative.

exercise 16

Put in *a little* or *little* or *a few* or *few* to make sense, in the
following sentences. Note where the sense changes
according to the words you choose.

1 Give me . . . meat and . . . potatoes, please.
2 I like . . . cream and . . . lumps of sugar in my coffee.
3 The poor woman has . . . money and . . . pleasures.
4 There is . . . too much salt in the soup and too . . . carrots.
5 . . . bread and . . . sardines make a good lunch.
6 We buy very . . . books because we have . . . time for
reading.
7 . . . people have . . . more money than they really need.
8 Would you like . . . more cake or . . . biscuits?
9 . . . people can keep healthy on . . . food and sleep.
10 . . . patience and . . . words of advice help more than
medicine, sometimes.
11 . . . men can act in an emergency when there is . . . time for
thinking.
12 . . . of you share my opinions so we have . . . in common to
discuss.
13 She has everything she needs, . . . money, . . . worries and
good health.
14 His grandmother does . . . visiting and meets . . . of her old
friends.
15 I'm going to order . . . bacon and . . . chips, for lunch.
16 . . . homes don't have a radio set although the family may
make . . . use of it.
17 You must learn . . . English every day, then you will make
. . . mistakes.
18 There has been . . . rain and there are . . . puddles in the
street.
19 Will you give me . . . money to buy . . . sweets?
20 . . . boys do all their homework. They only do . . . .

exercise 17

Use *no* and *not* in the following sentences to make the
nouns and verbs in *italic* type negative. Remember to use
the correct auxiliary verbs with *not*.

1   There are *wolves* in England.
2   We have *mice* in the house.
3   She *cooks* very well.
4   I had *dinner* yesterday.
5   Waiter! There is *salt* in my soup.
6   We have *money* in the bank.
7   She *goes* to the cinema often.
8   There are *apples* on these trees.
9   I can see there is *cheese* in this sandwich.
10 My friend speaks *English*.
11 I have *time* to speak to you now.
12 We *buy* sugar every day.
13 George *understands* everything I say in English.
14 That horse has *food*.
15 We eat *meat* on Fridays.
16 She eats *bread* between meals.
17 My knife *cuts* very well.
18 I *write* to all my friends.
19 The boys have *chocolate* in their pockets.
20 I *eat* cake very often.

no, not any

- We have already seen in the previous exercise that *no* is used to show that a noun is negative in number or quantity or that an uncountable noun is negative in degree.

- *Not any* combines both verb and noun negatively.
    We haven't any coffee in the house.

- NOTE: *Not any* combines both verb and noun in the negative and therefore sentences such as
    I don't have no friends

  make very bad English. We do not use them.

neither, nor

- *Neither* and *nor* are used to show that each of two nouns, pronouns, adjectives, prepositions, adverbs or verbs is negative. Thus:
    Wednesday is neither the first nor the last day of the week.
    Mr Brown neither smokes nor drinks.

- *Neither* precedes the first word in the pair and *nor* precedes the second. When the subject or object of a verb is negative the verb remains affirmative in form:
    Neither Mr Brown nor his wife is very tall.

  Notice, too, that the verb is singular since *Mr Brown* and *his wife* are really subjects of separate verbs, in the singular number. However, in common speech we frequently hear the plural verb when two singular subjects appear to share the same verb:
    Neither Peter nor John are at home this evening.

  Probably the speaker is thinking that
    both Peter and John are out this evening,

  and therefore confuses the plural with the singular. When the subjects are plural the verbs are also plural:
    Neither parents nor friends were there to help him.

exercise 18

By using *not any* make both verb and noun negative in
the following sentences.

1   I have no money today.
2   She had no time for play.
3   They do no homework at all.
4   There is no sugar in my tea.
5   We buy no potatoes.
6   There is no space behind our house.
7   She tells no lies.
8   I'm going nowhere.
9   We eat no meat on Fridays.
10 My brother speaks no English.
11 Peter brings no sandwiches with him.
12 Mary takes no sugar in her coffee.
13 There are no buses to Redhill Street.
14 I need no help, thank you.
15 There are no trains after midnight.
16 Mr Brown reads no periodicals.
17 I can find my glasses nowhere.
18 They talk to nobody during lessons.
19 I eat nothing between meals.
20 There are no more of these exercises.

exercise 19, exercise 20

Put in *neither* and *nor* to complete these sentences.

1 Grey is . . . black . . . white.
2 My father eats . . . beef . . . pork.
3 We . . . smoked . . . spoke all day.
4 Mary plays the violin . . . well . . . badly.
5 I like my boiled eggs . . . hard . . . soft.
6 The tramp . . . works . . . wants.
7 . . . he . . . she can speak Spanish.
8 John's spelling is . . . good . . . bad.
9 . . . Mary . . . Peter come to this school.
10 I . . . see . . . hear from Harry any more.

Join the two negative sentences in each pair by using
***neither* and *nor* to replace the *not* and *no* negative forms.**

EXAMPLE:

> *Today isn't <u>Monday</u>. It isn't <u>Friday</u>.*
> *= Today is <u>neither</u> Monday <u>nor</u> Friday.*

The words which are to become negative are in *italic* to
help you. Remember the verb becomes affirmative in
form in the new sentence.

1 We don't speak *Spanish*.   We don't speak *French*.
2 They *can't read*.   They *can't write*.
3 The film wasn't *exciting*.   It wasn't *interesting*.
4 He doesn't speak *quietly*.   He doesn't speak *clearly*.
5 That boy doesn't speak *kindly*.   He doesn't speak *politely*.
6 Our dog isn't *fierce*.   It isn't *disobedient*.
7 I don't *dance*.   I don't *sing*.
8 John doesn't work *hard*.   He doesn't work *very fast*.
9 He didn't come *early*.   He didn't come *late*.
10 She doesn't feel *unhappy*.   She doesn't feel *lonely*.

either, or

- *Either* and *or* are used where there is a choice of two possibilities. These two words are the affirmative forms of *neither* and *nor*. Consider the following sentences:

    A baby is either a little boy or a little girl. (A baby must be one or the other, it cannot be both).
    I shall see you either on Monday or Tuesday. (One or the other of these two days, not on both).

- *Either* and *or* may go with nouns, pronouns, verbs, adjectives, and adverbs in exactly the same way as *neither* and *nor* do.

- *Either* and *neither* are often used as pronoun subjects and objects of verbs and prepositions:

    Will you have tea or coffee? – It doesn't matter which, thank you. Either will be very nice.

Note that *or* and *nor* cannot be used as pronoun subjects or objects.

exercise 21

Put in *either* and *or* to complete the sense of these sentences.

1 The answer is ... right ... wrong.
2 I shall finish my work ... on Friday ... on Saturday.
3 Please, ... stop talking ... leave the classroom.
4 ... John ... Peter will help you with your work.
5 Nobody is ... completely bad ... perfectly good.
6 We write ... with a pen ... with a pencil.
7 I must ... spend less money ... earn more.
8 We are going ... to the theatre ... to the cinema.
9 A political party is ... in government ... in opposition.
10 I don't know very much about ... chemistry ... physics.

exercise 22

Put in *either* and *neither* to complete these sentences.
Remember that *either* and *neither* may be the subjects of
verbs or the objects of verbs and prepositions. Note that
neither = not either:

> Mr Brown doesn't eat either fish or eggs
> = Mr Brown eats neither fish nor eggs.

1 Will you have tea or coffee? . . . thank you.
2 Is Lisbon in Spain or France? In . . . , it's in Portugal.
3 Shall we have beef or lamb for lunch? . . . , I like both.
4 Did you have chocolate ice-cream or vanilla? . . . , we had
  strawberry.
5 Tom and Jane are coming . . . of them has arrived yet.
6 Must I pay cash or will you take a cheque? . . . will do very
  well, sir.
7 Which is the capital of the USA, New York or Chicago? . . . ,
  Washington is.
8 Both of the boys speak good English, but . . . speaks any
  Spanish.
9 I have heard both sides of the story and I don't believe . . . .
10 . . . of them is telling the truth.
11 Does . . . of you know Peter Smith?
12 No potatoes, nor beans, thank you. I never eat . . . of them.
13 I can't remember whether you are Mr Brown or
  Mr Black. . . . , I'm Mr Green.
14 . . . of these horses jumps well, they're both lazy.
15 I can see you . . . on Thursday or Friday. I'm sorry . . . day
  suits me.
16 Both Mary and Joan are clever girls. . . . could win the
  competition.
17 Will you buy the house or rent it? . . . , I don't like it.
18 Most people drink milk or coffee. Peter doesn't like . . .
19 Lemonade and tea are both refreshing. . . . is welcome on a
  hot day.
20 We didn't buy . . . butter or cheese as we needed . . . .

so do I,
neither do I

- These auxiliary verb constructions show that the speaker wishes to add to a statement that he has just made or which another person has just made.

- Constructions beginning with *so* show agreement with the preceding remark or participation in the action it describes. *So* constructions are used when making additions to affirmative statements. Consider:

  English people speak English. So do Americans.
  Peter has two sons. So has his brother.
  John must write his exercise again and so must you.

- *Neither* and *nor* show participation in a previous negative statement or that the subject also does not take part in the activity under discussion. Consider:

  We haven't seen Peter for a week. Neither has Mary.
  I can't speak Spanish nor can my wife.

  In the examples above notice that the two subjects (*We* and *Mary*, *I* and *my wife*) in each example share the same negative verb.

- NOTE: In *so* and *neither/nor* constructions the appropriate auxiliary verb comes first, before the subject (*so am I*). *Neither* and *nor* have no difference of meaning and they are interchangeable although *nor* seems preferable as a conjunction.

Fill in the blank spaces with a *so* . . . or *neither* . . . *nor* . . .
phrase. Remember the inversion!

1 You are all students and . . . am I.
2 Peter isn't very tall. . . . is John.
3 I'm sorry I can't come tomorrow. . . . my brother.
4 John doesn't know the way. . . . you.
5 Our cat never goes out at night. . . . ours.
6 Her father speaks good English. . . . mine.
7 I haven't been to the cinema for ages. . . . I.
8 You didn't know your lesson yesterday. Well, . . . you.
9 Uncle Peter gave me fifty pence. . . . aunt Mary.
10 George's brother collects stamps and . . . I.
11 Our summer holidays begin tomorrow. How wonderful,
   . . . ours.
12 John has a bicycle. . . . his sister Jane.
13 His bicycle has a large lamp on the front. . . . hers.
14 You will never finish in time if you don't hurry. . . . he.
15 You ought to write more clearly. . . . John.
16 Boys oughtn't to play truant. . . . girls, naturally.
17 You shouldn't copy the answers from Peter and . . . John.
18 The sun doesn't go round the earth, . . . it go round the
   moon.
19 I never drink coffee at night. . . . my wife.
20 British money seems difficult to me. . . . the weights and
   measures.

● NOTE: *So* = for that reason. Consider:
   I was tired so I sat down.
   The cat was hungry so I gave it some fish.

In this sense there is *no inversion* of subject and verb.

Negative
with inversion

Never	*hardly ever*	*seldom*
not only	*scarcely*	*rarely*, etc.

● These words and expressions are usually placed in front of the principal verb. Greater emphasis is obtained when the negative word or expression precedes the appropriate auxiliary verb which is followed by the subject and the required part of the principal verb. Consider:

    (a) *I shall never see my home again.*   (usual pattern).

    (b) *Never shall I see my home again!*
       (negative with inversion).

    (c) *We rarely go to the cinema nowadays.*
       (normal pattern).

    (d) *Rarely do we go to the cinema nowadays.*
       (negative with inversion).

The sentences at (b) and (d) have a much stronger negative sense. At the same time these sentences are too polished, dramatic and emphatic to be heard frequently in everyday conversation. They do occur frequently in written English and in careful, prepared speech when the emphatic effect is required.

exercise 24

Convert these normal negative sentences into emphatic negative sentences by means of inversion.

1 I have never seen such a beautiful picture.
2 The world has rarely contained so many great men all at one time.
3 We hardly ever hear such splendid singing by an amateur choir.
4 The king had scarcely left the room when the bomb exploded.
5 The people seldom saw these important men of affairs.

Question tags

- Many English sentences, especially in conversation, consist of an affirmative statement followed by an interrogative-negative construction. Consider:

    (a) *It is cold today, isn't it?*
    (b) *Yesterday was the tenth of the month, wasn't it?*

  Usually the question tag (at the end) is spoken on a falling tone since the speaker is not asking a question, but simply expects agreement with the statement in the affirmative part of the sentence. He expects the answer:

    (a) *Yes, it is* and
    (b) *Yes, it was* or *Certainly* or *Yes, I think so.*

- Negative statements are followed by simple interrogative forms of the auxiliary verb

    (a) *You aren't angry are you?*
    (b) *Mary doesn't dance well, does she?*

  Again the first speaker expects an answer which will agree with his negative statement:

    (a) *No, of course not* or *Certainly not* or *No, not really*
    (b) *No, she doesn't* or *No, I'm afraid she doesn't.*

  These negative statements to which speakers expect an answer in agreement are not really questions and so usually a falling tone is heard in the 'tag' part.

- Occasionally when the speaker is not very sure of the information in the affirmative or negative statement the intonation is as for an ordinary question.

exercise 25

Add appropriate question tags. Give good short form
answers to the sentences.

EXAMPLE:

> *It's too cold today, isn't it?*
> *Yes, it is, or I'm afraid so.*

1 Jack likes ice-cream, . . . ?   Yes . . .
2 We are learning fast, . . . ?
3 Jane comes by bus, . . . ?
4 You don't like cheese, . . . ?
5 We never eat meat, . . . ?
6 Paris is the capital of France, . . . ?
7 Mary makes all her own dresses, . . . ?
8 These boys haven't been here very long, . . . ?
9 We must try hard to succeed, . . . ?
10 You can speak Spanish well, . . . ?
11 Mary never goes to the cinema, . . . ?
12 She doesn't see very well, . . . ?
13 We haven't very much money, . . . ?
14 Poor Peter isn't very clever, . . .
15 John is a good footballer, . . . ?
16 I can borrow your pencil, . . . ?
17 People must pay taxes to the government, . . . ?
18 We all play tennis in summer, . . . ?
19 That little boy looks like Jack, . . . ?
20 Your brother is getting quite stout, . . . ?

exercise 26

Add a question tag and an answer to these statements.
Note that *never, hardly ever, rarely, almost never,* are
negative expressions so the tag is positive in form.

1 We never write a letter in red ink, . . . ? No . . .
2 The class is working hard today, . . . ?
3 Peter Brown hasn't arrived yet, . . . ?
4 That cat has been sleeping there for hours, . . . ?
5 Mary doesn't like milk chocolate, . . . ?
6 You haven't seen my new bicycle yet, . . . ?
7 We must do our best to pass the examination, . . . ?
8 You can't get a hundred and fifty pence for a pound
note, . . . ?
9 Children ought to be helpful to their elders, . . . ?
10 Mr Brown has never been to Rome before, . . . ?
11 Our dog never chases cats, . . . ?
12 You are beginning to find these exercises quite easy, . . . ?
13 Mary hardly ever cooks roast beef now, . . . ?
14 Americans and English people speak the same
language, . . . ?
15 You have been studying here for some time, . . . ?
16 Our friends almost never fall out, . . . ?
17 We haven't received our pocket money yet, . . . ?
18 That old house has been standing for hundreds of
years, . . . ?
19 You aren't sitting in a draught, . . . ?
20 Everyone ought to brush his teeth regularly, . . . ?

QUESTION
TAGS

exercise 27

Add a question tag and a reply to each of these
statements. Notice that *will you* is often used as a tag
when the statement is imperative (see No.12) and that it
goes with both affirmative and negative. Note, too, that
when *have* appears as a principal verb, the question tag is
also formed with *have*.

> *She has a new baby, hasn't she?*
> *They had lots of money, hadn't they?*

1 You won't forget our appointment, . . . ?
2 I shall if I don't make a note of it, . . . ?
3 Mary couldn't come a little earlier tomorrow, . . . ?
4 She didn't say so, . . . ?
5 We shan't be seeing you next week, . . . ?
6 No, you have arranged to go to the seaside, . . . ?
7 Peter has some good news for you, . . . ?
8 Yes, but you knew all about it, . . . ?
9 Naturally, but you don't mind, . . . ?
10 Of course not, but you won't tell the others yet, . . . ?
11 You can trust me to keep it dark, . . . ?
12 John, come here a moment, . . . ?   (imperative)
13 You must hurry to catch your train, . . . ?
14 Yes, or I shall be late, . . . ?
15 The boys will be in time for school, . . . ?
16 I think so. It won't take them long to dress, . . . ?
17 The children could help with the gardening, . . . ?
18 Don't play near the river bank, . . . ?   (imperative)
19 Peter hadn't met Mary before yesterday, . . . ?
20 Tom, give me a hand with this heavy box, . . . ?
(imperative)

exercise 28

Add suitable question tags to complete these sentences.

1 You wouldn't do a thing like that, . . . ?
2 Peter isn't coming today, . . . ?
3 You weren't thinking of asking him, . . . ?
4 I shall see him tomorrow, . . . ?
5 He won't have arrived before I go to school, . . . ?
6 Little girls must go to school, . . . ?
7 The postman hadn't been that day, . . . ?
8 I should have remembered that, . . . ?
9 We had been working like horses for a week, . . . ?
10 We were feeling tired, . . . ?
11 You will have finished by tomorrow, . . . ?
12 You hadn't been there before, . . . ?
13 You would like to go again, though, . . . ?
14 We should have gone to a better hotel, . . . ?
15 They were living in London at that time, . . . ?
16 No, I think they were travelling abroad then, . . . ?
17 We are talking about the same people, . . . ?
18 These trees look beautiful, . . . ?
19 Yes, but they'll have been cut down next autumn, . . . ?
20 They have been making the house very dark inside, . . . ?

Pronouns

Personal pronouns

● When a pronoun is clearly the subject of its verb we use the subjective, i.e., nominative forms:

  I, You, He, She, It, We, They.

● When the personal pronoun is the object of a verb or of a preposition we use the objective form. There are no separate case forms of the pronoun for the accusative and dative in English. Therefore we find it easy to use the term *objective* for any pronoun which is not the subject of a verb. The *objective* pronouns are:

  me, you, him, her, it, us, them.

Personal pronouns do not take adjectives before them.

exercise 29

Convert the nouns in the following sentences into personal pronouns, subjective and objective.

1   Tom and Mary often write to their uncle.
2   I am meeting Jane and Robert tonight.
3   My wife and I like these biscuits.
4   Peter sent these biscuits to my wife and me.
5   Jane is very fond of Tom.
6   Yes, and Tom is very fond of Jane.
7   My brother and I are going for a walk with our aunt.
8   That silver watch belonged to my grandfather.
9   Grandfather gave it to father on his twenty-first birthday.
10 The students are doing this exercise well.
11 People say that Mr Smith is very well off.
12 Miss Brown plays the piano beautifully.
13 The house belongs to my brother and me.
14 Mrs Jones made a cake for the children.
15 The children enjoyed the cake very much.
16 The two men talked about old friends for hours.
17 Mother always tells the children a story at bedtime.

Notes on personal pronouns

● When the personal pronoun is clearly the subject of its verb we always use the subjective form, particularly when the subject and verb are in the same phrase:

I want to see the manager, please.

● There is a strong tendency in colloquial English to use the objective forms when the pronoun is separated from its verb:

Who's there? – It's me, Peter.

Now this may seem wrong grammatically. However, the correct alternatives in the subjective forms sound so pedantic that very few people use them in ordinary conversation. The pedantic

It is I.

is generally avoided, and although some people insist on it, general usage is against them.

● When the pronoun is used predicatively, i.e. after verbs of state

be, seems to be, look like, appear to be, etc.

the objective is almost universally preferred.

● When the pronoun is a one word reply to a question it is, colloquially, objective:

Who wants an apple? – Me, please.

Such replies are, however, too curt to be used often and the subjective pronoun with the appropriate auxiliary verb makes a more satisfactory reply:

Who wants an apple? – I do, please.

● A common error among English people and others is that of using the subjective case after a preposition:

That is a secret between you and I.

This is quite mistaken. The only correct pronoun form after a preposition is *objective:*

This is a secret between you and me or *between us.*

Transferred indirect object

● Certain verbs nearly always have two objects, one of them direct and personal and the other indirect. Consider:

Father gave a present to Mary.

The direct object is *a present* and *Mary* is the indirect object. This sentence may also be written with the indirect object immediately after the transitive verb:

Father gave Mary a present.

Notice that we drop the preposition in the second form of the sentence.

● Common verbs which often have two objects are:

give, tell, offer, fetch and bring.

exercise 30

Rewrite these sentences putting the indirect object first after the verb. Note that the new sentence often sounds more natural to the English ear. (NOTE: drop *to* and *for*).

1 The doctor has given a pill to Robert.
2 John told the news to Peter.
3 Please fetch the newspaper for your father.
4 The waiter offered chicken and fried potatoes to the guests.
5 Will you please bring back a pot of jam for me?
6 My father wrote a long letter to me when I was on holiday.
7 We shall send a telegram to your parents at once.
8 Some students give a lot of their time to English lessons.
9 I'll fetch a cushion for you to sit on.
10 A baker makes bread for us to eat.
11 If you know, tell the answer to me, please.
12 These large pipes bring its water to the town.
13 John's father gives fifty pence pocket money to each of his children.
14 When you come back from school please bring your report to me.
15 The girls are sending some flowers to their teacher on her birthday.
16 Those ships bring our food to us from all over the world.
17 We must give all our attention to the lesson.
18 Our teacher tells historical stories to the class.
19 My wife is making a new dress for our younger daughter.
20 The gentleman offered a tip to the porter.

● NOTE: *Explain, suggest, describe* and *propose* are always followed by their direct objects,

  Explain the lesson to me.

Reflexive pronouns

● A verb is reflexive when its subject and object are the same person or thing. The reflexive form of the pronoun (myself, yourself, itself, ourselves, themselves) is the correct object.

I shave myself every morning.
Mary cut herself while she was carving the meat.

are clear examples of the use of the reflexive pronoun. Note the singular *-self* and plural *-selves* forms.

exercise 31

Put in the correct reflexive pronoun.

1 John cut . . . while he was shaving this morning.
2 Although Charles is only four years old he can dress . . . .
3 Old Mrs Black slipped on a banana skin but didn't hurt . . . .
4 Children always enjoy . . . at the seaside.
5 The food is on the table. Please help . . . to meat.
6 We came out of the swimming pool and dried . . . carefully.
7 Mary weighs . . . every morning on the scales.
8 Peter knows an old man who taught . . . to read and write.
9 Tomorrow is a holiday so I can please . . . about how I spend the day.
10 Little Charles is very dirty, he must wash . . . at once.
11 Our mother always worries . . . when her children come home late from school.
12 Glynis and Julia are learning judo so that they can defend . . . if necessary.
13 Mother birds look after their young until they are strong enough to feed . . .
14 Have a good journey and look after . . . .
15 Grandfather likes a good walk but he must not tire . . .
16 She is very poor and denies . . . food to give it to her children.
17 It is very cold outside so wrap . . . up well.

Emphatic pronouns

● Note the expressions *by himself, by themselves* and so on.
These examples will make them clear:

> *Peter lives here by himself* – alone, without company.
> *I made this table by myself.* – without help, alone.
> *The lift stopped at the third floor by itself* – automatically,
> without any action on my part.

NOTE: *The king himself will open the new bridge* – the king in
person . . .

exercise 32

Put in the correct emphatic pronoun.

1   I made this dress . . . .
2   The Queen . . . came down to see us.
3   The government . . . is in danger of falling.
4   The general told me so . . . .
5   Have some cake! I made it . . . .

Reciprocal pronouns

- Reflexive pronouns are not used in English when we wish to show that actions pass from one person to another and back again to the first. We use the phrase *each other* when two persons or things co-operate or reciprocate and the expression *one another* when the action is common to all members of a group.

    (a) *David and Jonathan loved each other like brothers.*
    (b) *People who speak the same language understand one another.*

- NOTE: While *each other* and *one another* are used for two and more than two respectively, the distinction is not strictly observed. *Each other* is sometimes used of a small number, three or four perhaps.

exercise 33, exercise 34

Put in the correct reciprocal, reflexive or emphatic pronoun.

1 Strawberries and cream go well with . . . .
2 The boy fell off his bicycle and hurt . . . .
3 You needn't help me, I can do this by . . ., thank you.
4 In a small village all the people know . . . .
5 Students must not talk to . . . during lessons.
6 Merchants have to trust . . . in business affairs.
7 Brothers very often look like . . ., don't they?
8 It is dangerous to leave little children near a fire all by . . . .
9 Pen friends are people who write letters to . . . .
10 Very often they have never seen . . . .

Put in the appropriate reciprocal emphatic or reflexive pronoun.

1 The children in this family all love . . . .
2 My brother and I write to . . . once a week.
3 The two sisters tell . . . all their secrets.
4 Our friends always invite . . . to their birthday parties.
5 Peter and Mary have no secrets because they trust . . . .
6 We needn't serve lunch for the boys. They can help . . . when they come in.
7 George and his wife help . . . with the housework at weekends.
8 The two brothers hardly recognised . . . after such a long time.
9 At Christmas we all buy presents for . . .
10 Children, go and look at . . . in the mirror! You should be ashamed of . . . .

Interrogative pronouns

● *Who* refers to persons of both sexes, singular and plural number. We use it when we ask a question about a person, concerning his personal identity. The answer to the question usually gives a person's name or personal position in a family or organisation. Consider:

> *Who is that tall man?*
> *He is Peter's father.* or *He is Mr White, the headmaster.*

● *What* refers to persons of both sexes and numbers when we ask a question concerning the profession, rank, nationality or social position of a person,

> *What is your father? – He is a doctor.* or *He is a Scotsman.*

● *What* is also used to ask questions such as:

> *What's the time? What do you want? What are you doing?*

● *Which* asks a question concerning people or things. It is used for both male and female and singular and plural.

● *Which* is selective. It asks questions, but the choice of answer is limited by the terms of the question. Consider:

> *Which do you prefer, tea or coffee?*
> *Which of Peter's children is the cleverest?*
> *Which of the students have lunch at school?*
> *Which way does the sun travel?*

To each of these questions there are very few possible answers (indeed, to the last there is only one possible answer). The person who replies to the question knows that he must select his reply from a limited category of persons or things, that he must name one or a few objects from a limited group.

> (a) *What is the most important mineral?*
> (b) *Which is more useful, gold or iron?*

To (a) you may reply with the name of any mineral you think is the most useful. To (b) you must name either gold or iron in your answer.

● *Whom, whose: Whom* is used of persons in questions, as the object of the verb.

> *Whom do you wish to see? Whom shall I marry?*

In conversation, *Who* is very often used instead of the grammatically correct *whom* and it is generally tolerated, except after a preposition. Then *whom* must be used.

● *Whose* is the possessive case question pronoun for persons.

This is a pretty garden.   Whose is it?   Whose child are you?

exercise 35

Give a suitable answer to the following questions. Use short form auxiliary verb constructions whenever possible,

Peter does; John has; our teacher will.

1   Who is the pretty girl in blue?
2   What is Mr Brown?
3   Who is the Prime Minister?
4   Who cooks the meals in your house?
5   What is your name?
6   Who wrote *Romeo and Juliet*?
7   What other plays did he write?
8   What's the date today?
9   Who teaches you English?
10   What are the people of Persia called?
11   Who wears top hats nowadays?
12   Who is that tall man in the corner?
13   What is he?
14   What do you want to be when you leave school?
15   Who helps you with your homework?
16   What did you say?
17   Who knows the answer?
18   What do you know?
19   Who is your doctor?
20   What is the biggest ship in the world?

exercise 36

Give questions to which the following are suitable
answers.

1 That's Peter's uncle.
2 He's an engineer.
3 I want to be a doctor.
4 She's a typist in an office.
5 They are Italian.
6 We generally speak English.
7 It's the seventeenth (of the month today).
8 Yes, one is an engineer, the other is a lawyer.
9 The man on the left is Mr Brown.
10 She's the girl I'm going to marry.
11 I'm studying mathematics.
12 It's a sewing machine.
13 My cousin Mary told me.
14 They're made of wood.
15 Yes, the headmaster gave me permission.

PRONOUNS

exercise 37

Notice that when the interrogative pronoun is the subject
of its verb, that verb remains affirmative. Use *who, which*
or *what* to fill in the blanks in the following sentences.

1 . . . is the heavier, a kilo of gold or a kilo of feathers?
2 . . . are the two longest rivers in Europe?
3 . . . is the highest mountain in the world?
4 . . . of the boys is the eldest son?
5 . . . is the new baby's name?
6 . . . will you take, madam, the blue or the red one?
7 . . . is the price of this house?
8 . . . do you prefer, tea or coffee?
9 . . . lives in that old house?
10 . . . is better, the cinema or the television?
11 . . . are more comfortable, boots or slippers?
12 . . . of these students work hard?
13 . . . looks after your home?
14 . . . of these books do you want?
15 . . . shall I give you, tea or lemonade?
16 . . . girls in this class haven't done their homework?
17 . . . kind of work can you do best?
18 . . . can you buy cheaper, butter or margarine?
19 . . . is the climate like in your country?
20 . . . tells you what to do in class?

exercise 38

Fill in the blanks in the following sentences with either
whose, whom or *who*. Supply short answers,

EXAMPLE:
1 *Peter's.*
2 *The manager.*

1 ... book is this? I found it on the floor.
2 ... do you wish to see?
3 ... did you ask about our holidays?
4 ... book did you find?
5 ... have you told about this?
6 ... dog bit you?
7 ... have you invited to the party?
8 ... birthday is it tomorrow?
9 ... is the grey car standing outside?
10 ... did you meet on the way to school?
11 ... wife is she?
12 ... can we get to look after the garden?
13 ... portrait is that hanging on the wall?
14 ... sister works in our office?
15 ... should I thank for these lovely flowers?
16 ... idea was it to send them?

Interrogative pronouns with prepositions

- *Whom, which* and *what* are grammatically correct forms to use after a preposition.

  > *To whom are you speaking?*
  > *From what is paper made?*
  > *Through which countries does the Rhine flow?*

  In these sentences the construction (preposition followed immediately by the interrogative pronoun) is very formal. In natural, free conversation we prefer the following patterns:

  > *Who(m) are you speaking to?*
  > *What is paper made from?*
  > *Which countries does the Rhine flow through?*
  > *Who(m) are you writing that letter to?*
  > *What will Peter use these old bricks for?*
  > *Who(m) is the letter for?*

  See also the sections on End Prepositions and Adverbs, pp. 108 ff.

- *Whose* is also used with prepositions in exactly the same way.

  > *To whose kindness do I owe this invitation?* is formal.
  > *Whose kindness do I owe this invitation to?* is less formal.

- In conversation, the interrogative *Whom* . . .? often becomes *Who* . . .? This is grammatically incorrect but in ordinary informal conversation it is accepted by most people and preferred by many.

- The *whom* . . .? type of construction is not used in speech except in very formal English when we utter it in the appropriate tone of voice!

- NOTE: When the interrogative pronoun is the subject the verb remains affirmative in form.

  > *What made John angry?*   but   *What did Peter do to make John angry?*
  > *Which dress suits her best?*   and   *Which dress do you like best?*

exercise 39

Insert appropriate interrogatives (*who* or *whom, which, what, whose*) and prepositions or particles. Notice where a change of preposition or interrogative may cause a change in meaning. Give suitable answers to the questions.

1 ... are you looking ...?
2 ... does he work ... now?
3 ... kind of school do you go ...?
4 ... room will our guest sleep ...?
5 ... time shall we meet ...?
6 ... did you ask ..., madam, the pink ones or the yellow?
7 ... is that beautiful cake ...?
8 ... are you phoning ...?
9 ... house are you staying ...?
10 ... day do they want to come ...?
11 ... town did you spend your holidays ...?
12 ... did you go to the cinema ...?
13 ... office does she work ... now?
14 ... does this pencil belong ...?
15 ... can we use old wood ...?
16 ... of us is the letter ...?
17 ... are you reading?
18 ... dinner is that steak ...?
19 ... do you buy your bread ...?
20 ... farm did you spend the weekend ...?

Connectives: *what*, *where*, *when*, *why* and *whose*

- Note that when these words are used as conjunctions the subject and verb are not inverted. Thus:
    - (a) *I asked Peter where he was going.*
    - (b) *The little boy told me why he was crying.*
    - (c) *Mary wants to know when you will be back for lunch.*

None of these sentences is a question, although we can easily see interrogation in them. The sentences are really reports of questions and must not be spoken or written as questions. (See also Reported Speech: Questions p. 348.)

exercise 40

Put in phrases beginning with *what, where, why* or *whose*. Use your imagination to make sensible sentences,
The girl in the shop asked me what I wanted to buy.

1   The girl in the shop asked me what . . .
2   I wanted to speak to Mr Brown but didn't know where . . .
3   Mary can never remember when . . . in the history lesson.
4   Our teacher asked John why . . .
5   I'm afraid I don't know where . . .
6   No, I have no idea why . . .
7   Who knows what . . .
8   Nobody knows when . . .
9   The boys are discussing where . . .
10   Yes, I can tell you why . . .
11   Certainly, anybody will tell you where . . .
12   Of course, everybody knows what . . .
13   Listen carefully while the teacher is explaining why . . .
14   I can't really say when . . .
15   We can't understand why . . .
16   The doctor will soon tell us what . . .

Relative pronouns

Defining relative pronouns

- *Who* – Subject (for persons, singular and plural)
  Whom – Object of verb or preposition (persons, singular and plural)
  Which – Subject and object (for things, singular and plural)
  That – Subject and object (for persons and things, singular and plural)
  Whose – Possessive relative (persons, singular and plural)
    - (a) *Girls <u>who</u> work in restaurants are called waitresses.*
    - (b) *The towel <u>which</u> you gave me wasn't very clean.*
    - (c) *A man <u>that</u> flies an aeroplane is a pilot.*
    - (d) *Papers <u>that</u> contain important information must be locked up.*

- The relative clauses each describe and define the nouns immediately before them (the antecedents of the relative pronouns). The sentences refer to a certain category of girls, a particular towel, a specific sort of man, special papers.

- We do not use commas to separate a defining relative clause from the rest of the sentence, because it is necessary to the sense of the sentence.

- *That* is the most common of all relative pronouns because we use it in place of any of the other defining relatives (except *whose*) without any loss or change of meaning. In the examples above, *that* may replace *who* and *which* without any difference to the sense of the sentence as a result.

- *That* cannot be used as the object of a preceding preposition. In this case, such forms as *by whom, of which, for which*, etc. must be used:
    The man of whom she spoke is her uncle.
    She gave me a pen with which to sign my name.

exercise 41

Supply the correct form of the relative pronoun to
complete these sentences. Do not use *which*.

1 The dog . . . bit me wasn't mad, fortunately.
2 She ordered a meal . . . didn't cost too much.
3 Mary is the girl . . . married Peter's brother.
4 This is the tram . . . goes to Duke Street.
5 Do you know the little kiosk . . . stands at the corner?
6 Is that the one . . . sells newspapers?
7 We want a dog . . . will look after the house.
8 Mr Smith is the man . . . works in the next office.
9 The building . . . is going up in Black Street is to be a
   school.
10 A gentleman . . . works in a government office told me.
11 Boys . . . make a noise in the early morning are a nuisance.
12 Men . . . work is good receive high wages.
13 We used to have a table . . . had five legs.
14 Privates are soldiers . . . have no stripes.
15 John had a dog . . . could walk on its hind legs.
16 Children . . . behaviour is bad may be punished.
17 What do you call women . . . look after sick people?
18 Will you call the waiter . . . usually serves this table,
   please?
19 The doctor . . . usually attends Mrs Brown is away on
   holiday.
20 Captain Scott was the first Englishman . . . went to the
   Pole.

Object relative pronouns

- *Whom* – Object of verbs and prepositions (persons,
  singular and plural).
  Which – Object of verbs and prepositions (thing, singular
  and plural).
  That – Object of verbs only (persons and things, singular
  and plural).

  NOTE: The relative must follow its antecedent
  immediately.

  > *The lady (whom) I expected hasn't come in yet.*

- In the sentences above the defining relative pronoun is not
  the subject of the verb in the relative clause. It is the object
  and is very often omitted from the sentence altogether,
  especially in spoken English:

  > *The lady I expected hasn't come yet.*

- *That* is regularly preferred to *whom* and *which* in object
  clauses, if the defining relative pronoun is retained:

  > *The boy (that) I saw yesterday . . .*

  That cannot be the object of a preposition so *whom* and
  which must be used:

  > (a) *The people with whom I work are all very friendly.*
  > (b) *This is the record about which John spoke.*

  Compare:

  > (a) *The people* $\left\{ \begin{array}{c} that \\ whom \end{array} \right\}$ *I work with . . .* and
  > (b) *This is the record* $\left\{ \begin{array}{c} that \\ which \end{array} \right\}$ *John spoke about.*

  That is strongly preferred after superlatives:

  > *We always buy the best materials (that) we can find.*
  > *Mary is the prettiest girl (that) I have ever seen.*

  It is also preferred after certain words and constructions:
  all, any, few, little, no, none, much, only, and their
  compounds. Examples of this usage are:

  > *I can't lend you the only pen (that) I have.*
  > *We didn't see anything (that) we wanted in the shop.*

  That is used only in defining relative clauses.

exercise 42

Restate these sentences by changing the relative pronoun or by omitting it. Do not use *which*.

1 The man whom I telephoned was out.
2 The letter that I wrote to him hadn't arrived.
3 The roses which you gave Mary were beautiful.
4 A tree that I saw this morning is in bloom already.
5 Food that she likes makes her fat.
6 Our teacher gives us explanations which we can understand.
7 Every penny which Peter spends is marked down in his little book.
8 I met an old friend whom I hadn't seen for years.
9 The eggs that I had for breakfast were too hard-boiled.
10 The salary that John earns doesn't pay for his clothes.
11 Songs that people sing at Christmas are called carols.
12 David wasn't very pleased with the suit which his tailor made.
13 Many people felt angry at the remarks that the speaker made.
14 He gives all the money which he receives to charity.
15 Goods that we send by air arrive fresh at their destination.
16 Most of the people that we teach here like their lessons.
17 Mary always gives me a piece of cake which she makes herself.
18 The news that the radio announced surprised everybody.
19 Some information that my wife received made her very happy.
20 The gentleman whom I wanted to see was not at home.

Defining relative + preposition

● The defining relative preceded by a preposition is very
formal. In easy speech we prefer the idiomatic
constructions shown below.

    (a) *The method by which we make this is a secret* = The
       method (that) we make this by is a secret.

    (b) *The girl to whom I spoke comes from Spain* = The girl
       (that) I spoke to comes from Spain.

Notice that the defining relative generally becomes *that*
and, as it is not the subject of its own clause, may
disappear from the sentence. The preposition is placed (a)
at the end of the relative clause after the intransitive verb,
(b) after the object of the transitive verb.

Non-defining relatives

● *Who*— subject of a verb (persons, singular or plural).
Whom— object of a verb or preposition (persons, singular
and plural).
Whose— possessive (persons, singular and plural).
Which— subject and object of a verb or preposition, (thing
singular and plural).

● The non-defining relative introduces a clause which
provides some additional information about its
antecedent, but does not define it.

● This supplementary or parenthetical information is
between commas to separate it from the main sentence:

    My wife's mother, who lives with us, *is a charming lady.*

● NOTE: The relative must always follow its antecedent as
closely as possible.

● The *non-defining* relative pronoun *cannot* be dropped out of
the sentence. It is a necessary part of the non-defining
relative clause. *That* is rarely used as a non-defining
relative.

exercise 43

Restate these sentences by changing the place of the preposition and by changing the relative to *that* or by omitting the defining relative from the new sentence.

1 People to whom I send letters always reply.
2 The room in which Peter works is very small.
3 Goods for which we have paid have not been delivered.
4 The lady to whom I introduced you is my aunt.
5 Lessons to which you do not pay attention will not help you much.
6 Houses for which people pay high prices aren't always well built.
7 The school to which she went stood on a hill.
8 Factories are large buildings in which we manufacture things.
9 The writers from whose works he quotes are all French.
10 People from whom they obtain information are often criminals themselves.
11 The gentleman through whom he got his situation is an old friend of the family.
12 Firms with whom we do good business receive special attention.
13 Those to whom one gives advice seldom take it.
14 The mistake to which he refers is on the fourth page.
15 Peter dislikes meeting people with whom he has nothing in common.
16 Dr Brown asked the patient to describe the pain from which he suffered.
17 The people for whose benefit he worked never appreciated his efforts.
18 His parents have made great sacrifices for which he should be grateful.
19 Can you tell me something about this man for whom I shall work?
20 Nobody can make us buy things for which we have no use.

exercise 44

Supply the correct non-defining relative pronoun to complete the sentence.

1 John's sister, of . . . we are very fond, plays tennis well.
2 My mother, . . . you never met, was born in India.
3 A gentleman, . . . I had never seen before, smiled at me.
4 Two tables, . . . were beautifully polished, stood in the middle of the floor.
5 Mr Black, . . . opinion I value, told me to look for a new job.
6 The children, . . . are usually good, were naughty last night.
7 My doctor, from . . . I have few secrets, is a close friend of mine.
8 Ships, on . . . Mary always feels sick, seem romantic to her brother.
9 Mrs Brown loves good pictures, of . . . she has a few.
10 Chocolate, for . . . I have a great liking, is going up in price.
11 Miss Brown, in . . . office there are six telephones, refuses to have one at home.
12 An old lady, . . . looks younger than her years, takes care of our house.
13 The following month, . . . began wet and cold, was the hottest for ten years.
14 Jane says that the new book, of . . . I forget the author's name, is quite interesting.
15 Although he has money, with . . . he can buy most things, he is rather unhappy.
16 Mr Brown, of . . . you have heard me speak, grows beautiful roses.
17 Mary, . . . father and mine are brothers, looks like my younger sister.
18 John's parents, for . . . hospitality we are grateful, invited us to stay for a month.
19 A nice old man, . . . reminded me of my father, came up and spoke to me.
20 A young man, . . . spoke very politely, asked Mary to dance with him.

exercise 45

Restate each pair of sentences as one complete sentence
by turning the second one into a non-defining relative
clause.

The relative must follow its antecedent closely.

NOTE: *Mary loves chocolate. She is my younger sister.*
= **Mary, who is my younger sister, loves chocolate.**

1 The cat sat on my lap. It was a black one.
2 On Tuesday he paid his bill. It was 23rd June.
3 Mary is a pretty girl. She studies mathematics.
4 George couldn't see very well. He had forgotten his
   glasses.
5 Chocolate makes her fat. She is very fond of it.
6 The weather is quite warm. We expected it to be cold.
7 John's brother plays cricket. He studied at Oxford.
8 Mrs Smith makes good cake. She lives next door.
9 The Queen is a very great person. I have never seen her.
10 Even Mr Black sometimes makes mistakes. We respect him
   greatly.
11 Tea comes from India. It's a very refreshing drink.
12 The Bible is a very common book. It is published in nearly
   every language.
13 Peter's father helped us. We have known him for ages.
14 Our dog bit the postman. It is usually very quiet.
15 The postman came to the back door. He is new in the
   district.
16 Mary's birthday is tomorrow. I had almost forgotten.
17 In February we shall be very busy. It is the shortest month.
18 Jane speaks three languages. She went to our school.
19 Mrs Green visits us often. You met her yesterday.
20 John's birthday is in May. It was on a Monday last year.

Relative pronouns and prepositions

- **Consider these formal constructions:**

    (a) *The box, <u>in</u> which John kept his private papers, was
    found in the table drawer.*

    (b) *The doctor, <u>in</u> whom we have complete confidence, came
    to the town last year.*

    (c) *Mary, <u>to</u> whom I am taking these books, is John's cousin.*

- In these formal examples all of the verbs in the relative
  clauses are transitive and it is easy to re-cast the sentence
  in a more conversational, lighter form by moving the
  preposition so that it follows the direct object of the relative
  clause. Many people feel that this informal construction is
  more suitable for everyday talk on ordinary matters. The
  sentences are:

    (a) *The box, which John kept his private papers <u>in</u>, was
    found in a table drawer.*

    (b) *The doctor, whom we have complete confidence <u>in</u>, came
    to the town last year.*

    (c) *Mary, whom I am taking these books <u>to</u>, is John's cousin.*

exercise 46

**Restate the non-defining relative constructions so that the
preposition comes at the end of the clause.**

1 Peter, with whom I was at school, works in our office.
2 Members of Parliament, by whom we are governed, are
  ordinary men and women.
3 Your information, for which I am grateful, is very helpful.
4 Mary, of whom I am very fond, is an old school friend.
5 The owner of the restaurant, to whom we complained,
  gave us our money back.
6 Newspapers, in which we read the latest reports, are
  surprisingly cheap.
7 John, to whose party we are invited, lives in Nile Street.
8 Dogs, against which I have nothing, must not enter the
  dining room.
9 The ship's captain, at whose table they dined, was a very
  experienced sailor.
10 Large dogs, of which she used to be afraid, are her
  favourite animals.
11 Jane, to whom I told the news, passed it on to her
  husband.
12 Gentlemen, from whom we expect politeness, ought not to
  lose their tempers.
13 The oldest inhabitant, in whose cottage we spent the
  night, was ninety-eight.
14 Public opinion, to which many people pay no attention, is
  often important.
15 Mr Brown, to whose son I am engaged, knew my father.
16 The cost of living, on which salaries are based, goes up and
  down.
17 Mary's cooking, to which I owe my health, is superb.
18 Goodluck charms, in which we don't believe, cost a lot.
19 Miss Green, from whom you have your music lesson, is
  getting married soon.
20 A triumph, for which he got the credit, gave him the
  captaincy.

Possessive adjectives, possessive pronouns

- The possessive adjectives qualify nouns or, occasionally, the pronouns *one* and *ones* which must appear in the sentence with them. The possessive adjectives are:

  my, your, his, her, its, and *our, your, their*.

  The possessive pronoun takes the place of both the possessive adjective and the noun it qualifies. It stands by itself as subject or object of a verb or after a preposition. The possessive pronouns are:

  mine, yours, his, hers, and *ours, yours, theirs*.

  Notice that *its* is not used as a possessive pronoun.

of + possessive pronoun

- The possessive adjective with a singular countable noun often gives the impression that we possess only one of these things:

  I am going to see my friend. does not sound quite so natural as: *I am going to see my mother*.

  because, while my friend is one of a number of friends, my mother is, naturally, my one and only mother. When we wish to speak of one person or thing which is part of a larger group we prefer the pronoun construction: a friend *of* mine, a cousin *of his*, and, with a plural number some friends *of mine*, three cousins *of ours*, some old letters *of yours*, etc.

- Notice that we do not use this construction when talking of members of the immediate family, except impatiently, critically or perhaps affectionately:

  That brother of mine is always getting into trouble!
  That old mother of mine cooks like an angel.

exercise 47

Put in suitable possessive pronouns and possessive adjectives to complete the sense in these pairs of sentences. Wherever possible use more than one combination

EXAMPLE:

My house, your house, his house, our house, their house, etc.

1 . . . house is round the corner. . . . is in the next street.
2 Mary is wearing . . . new dress. I shall put . . . on tomorrow.
3 . . . classroom is on the first floor . . . is on the second floor.
4 What's . . . name, little boy? . . . name is Peter. What's . . .?
5 . . . brothers have motorcycles. These red ones are . . . .
6 This isn't . . . book. The red one is . . . .
7 May I borrow . . . ruler, please? I can't find . . . .
8 Will you lend her . . . eraser, please? She has lost . . . .
9 We paid . . . fares to the conductor. Our friends paid . . . separately.
10 Mary wants to borrow a needle. She can't find . . . .
11 The Browns often invite us to . . . house. They often come to . . ., too.
12 We like . . . better than . . . because . . . has central heating.
13 I shall need . . . umbrella today. Mother is taking . . . with her, too.
14 Is that . . . dog, Peter? No, it's . . ., it isn't . . . .
15 Give me . . . word to keep it a secret. I'll give you . . . .
16 All right, if you give me . . ., I'll give you . . . .
17 John always eats . . . sandwiches quickly. Mary gives him . . . as well.
18 May I use . . . telephone, please? . . . is out of order.
19 Certainly, . . . house is . . . house. What's . . . is . . . .
20 I don't want to borrow . . . coat. I want to find . . . .

exercise 48

**Change these sentences and use the *of* + possessive
pronoun construction.**

1 I am going to see my friend.
2 Mary's coming here to meet my cousin.
3 May I introduce you to my old school friend?
4 Our teacher always likes to meet his old pupils.
5 Sergeant Brown is my old comrade.
6 Some of our friends are paying us a visit tomorrow.
7 She gave the poor old man one of my old jackets.
8 May I borrow your book please?
9 No, you already have two of my books.
10 They have gone out with their friends.
11 Today I am meeting some of my compatriots.
12 My father often tells us about his shipmates.
13 The girls were talking to some of their relatives.
14 Can't you move your old car out of my way?
    (that old car . . .)
15 Take your old bone-shaker off the road!   (that old . . .)
16 I see my brother is late for school again!
17 John sometimes borrows one of my pencils.
18 Mary is showing me some of her photographs.
19 Ask her to give us some of her wonderful coffee.
    (that wonderful . . .).
20 Your friend is my friend.

Possessive case: the apostrophe

- We form the possessive case of nouns by adding—'s to singular nouns and apostrophe (—') to plural nouns. Notice that we make these additions to the *possessor* and not to the possession itself:

    The brother of John – John's brother.
    The brothers of John – John's brothers.

    The possessor in each example is singular and takes the singular form (—'s) whether he possesses one thing or more than one.

- When the possessors are plural in number we add (—') to them:

    The wives of his brothers = His brothers' wives.
    The house of my parents = My parents' house.

    The possessors are plural so we add (—') regardless of whether the thing they possess is singular or plural.

- NOTE: *the baker's (shop), the Browns' (house).*

- A few nouns do not make their plural in—'s. The most common of them are:

    man/men,
    woman/women,
    child/children,
    gentleman/gentlemen.

    These plural nouns form their possessive case in—'s in the same way that singular nouns do.

exercise 49

Add (—'s) or (—') correctly to the nouns in brackets to
make the possessive case. Note that the sentences cannot
remain as they are.

1 Peter is (John) brother.
2 Mary is his (sister) name.
3 The (Boys) High School closes today.
4 We buy meat at the (butcher) shop.
5 This (woman) children don't go to school.
6 The (men) work makes them tired.
7 Please leave your coats in the (gentlemen) cloakroom.
8 The (children) toys amuse them very much.
9 That (farmer) horses are too old for work now.
10 These (women) husbands are all fine men.
11 There is a new typist in my sister (Helen) office.
12 I always get my books at that big (bookseller).
13 I don't know (Peter) telephone number.
14 I can give you his (parents) address.
15 What are a (policeman) duties?
16 Will you meet me outside the (Students) Club?
17 Can you tell me the way to the (Browns) house, please?
18 We went to London to visit my (father) sister.
19 We stayed at my (aunt) house for ten days.
20 Later we stayed at a Young (Men) Hostel for a time.

● The apostrophe, generally speaking, can only be used when the possessors are persons or animals. Inanimate things cannot really possess or own or have anything. Consider:

   (a) *The boy's bicycle*
   (b) *the horse's tail* and
   (c) *the walls of the house*

The phrase (c) cannot be written in the apostrophe form because the house is inanimate.

● Some expressions of time take the apostrophe form:

   a month's salary, a night's rest, three days' work, half-an-hour's walk.

● There is a tendency, however, to put *a* before plural time expressions and use them as adjectives:

   a three day job, a ten minute walk, a fifty minute lesson.

● Note that such constructions are singular in form and take a singular verb:

   A twenty minute walk every morning helps to keep me fit.
   The three year course in mathematics is a very hard one.

The same construction is used for distance, weight, value, volume or capacity, and other measurements:

   a five mile run
   a thousand kilometre race
   a three ton lorry
   a fifty kilo sack of sugar
   a ten-pound note
   a twenty litre tank
   a two gallon jar and so on.

The construction is now adjectival before the noun and adjectives have no plural form in English – *a five-pound note, a ten-penny piece, a threepenny stamp.* The hyphen is often omitted.

exercise 50

Use (—'s) and (—s') in the following sentences to replace
the *of* forms where appropriate.

1 The father of the boy is very tall.
2 He goes to work with the brother of my wife.
3 They usually travel to work in the car of a friend.
4 The car belongs to the employers of their friend.
5 They generally sit in the back of the car.
6 Their friend sits in the seat of the driver.
7 In the garden of our house we have cherry trees.
8 Peter studies at the College of Engineers.
9 At present he is having a holiday of two months.
10 The sister of John plays the piano beautifully.
11 She plays the music of Chopin very well.
12 I like listening to the sound of a good violin.
13 I agree, but only to the playing of a fine musician.
14 Peter will have his salary of a month tomorrow.
15 It is a walk of three minutes to the bus stop.
16 The teeth of the dog are beginning to fall out.
17 The farm of my grandfather was quite a large one.
18 The handle of the knife is made of silver.
19 The palace of the king is a splendid building.
20 The heads of the governments are meeting in Paris.

POSSESSIVE CASE:
THE APOSTROPHE

- Joint possession is indicated by the apostrophe on the second or last of the possessor's names only:

  Peter and Mary's children.
  David and Jonathan's friendship.

- When a number of individual possessors of separate things are mentioned each takes its own apostrophe:

  Peter's and John's sons (Peter's sons and John's sons).
  Galileo's and Columbus' discoveries (the scientific discoveries of Galileo and the geographical discoveries of Columbus).

- When classical names end in —*s* we do not usually add an —'*s* but simply place the apostrophe behind the —*s* at the end of the name:

  Achilles' heel, Socrates' philosophy, but *Strauss's waltzes.*

- Note that more than two apostrophe forms written together make a puzzling sentence, even for a native of England:

  My wife's mother's friend's house

  is overdone and is better written as:

  My mother-in-law's friend's house.

exercise 51

Restate these sentences by stating the possessive in the —'s or —' form.

1 The friends of mother and father are coming to dinner.
2 The discoveries of Pasteur and Fleming are very important.
3 Mary says that she is a cousin of Peter.
4 May I invite a friend of John to tea?
5 The inventions of Edison and Marconi are still in daily use.
6 Please send my letters to the office of Smith and Black, in London.
7 That is the house of Uncle David and Aunt Margaret.
8 The family of Mr and Mrs Brown all live at home.
9 The paintings of Picasso seem strange to me.
10 The duet of Margaret and Robert received great applause.
11 The weddings of Mary and Margaret both take place today.
12 My invitation comes from a friend of Mr Brown.
13 Mr Brown is an old classmate of my father.
14 There are always some pets of the children in the house.
15 Here are the morning newspapers of the gentlemen.
16 I think that the statues of Epstein are very impressive.
17 The arguments of Socrates are very interesting.
18 The house of his mother-in-law is very comfortable.
19 In the old days the wireless set had a whisker of a cat, they say.
20 The name of that old man is Robert Green.

Introductory *there*

- *There is* and *there are* introduce the subject of the verb *to be* when we have not defined it. Consider:
    - (a) *The boys are in the garden*   (the boys are defined).
    - (b) *There are boys in the garden.* (the boys are not defined).
    - (c) *Boys are in the garden.*   (undefined boys).

  Notice that while (c) is possible grammatically, it is very unusual.

- *There is, are, has been, have been, will be,* etc. forms simply denote the existence of the subject without defining or identifying it. *There* is not stressed when spoken.

- *There is/are* forms often introduce nouns which are followed either by the present participle (*-ing*) or past participle of a principal verb. The following examples show this construction:
    - (a) *A dog was sleeping on the floor.*
    - (b) *There was a dog sleeping on the floor.*
    - (a) *Twenty people were hurt in the accident.*
    - (b) *There were twenty people hurt in the accident.*

- In the examples (a) *was sleeping* and *were hurt* are quite clearly forms of the verb while in sentences of the type at (b) the participles may sometimes have an adjectival sense and at other times keep their meanings as verb forms.

exercise 52

Restate the following sentences using *There* to introduce them with a suitable form of *to be*.

    (a) A newspaper was on the table. – There was a newspaper on the table.

    (b) A fox has been in the chicken-run. – There has been a fox in the chicken-run.

NOTE: The subject follows the verb *to be* when *there* is used. (Note possible changes of the meaning.)

1   A brown horse is in the field.
2   Two policemen are in plain-clothes.
3   A Mr Smith is on the telephone for you.
4   Eleven boys are in a football team.
5   An old man is at the front door.
6   A pretty vase is on the table.
7   Some people are in the restaurant.
8   Nobody is in the house.
9   Nothing is in my pocket.
10   Some dirt is on your hands.
11   A cat is on the window-sill.
12   Some food is on the table.
13   A bottle of milk is on the doorstep.
14   A bus is at the corner of the street.
15   Many people are in London.
16   Two girls are in the car maintenance class.
17   Too many passengers are on this bus.
18   Three nests are in that tree.
19   Some water is in my glass.
20   Six members are in our family.

exercise 53

Convert the following sentences by using *there* and the appropriate part of the verb *to be* to introduce the subject.

1 A man was standing at the corner.
2 Two policemen were watching him.
3 An old lady is looking out of the window.
4 A hundred cats are fighting in our garden.
5 Three of them are hiding in the apple tree.
6 Some children are waiting to see their teacher.
7 Many foreign people are visiting London.
8 A man is knocking at the door.
9 A few people were invited to tea.
10 Fifty thousand people were watching the match.
11 Many people were drenched in the heavy rain.
12 No damage was done to my car in the accident.
13 Many people were employed in that factory.
14 A lot of money was spent on new roads.
15 A cat was washing itself under the table.

Here you are! There you are!

● These expressions are commonly used as short answers to a request for something.

> *Can you lend me a pencil, please? – Yes, here you are!*
> *Where is the manager's office, please? – There you are,*
> *second door on the right.*

Here you are is used when the speaker refers to something which is close to him or in his hand perhaps, and *there you are* when he points out something some distance away. Note also *here it is, there they are* and so on in answer to questions relating to place:

> *Where are my spectacles? – There they are, on your nose!*

exercise 54

Answer these questions using *here/there* short answers.

1 Where's your book?
2 May I have a glass of milk?
3 Two kilos of sugar, please.
4 Have you change for a five-pound note, please?
5 Where's your teacher? ..., over there.
6 Give me a match, please. ..., on that table.
7 Where are the children today? ... out in the garden.
8 Will you lend me a pencil, please? Of course, ...
9 Can you identify the thief? Yes, ..., going downstairs.
10 Where's my newspaper? ..., on the chair.
11 Is John in the picture too? Yes, ... at the back.
12 Show me these shoes in size 40, please ..., please try them on.
13 That will be forty pounds please. Very well, ...
14 John is very late today. Oh, ..., now. Hello, John.
15 Give the child some chocolate, please. Certainly, ...
16 Does the bus to Trafalgar Square stop here? Yes, ..., across the street.

Introductory *it*

- We often use *it* as a pronoun to introduce the subject of the verb *be* when the purpose of the sentence is to define the subject,

    Who wrote Hamlet?   It was Shakespeare, I'm sure.
    Who's in the kitchen?   It's only Mary looking for a snack,
    or It's the children saying goodnight to the cat.

    NOTE: *It* is both singular and plural and refers to people, animals, and inanimate objects.

- *It* sometimes has no meaning of its own and serves simply to introduce impersonal verbs or to stand with a verb in place of the subject, especially when the subject is made up of a phrase or clause:

    That John speaks three languages is true = It is true that John speaks three languages.

    Both forms are heard; the first often introduces an objection:

    That he speaks three languages is true but none of them is the one we need.

- *It* introduces some expressions of
      (a) time
    and
      (b) distance.

    It's a week since I saw Peter.
    It is two miles to the next village.
    It's three years since I had a holiday.

    Notice that whether the time and distance are expressed in plural numbers or singular ones *it is* remains unchanged. *It is* serves for both singular and plural introduction.

- *It* is used to introduce verbs of state such as:

    seem, feel, appear, sound, look, sound like, and so on.

● The personal pronoun after an introductory *it* is usually objective in form. Ideal grammar might demand the subjective form; common speech prefers the objective:

> *Who's there? It's me* or *It's us.*

A few very strict speakers might reply:

> *It is I* or *It is we.*

but in modern colloquial English the subjective form after introductory *it* seems pedantic and even comical sometimes, at least in common speech.

● However, when the introductory phrase precedes a relative clause in which the relative pronoun stands for the personal pronoun in the introductory clause, the two pronouns agree in their case forms:

    (a) *It is they who love us that punish us most.*
        It was she who called the police.
    (b) *It was them that (whom) I wanted to see.*
        It was her that (whom) I wrote to you about.

In the examples in (a) the relative pronouns are correctly expressed in the subjective form and their antecedents sound better in agreement with them in the subjective form. In the examples in (b) the relative pronouns are objective and their antecedents agree with them in their objective forms.

● While the objective form is sometimes tolerated in speech in (a) type sentences, especially when *that* is the relative pronoun, one prefers the grammatically pleasing forms in the examples.

exercise 55

Add *it is, was, has been, etc.* to complete the following sentences.

1   . . . on my first visit to Greece that I went to Athens.
2   . . . unusual to see gentlemen in top hats nowadays.
3   . . . difficult to work well when you are tired.
4   . . . strange that John didn't tell us of his marriage.
5   . . . odd that you never noticed the difference between the boys.
6   . . . not unknown for there to be shortage of water in England.
7   . . . funny to see the faces some men make when they are shaving.
8   . . . a shame to waste good food. Eat it up!
9   . . . five miles to the nearest village, as the crow flies.
10   . . . usual to remove your hat when you enter a church.
11   . . . half an hour's walk to John's new house.
12   . . . a long time since we last met.
13   . . . uncommon to see a pair of horses in London streets.
14   . . . three weeks since the last time you wrote to me.
15   . . . a pity that nobody came to meet you at the station.
16   . . . cold at this time of year in Sweden.
17   . . . not far to Oxford, about forty miles I think.
18   . . . not fair to give him five pounds and me only three!
19   . . . wet last winter, wasn't it?
20   . . . too cold to go out last night, so we stayed at home.

exercise 56

Complete the following sentences by adding *it is, was,* *etc.* and a personal pronoun,

> *It was they who told us the news.*

In some of the sentences all or most of the personal pronouns will make good sense, provided that the case is correct. Questions are formed by inversion: *Is it?* followed by a noun or pronoun.

> *Is it Mary who is late?*
> *Was it you who told John about the accident?*

1   . . . who broke the china vase.
2   . . . that we wanted to see.
3   . . . that brought him the good news.
4   . . . that I spoke to on the telephone.
5   . . . who told me about your engagement to David.
6   . . . that Peter gave your telephone number to.
7   . . . that Mr Brown meant when he spoke about naughty boys.
8   . . . who went to St James's School, not the Jones children.
9   . . . that I knew well, not his brother.
10   . . . that we visited in London last year.
11   . . . that objects to cigar smoke, not her mother.
12   . . . who work hardest that earn most money.
13   . . . that the letter is addressed to.
14   Since I am in the wrong . . . who ought to apologize.
15   When she needs help . . . that she comes to.
16   . . . that you were expecting at the party last night?
17   . . . that informed us of the change in your plans.
18   . . . who spares the rod that spoils the child.
19   . . . that you took a photograph of at the seaside?
20   . . . who had his picture in the newspaper?

Adjectives

- Adjectives usually form their comparative degrees, by adding —*er* to the positive, while —*est* makes the superlative form. The following table sets out a few examples.

Positive	Comparative	Superlative
old	older	oldest
new	newer	newest
bright	brighter	brightest
large	larger	largest

The —*er* and —*est* endings for comparative and superlative degree are added to all adjectives of one syllable:

larger, greater, smaller, oldest, highest, longest.

- Adjectives of two syllables ending in —*ow*, —*le*, —*er*, —*y* also take the —*er* and —*est* endings (see note 6 below)

yellowest, simpler, cleverer, prettiest, heavier.

- Some two-syllable adjectives with the accent on the first syllable take —*er* and —*est* endings for the comparative and superlative forms:

rottenest, commoner, stupidest.

But *more* and *most* can also be used with them;

most common, more stupid.

- Two-syllable adjectives ending in —*ful* and —*less* generally take *more* and *most*:

most useful, more helpful, more reckless, most faithful.

When the adjective ends in —*ing* use *more/most* constructions only:

more willing, most thrilling, more promising.

- Past Participles, when used as adjectives, take *more* and *most*:

more wanted, most wanted, more upset, most upset.

- Some adjectives form their comparative and superlative degrees irregularly. The most common of them are shown below.

Positive	Comparative	Superlative
good (well)	better	best
bad	worse	worst
*little (of quantity, degree)	less	least
*some	more	most
*some	less	least
*much	more	most
*many	more	most

(*see countable and uncountable nouns, p.2).

- Some adjectives form their comparative and superlative degrees in two ways:

  old, older, oldest and *old, elder, eldest*.

The second way is used in referring to the members of a family and defines their place in it. Consider:

  The eldest son is five years older than his youngest brother.   The eldest son is the first-born.
  My elder brother is two years older than I am and a year younger than my eldest brother.   My elder brother was born before me.

far, farther, farthest. These forms are generally used when we refer to distance.

  The North Pole is the farthest point north in the world.

further generally means additional or extra

  I gave him twenty pounds for his fare and a further ten pounds for expenses.
  I need further information before I make a decision.

farther never means additional or extra and we must not use it in that sense.

● Notice that positive adjectives ending in—*y* change the *y* for *i* when they become comparative or superlative:

> *happy, happier, happiest*
> *funny, funnier, funniest*

except when the final *y* is preceded by a vowel:

> *gay, gayer, gayest.*

● *good, well:* Well generally refers to one's health and is generally used predicatively, i.e. after the verb *be* or similar verbs of state such as *look, seem* and *feel.*
Consider:

> *John had a bad cold last week but he is quite well now.*
> *How are you, Peter? Very well; thank you.*

The comparative and superlative forms are *better* and *best.*

> *He wasn't well yesterday but he is better today.*
> *Grandfather feels best in the mornings after breakfast.*

Notice however that *better* often means cured.

> *I am sorry to see you so ill. I hope you will be better soon.*
> *The doctor says that I must go to hospital to get better* – to be cured.

good, better, best: Consider the examples:

> *Bobby is a good little boy today. Yesterday he was naughty, but today he is better. He is on his best behaviour.*
> *These cows give good milk. Milk is good for children.*

good refers to quality and is used both before the noun and predicatively. Consider:

> *The students in this class are good.* = polite, intelligent, studious, etc.
> *The students in that class are well* = healthy, in good health; they are not ill or unwell.

● Pronouns after *as* and *than.*

> *Peter is older than me. I'm as tall as him.*

In these two sentences the personal pronouns after *than* and *as* respectively are in the objective form. Most people

prefer the objective form although a few insist that only the subjective forms, *I* and *he*, are really correct. In the two sentences given above no change of meaning can result from the use of either form of the pronoun and while the subjective form may seem more stylish it is the objective that popular speech and writing use most.

● However, in certain types of sentences we must take care to use the grammatically correct form of pronoun to avoid confusion of meaning:

    (a) *Peter likes John better than me* = Peter likes John better than he (Peter) likes me.
    (b) *Peter likes John better than I (do)* = Peter likes John better than I like John.

Although sentences of type (a) are often ambiguous, we hear them very often. It is much better to use type (b) when the two subjects (Peter and I) share the same verb. In (b) the addition of the appropriate auxiliary helps to remove all doubt from the sentence.

    (a) *Mary loves him more than (she loves) me.*
    (b) *Mary loves him more than I (do).*
    (c) *She likes him as much as (she likes) me.*
    (d) *She likes chocolate as much as he (does).*

● In sentences of the (a) type, in which there are a transitive verb and objective case pronouns as the object of that verb, confusion of meaning can be avoided by repeating the subject with its appropriate auxiliary:

    You helped him more than you did me.
    He punished me more than he did them.
    We like him as much as we do her.

This construction is particularly useful when there is a change in the forms of the verb:

    I will help you as I did your brother   (Future and Past).
    They will pay us more than they did you   (Future and Past).
    He makes me work harder than he will (make) *you*   (Present and Future).

● After the comparisons with *as* and *than*, whether of adjectives or adverbs, a new subject can be introduced:

> *He studies more than you ever did.*
> *She speaks English as well as he does.*

● Participial adjectives (*pleasing, worrying, pleased, worried*) generally form their comparatives with *more* and the superlative with *most*.

> *Mother is most annoyed when we come in late for meals.*

Positive degree

● The positive degree of the adjective shows similarity of quality, quantity, degree and so on between nouns and pronouns.

> *Peter is as strong as a horse.*

● When we wish to show inequality between the nouns instead of saying *as sweet as honey* we say: *not as sweet as honey* and *not as tall as John, not as old as her husband.* You will sometimes hear *so* instead of the first *as* in negatives.

● In English the adjective has only one form, that is to say, gender, number and case do not affect the adjective.

exercise 57

Put in *so* or *as* in the following sentences.

1   Today isn't . . . cold . . . yesterday.
2   Mrs Brown is almost . . . tall . . . her husband.
3   Mr White doesn't feel . . . ill today . . . he did yesterday.
4   There are apples on our tree . . . large . . . a fist.
5   Genoa isn't quite . . . far from London . . . Milan is.

Comparative degree

- We use the comparative degree of the adjective to show clearly that there is inequality of quantity, quality, degree and so on between nouns and pronouns. Consider the following:

    John isn't so tall as Peter (Positive).

We can give the same information by saying:

  (a) *John is shorter than Peter*, or
  (b) *Peter is taller than John*.

The comparative is formed by adding —*er* to the positive form of the adjective: *old, older, young, younger* and so on, or by putting *more* before the positive degree: *more careful*, etc. *Than* is the correct connecting word to use in making a comparison of inequality.

exercise 58

Restate each of the following negative sentences twice, using comparative adjectives in their construction.

EXAMPLE: **A pony isn't so large as a horse.**

  (a) **A pony is smaller than a horse.**
  (b) **A horse is larger than a pony.**

1 February isn't so long as March.
2 Winter isn't so warm as summer.
3 John's father isn't so young as his mother.
4 Paris isn't so far from London as Berlin is.
5 Lemons aren't so sweet as oranges.
6 Cream cake doesn't cost so much as fruit cake.
7 Peter doesn't eat so much as John.
8 Dogs don't swim as fast as otters.
9 Mary's books don't look so new as Jane's do.
10 Robert doesn't buy so many apples as I do.

Superlative degree

● When we compare a number of nouns, that is three or
  more, we apply the superlative degree of the adjective to
  the one that exceeds all the others in some quality,
  quantity, degree and so on.

> John is taller than either of his brothers
> = *John is the tallest of the three brothers.*
> Mary is younger than any other girl in the class
> = *Mary is the youngest girl in the class.*

exercise 59

**Restate the following sentences using the superlative
adjective, as in the example above.**

1 A diamond is harder than any other stone I know of.
2 Roses have a sweeter smell than all the flowers in the
  garden.
3 Peter likes horses better than any other animal on the farm.
4 Peter's brother is younger than all the other captains in the
  army.
5 Moscow is colder than any other capital in Europe.
6 Bjorn Borg is more determined than any other tennis
  player.
7 Football is more important than any other sport.
8 The queen bee is more important than the other bees.
9 The President is more powerful than any other man.
10 This ring is more expensive than any other in the shop.

exercise 60

Put in the correct form of the adjective, i.e. positive (p), comparative (c), or superlative (s) with the correct connecting words (*as, so, than*).

1 A donkey isn't . . . a horse.   (intelligent p)
2 You must drive your car in a . . . manner in future.   (careful c)
3 A pen without ink is . . . a car without an engine.   (useless p)
4 The Taj Mahal is one of . . . buildings in the world.   (beautiful s)
5 Saturday is the . . . day of the week for me.   (tiring s)
6 John's handwriting is bad but mine is . . . .   (bad c)
7 All change here! This is the . . . that this train goes. (far s)
8 Some jobs are . . . others.   (dangerous c)
9 John speaks . . . English . . . I do.   (good c)
10 The firm does . . . business now . . . it used to.   (little c)
11 There is . . . competition in the market today.   (some c)
12 Onion soup makes the . . . supper I know.   (tasty s)
13 I should like you to meet Robert, my . . . son.   (old s)
14 Bill and Tom are Robert's . . . brothers.   (young c)
15 The police have received . . . information about the missing jewels.   (some c)

Adjectives as nouns

● Sometimes an adjective is used as a noun, as the subject or object of a verb. The adjectival noun is never used to refer to one individual. Consider:

(a) *The poor are always with us.*
(b) *The sick need special care.*
(c) *Do not speak ill of the dead.*

In (a) and (b) the verb is plural. The subjects of these verbs are plural in sense since they refer to all those who are poor and all those who are sick, in a general way, as categories of people. In the same way, *the dead* refers to all those who are dead as a general classification.

NOTE: Adjectival nouns are nearly always plural and general in sense, when we use them in this way, but do not take a final —s.

exercise 61

Rewrite the following sentences, replacing the phrases in brackets with an adjectival noun,

(All the poor people) received a gift of money. = (The poor) received a gift of money.

1 (Anybody who is sick) needs medical advice.
2 (Lazy people) do not deserve to succeed.
3 (Deaf people) can often read one's lips.
4 (All the wounded soldiers) went to hospital next day.
5 (People who are young) are more active than (old people).
6 (Rich people) often have as many troubles as (poor people have).
7 There is a Latin phrase which says that we must not speak ill of (those who are dead).
8 (People who are blind) can learn to read with their fingertips.
9 (Unusual happenings) often interest journalists.
10 There is a saying that only (good people) are always happy.

so, such

- *So* goes with adjectives and adverbs to indicate a very superlative degree or quantity:

  (a) *John is so tall (that) he can touch the ceiling.*
  (b) *A microbe is so small (that) we cannot see it with the naked eye.*

  Notice the phrase underlined in each example. It shows in (a) a consequence of excessive tallness and in (b) a consequence of excessive smallness.

- *Such* goes with plural countable nouns and with uncountable nouns.

- *Such a* goes with singular countable nouns. These expressions indicate a very superlative quality in the noun they precede. Consider:

  (a) *Peter is such a lazy fellow (that he never does his homework).*
  (b) *We had such fine weather (that) we were all tanned brown with the sun.*
  (c) *They were such good boys (that) I was almost never cross with them.*

  Again, notice that the consequence clause is underlined to draw your attention to the construction *that . . . .* Very often, especially in conversation, *that* is dropped from the sentence.

exercise 62

Put in *so, such* or *such a* and supply a good consequence to complete the sentence.

1 Mary is . . . polite that . . . .
3 Shakespeare wrote . . . well that . . . .
3 Peter talks . . . nonsense that . . . .
4 I feel . . . happy that . . . .
5 John has . . . wonderful presents that . . . .
6 The teacher used . . . difficult words that . . . .
7 I have . . . many things to do that . . . .
8 George is . . . liar that . . . .
9 Last night I was . . . tired that . . . .
10 They are . . . good children that . . . .
11 Our opinions are . . . different that . . . .
12 It was . . . rainy day that . . . .
13 The dog was . . . big one that . . . .
14 John was . . . strong fellow that . . . .
15 She gave me . . . little piece of chocolate that . . . .
16 The new school will be . . . large building that . . . .
17 The apples were . . . good ones that . . . .
18 She was talking . . . fast that . . . .
19 A horse is . . . fine animal that . . . .
20 Nightingales are . . . beautiful singers that . . . .

● NOTE:

> *I've never met such a fool before* = a fool like this one.
> *She's never eaten such things* = things like these/those.
> *He would never do such a thing* = a thing like that.

how ...! what ...!

- *How* goes with an adjective or an adverb,
    How cold it is today!   How sweetly she sings!

How also goes with a verb,
    How John loves arithmetic!

What a ... precedes singular countable nouns.
    What a day it was!   What a kind thing to do!

What precedes plural countable nouns and uncountable nouns.
    What fools we were!   What stupidity it was!

These exclamations express surprise, excitement, pleasure, regret and so on. The tone of voice changes according to the speaker's feelings.

exercise 63

Fill in the blanks using *how, what* or *what a*.

1   ... charming person she is!
2   ... kindly she talks to everybody!
3   ... polite boy your son is!
4   ... clever men the ancient Greeks were!
5   ... well John tells a story!
6   ... interesting he makes it sound!
7   ... large city London is!
8   ... traffic runs in the main streets!
9   We ate bread and cheese but ... bread, ... wonderful cheese!
10 ... we enjoyed that meal!   ... appetites we had!
11 ... energy that man has!   ... hard he works!
12 Hello, Peter!   ... good luck to meet you here!
13 ... lucky I am to see you this morning!
14 ... pretty tune!   ... pleasant it sounds!
15 We went to a concert.   ... beautifully they played!

still, yet, already

- *Still* is generally used in affirmative contexts. *Yet* is used in negative and interogative sentences. Consider:

  > *It was raining at lunch time and it is still raining. The rain hasn't stopped yet.*
  > *Is John out of bed yet?   No, he isn't awake yet. He is still asleep.*

- *Still* indicates that certain actions and states have not come to an end. *Yet* often shows that, so far, they have not occurred.

- *Already* is used in sentences that tell what has happened or has been completed before the time of speaking. Consider:

  > *I was still waiting for the train to leave. The signal had not changed to green although we were already twenty minutes late.*

- *Already* also expresses surprise that an action has been completed so quickly, that an event has occurred so soon. Consider:

  > *How time flies! It's ten o'clock already.*
  > *Have you finished your homework already? It's only ten minutes since you sat down to begin.*

exercise 64

Put in *still*, *yet* and *already*.

1   My goodness, look at the time! It's nine o'clock . . . and I'm
    . . . at breakfast.

2   Have you finished my book . . . ?   No, I'm . . . in the
    middle of it.

3   The family haven't gone on holiday . . . .   We are . . . at
    home and it is . . . late in the season.

4   The doctor says you mustn't get up . . . . You are . . . too ill
    to get about.

5   Are you ready to come in to dinner . . . , John?   What! Is it
    dinner time . . . ?

6   No, not quite. You needn't come in . . . . You . . . have ten
    minutes.

7   Hello, I didn't expect to find you here . . . . I thought you
    would . . . be on the way.

8   Why aren't the children in bed . . . ? They are up because
    they haven't finished their homework . . . .

9   The bill was for three hundred pounds. I have . . . given
    him two hundred and I . . . have to pay a hundred.

10 I can't pay him . . . because I . . . have to find a customer for
    the goods.

11 It wasn't . . . five o'clock on that afternoon but . . . it was
    very dark.

12 Have you replied to Mary's letter . . . ? No, I'm trying to
    find time for that. It's three days late . . . .

13 After only three years in the army, he was . . . a captain
    and rising, although he isn't a general . . . .

14 I'm in a hurry! I ought to be at school . . . but I'm . . . at the
    station. The train hasn't come . . . .

15 I'm waiting for the coffee I ordered. The waiter hasn't
    brought it . . . . I've been here an hour . . . .

16 You ought not to be here . . . . We expected you tomorrow
    and are . . . preparing your rooms.

17 Peter is . . . in love with Mary and would have married her
    if she hadn't . . . married somebody else.

● *Still* is often heard in negative or interrogative sentences when the speaker confirms a previous negative statement or repeats a question to which he has previously had an affirmative answer and expects that this time too, the answer will be affirmative. Consider:

(a) *I didn't believe him yesterday and <u>still don't</u> believe him.*
(b) *He told me a lie then and he <u>still isn't</u> telling the truth.*
(c) *John didn't smoke when he was in the army and he <u>still doesn't</u>.*
(d) *Our guests were to arrive at seven o'clock but they <u>still hadn't</u> come at eight.*
(e) *Do you <u>still have</u> English lessons at school?*
(f) *Does your mother <u>still live</u> in that little, white house?*
(g) *Have you <u>still got</u> your old school books?*

NOTE: In these questions, (e), (f) and (g), the speaker asks whether there has been any change since the previous time of asking (f), for example, could be written:

Does your mother continue to live in that little white house?

● *Yet* could not be used in place of *still* since *yet* asks whether an action has, in the meantime, occurred; *still* enquires whether an action, already begun, continues at present. Thus,

Is Mary talking yet?

is a perfectly polite question about a baby girl's progress (Has she begun to talk yet?) and

Is Mary still talking?

may be a less polite enquiry about an older Mary (Hasn't she stopped talking yet!).

- Note that in questions about continuity (see examples (e), (f), and (g) on page 100) the word *still* takes its place between the subject and the main verb:

    Does Mary still spend all her time at home?

- In statements that prolong previous negation (see examples (a), (b), (c) and (d) on page 100) *still* precedes the whole of the verb, taking its place after the subject but before the auxiliary verb:

    That lazy fellow has never worked – and he still isn't looking for a job.
    I've looked everywhere for John's address – but I still can't find it.

- *Yet* generally takes an end position after the verb:

    The train hasn't left yet.

When there is an object *yet* follows it:

    Has Peter given Charles his book yet?

In negative sentences *yet* may be placed between the auxiliary and principal verbs.

    Your letter has not yet arrived.
    We had not yet decided (not yet = not so far; not up to the time of writing).

exercise 65

Put in *still* and *yet*. Notice where the use of either word might change the meaning of the phrase. Give suitable answers to questions. (Nos. 1, 2, 3, 5, etc.)

1 Does your father . . . keep horses?
2 Is Peter's sister married . . .?
3 Have you telephoned the office . . .?
4 No, I . . . haven't spoken to the manager.
5 Can Peter . . . swim as well as ever?
6 John didn't like hard work in his youth and he . . . doesn't.
7 Will you . . . be there when Mary arrives?
8 Shan't we . . . be friends, even when we are old?
9 The line was engaged last time I phoned and they are . . . speaking.
10 The manager hasn't come in . . . so the workmen are . . . waiting for instructions.
11 Shall I . . . be doing exercises a year from now?
12 Even after our teacher's explanation I . . . didn't understand.
13 Don't people . . . drink a lot of tea in England?
14 I couldn't sing when I was a boy and I . . . can't sing a note.
15 Did he . . . persist after he was shown his mistake?
16 She didn't do her homework yesterday and she . . . hasn't done it.
17 Can't the public . . . attend debates in Parliament?
18 We have been learning English for a few months but we don't know everything . . . .
19 Must we . . . go on learning after we leave school?
20 I've done my exercise three times and it . . . isn't right.

Pre-verb adverbs

● The pre-verb adverbs:

> *hardly, nearly, almost, quite, scarcely*

and the frequency adverbs:

> *often, sometimes, always, never, generally, usually, just*

are normally placed after the simple tenses of *to be*, before the simple tenses of other verbs. In compound verbs they are placed after the first auxiliary.

> *We usually have fish for lunch on Fridays.*
> *John has never lived in a large town before.*
> *I had hardly begun breakfast when the postman came.*

exercise 66

Put in the given pre-verb adverb in the correct place.

1 We have fish for breakfast.   (never)
2 John goes to school by bus.   (generally)
3 He plays football on Saturdays.   (always)
4 It is so dark that I can see.   (scarcely)
5 The man is so ill he can walk.   (hardly)
6 I'm sorry, Mr Brown has gone out.   (just)
7 I missed the train this morning.   (nearly)
8 Hush! The baby is asleep.   (almost)
9 I agree. Peter is right.   (quite)
10 My grandfather has been abroad.   (never)
11 Peter forgets to wind his watch up.   (sometimes)
12 In fact, he forgets to put it on.   (often)
13 Mr Brown meets his old friends now.   (rarely)
14 The London train is late.   (seldom)
15 I travel on it.   (hardly ever)
16 It is full of passengers.   (usually)
17 We have to stand in the corridor.   (sometimes)
18 We go to bed after midnight.   (scarcely ever)

- *Nearly, almost, hardly, quite, only* and *just* precede the principal verb or follow *to be* when they are used as adverbs of degree controlling the verb. Their places in the sentence may vary according to the words they control or modify:

  We nearly fell all the way down the steps.   (we didn't fall)
  We fell nearly all the way down the steps.
  (we fell a long way)
  Only Mary came to see me.   (nobody but Mary came)
  Mary came to see me only.   (me, nobody else)

- *Sometimes, often, frequently, occasionally* and *usually* behave as frequency adverbs but may vary their positions as adverbs of time do.

  We sometimes go to the theatre.
  (not often, but sometimes)
  Sometimes we go to the theatre.   (and sometimes not)
  We go to the theatre sometimes.   (but rather seldom)

- Except when the pre-verb and frequency adverbs are movable in the way you have seen above, they follow auxiliary verbs and special finites i.e. *must, can, may*, etc. in order to precede the principal verb. Notice that auxiliary types *used to* and *have to* take these pre-verbs before them:

  We always used to walk to school.
  We often had to run, in fact.

We prefer to put the pre-verb between *ought* and *to*.

  You ought never to say such things.

With the exception of the negative pre-verb adverbs (*never, hardly ever, almost never*, etc.) *ought to* sentences often take the frequency adverb at the end of the phrase or sentence:

  We ought to clean our teeth often.
  You ought to write to your parents sometimes.

● The pre-verb adverb precedes the verb *to be* in an emphatic sense.

> *Peter is very smart today. Yes, he always is.* (well dressed)

The pre-verb adverb may precede the auxiliary verbs in short answers:

> *Do you have coffee for breakfast? Yes, I often do.* (rather emphatically), or *Yes, I do, usually.*

In such short answers the negative (*hardly ever, rarely, scarcely, never, seldom,* etc.) always precedes the auxiliary:

> *Can you remember the names of the kings of England? No, I never can.*
> *Does John use his bicycle much? No, he hardly ever does.*

These frequency adverbs always sound most natural when they come immediately before the verb. When the verb is in two parts (I shall come) the frequency adverb takes its place before the main verb. (Peter has never eaten meat).

When there are two or more auxiliaries in the verb, the frequency adverb usually follows the first of them.

> *Such a wonderful story had rarely been heard before.*

When *have* is the principal verb (have = possess, own) the frequency adverb naturally takes its place before *have* or its participles:

> *We never have more money than we need.*
> *She has never had such a wonderful holiday before.*

When *be* is constructed with auxiliary verbs (*shall, will, would, should, have, had*) the frequency adverb follows the auxiliary and precedes *be*:

> *I shall never be late again.*
> *We had often been there before.*

exercise 67

Put the frequency adverb in its correct place in each sentence that is to say (a) after the auxiliary in a compound verb or (b) before the simple tenses of verbs except *to be*.

NOTE: *Have you ever . . .? Do you ever . . .?* etc. in open questions.

1 Peter works overtime.   (sometimes)
2 He arrives home before ten o'clock.   (always)
3 We walk to work in the morning.   (often)
4 He has been ill all his life.   (never)
5 We see an eagle in England.   (rarely)
6 They leave the mountains of Scotland.   (hardly ever)
7 We drink wine with our meals.   (seldom)
8 My father sends me a cheque on my birthday.   (generally)
9 Have you ridden a camel?   (ever)
10 I can imagine you on a camel's hump!   (just)
11 My brother rings me up on Tuesday evenings.   (usually)
12 Does she do her homework?   (ever)
13 Yes, but her sisters help her.   (often)
14 The boys have their lessons in the garden.   (sometimes)
15 It rains here in the summer months.   (never)
16 I shall remember your kindness to me.   (always)
17 Shall I learn to spell correctly?   (ever)
18 People ride tricycles nowadays.   (rarely)
19 We see horses in the streets of London.   (hardly ever)
20 The clock had struck ten.   (just)

● The frequency adverb precedes the auxiliary in the end
position, that is to say, when the sentence ends with an
auxiliary verb (a) to avoid repetition of a principal verb or
(b) for emphasis:

Mary always got up early but I seldom did.
My brother never goes by bus but I always do.
They said they hoped to meet us again but I knew they never
would.

exercise 68

**Complete the following sentences by adding the given
frequency adverb followed by the appropriate auxiliary
verb.**

1 Are you often late for work?   Yes, I'm afraid I
   . . . .   (often)
2 I always take a shower in the morning but George . . . .
   (hardly ever)
3 He often promised to come but he . . . .   (never)
4 John could never come on Saturdays but Peter . . . .
   (occasionally)
5 She can type in English although she . . . .   (seldom)
6 He often said he would punish us but . . . .   (rarely)
7 Peter sometimes works overtime but John . . . .   (hardly
   ever)
8 John will learn if he tries hard, but I . . . .   (never)
9 The boys had never seen an elephant before but their
   father . . . .   (occasionally)
10 If I can help you, please ask.   You know I . . . .   (always)

Prepositions, adverbial particles

● **1** These prepositions are words like: *from, to, into, up, down*, that show direction of movement:

> *Come into the house.*
> *Go up the hill.*

● **2** Other prepositions such as *at, on, in, behind, in front of*, show location.

> *I met him at Mary's house.*
> *There are cigarettes in the box.*
> *The box is on the table.*

We can say then that a preposition stands in front of a noun, a pronoun or a noun phrase to give

(a) direction of movement to the action of the verb or
(b) to indicate static location:

> (1) *The manager went* (a) *to his office and* (b) *sat at his desk.*
> (2) *I had a letter* (a) *from my brother who lives* (b) *in London.*

● **3** Adverbial Particles do very much the same kind of work as prepositions but may stand alone without a following noun, noun phrase or pronoun, as adverbs. They tell us how, where or in what direction or position an action takes place.

Prepositions	Adverbial Particles
It's very cold outside the house	*Don't stay outside – come inside.*
Go into the kitchen.	*Please go in.*
We came out of the cinema early.	*Has John gone out?*

● **4** As you have seen, words which appear to be one and the same may in fact have two different functions. The following words can be used both as prepositions and as adverbial particles and show direction of movement or location:

> *off, on; in, inside; out, outside; up, down; across, through; over, under; along, by* and *past.*

At, from, to and *with* cannot be used as adverbial particles.

● **5** Adverbial particles take their places immediately after intransitive verbs:

> *He stood outside in the rain.*
> *They set off soon after breakfast.*

● **6** When the verb is transitive the adverbial particle may be placed either before or after the object noun or noun phrase.

> *He paid back all the money.*
> *He paid all the money back.*
> (See also note **4** on page 136).

When the object of a transitive verb is a pronoun, the adverbial particle must follow it: (see note **4**(b) page 137).

> *They broke the old cars up.* ⎫
> *They broke up the old cars.* ⎬ *They broke them up.*
>
> *The policeman held out his hand.* ⎫
> *The policeman held his hand out.* ⎬ *He held it out.*

● **7** Prepositions stand in front of the noun, noun phrase or pronoun: (but see **9, 10** and **11**).

Verb	Preposition	
He swam	*across the river.*	*He swam across it.*
They walked	*round the garden.*	*They walked round it.*
He called	*on Mr Smith.*	*He called on him.*

● **8** (See **4** and **6**)

> *He went up the ladder.*　(*Up* is a preposition here)
> *We went up it.*
> *The postman brought up my letters.*　(*Up* is an adverbial particle here).
> *He brought them up*　(to my room)

● **9** A preposition comes at the end of the clause: when it governs a relative pronoun that is

(i) expressed.
> *This is the house that we stayed at.*
> *They know the people whom you work for.*

(ii) omitted.
> *That's the bed I slept in.*
> *He's the man I'm talking about.* (see also Object relative Pronouns page 61).

NOTE:
> *To whom were you writing?*
> *Who(m) were you writing to?*

Who were you writing to? is so common that it is accepted in speech but *whom* should always be used in formal English.

● **10** A preposition stands in the end position when it governs the interrogative pronoun.

> *What do you want it for?*
> *What town does she come from?* (see Interrogative Pronouns page 51).

● **11** Adverbial particles and prepositions which are themselves elements of transitive phrasal verbs frequently take the end position in passive voice constructions.

> *The matter will be looked into.*
> *Negotiations were broken off.*
> *This proposal was turned down.* (See Passive Voice, page 322 ff).

Direction of movement

Throughout this section the word *particle* means
preposition or adverbial particle. Here are some particles
that indicate movement in one direction or another:

to	down	out	towards
into	through	of	forward(s)
from	along	round	backward(s)
on	by	around	upward(s)
off	past	back	downward(s)
up	out	throughout	

into: from an external position to an internal one.

> *I knocked on the door and went into the room.*

out of: from an internal to an external position.

> *He got out of bed and took some clothes out of the wardrobe.*

on and ***off:***

> He got $\begin{Bmatrix} on \text{ (to)} \\ off \end{Bmatrix}$ *the bus (ship, plane, bicycle, horse etc.)*

the *to* is often omitted after *on.*

by and ***past***

> *They always go* $\begin{Bmatrix} (by) \\ (past) \end{Bmatrix}$ *the post office*

(They don't go in – they pass it on the outside)

through:

> *I can see the crowd through the window.*
> *I can't see anything through a closed door.*

throughout: to/in every part of

> *The epidemic spread throughout the whole country.*
> *The BBC broadcasts throughout the world.*
> *The heart pumps blood throughout the body.*

forward(s) backward(s) upward(s) downward(s): there is a
tendency towards dropping the —s from these words.
However the expression *backwards and forwards* with the —s
is still frequently heard.

Location

● These particles indicate position and place, that is to say,
static location:

at	on	in	above
below	over	under	by
beside	underneath	below	beneath.

over = in a higher inclined position.

> The doctor bent over the injured man.
> John leaned over his desk to reach the telephone.

over = more than

> Students over sixteen years of age may have extra English
> lessons.
> That car costs over six thousand pounds.

below = lower down:

> My brother's flat is the one below yours
> From the mountain we watched the valley below us.

under = lower, but directly.

> I wear a pullover under my jacket.
> How long can you swim under the water?

under = less than.

> Mary is under twenty-one but she has a passport.
> John isn't tall – he's well under six feet.

underneath = in a lower position (often covered or hidden
by whatever is over it)

> There was a lot of dust underneath the carpet.
> Our neighbour's cat often sleeps underneath our car.

beneath and **underneath** are similar in meaning but
beneath is also used figuratively meaning 'too low', 'too far
below.'

> It is beneath my dignity to tell lies.
> Your dishonest suggestion is beneath my consideration.

Time

as	around	through	till
to	in	throughout	by
past	within	from . . . to	by the time
about	during		

The holiday was <u>over</u>.
  (finished, ended)

The seven days will be $\left\{\begin{array}{c} up \\ \underline{over} \end{array}\right\}$ *tomorrow.*
  (will have expired).

I'll see you <u>in</u> a week's time
  (a week from today).

You must pay the bill <u>within</u> a week
  (before the week expires).
  (before the week is *up*)

We shall arrive <u>by</u> two o'clock
  (perhaps before but not later than two o'clock)

We shall stay here <u>till</u> five o'clock, then we shall go home.

Topics and Subjects

about
on
of

A book about cats.
A story about a boy and a dog.
A lecture on the Early Romans.
An article on the Middle East.
A collection of photographs.
A set of foreign stamps.

on seems more usual when formal talks, lectures and writings are mentioned.

a book	on	*Problems in Society*
a talk		*the Uses of Psychology*
a lecture		*Causes of Inflation*
a report		

about seems to go better with less formal matters.

We chatted <u>about</u> the weather.
He told us <u>about</u> his new job.
There is an article <u>about</u> atomic energy in the newspaper.

However, *about* and *on* are frequently interchangeable.

of = containing:

a book of poems
a collection of stamps
a series of articles
a set of Shakespeare's works

NOTE:

$A\ book \begin{Bmatrix} on \\ about \end{Bmatrix} poetry$

$A\ book\ giving\ information \begin{Bmatrix} on \\ about \end{Bmatrix} poetry$

A book of poems

A collection of poems in a book.

Materials and ingredients

The particles are:
of
from
out of
into
with
without

of is generally used when the materials have not changed much:

A bottle is made of glass (it is a glass bottle)

from indicates that the materials are not now in their previous state:

Glass is made from sand. (but it can never be sand again)

out of sometimes suggests a makeshift, improvised construction:

He built a boat <u>out of</u> old wine barrels.
I made my first car <u>out of</u> three old ones.

into is the word that tells us what happens to materials:

They are made <u>into</u> something else.

What can you make $\left\{\begin{array}{l} \textit{with} \\ \textit{out of} \\ \textit{from} \end{array}\right\}$ *milk?*

You can make it into cheese.
Can you make cheese without milk?
No, cheese must be made from milk.
We make bread with flour, water and yeast.
You can't make bricks without straw.

Purpose and destination

>   *What . . . for?*
>   *Who . . . for?*
>   *Where . . . for?*

This kind of question asks about purpose or destination.

>   *What's that little sharp knife for?   It's for peeling potatoes with.*
>   *What's the money on the table for?   It's for the telephone bill.*
>   *Who's the letter for?   It's for Mary, not for you.*
>   *When does your ship leave for Cadiz?   She sails for Spain on Tuesday.*
>   *Which is the bus for Henley?*

See: Infinitive to express purpose or reason page 229.

Motive, cause and reason

because of

>   *Why . . .?* questions are often answered with *because of*
>
>   *John was absent from class because of his bad leg.*
>   *I couldn't sleep because of the noise.*

on account of = because of, and seems more formal.

>   *On account of Mr Brown's retirement we shall require a new manager.*

out of = from feelings of.

>   *Everyone came to see the new baby out of friendly interest.*
>   *We went to hear the speech out of curiosity.*
>   *The poor old soul almost wept out of gratitude for our help.*
>   *Out of respect for his great age, we did not interrupt him.*

owing to = as a consequence of.

>   *The train arrived late owing to bad weather.*
>   *Our plan to visit Australia was cancelled owing to my illness.*
>   *There's a shortage of water, owing to a long, dry winter.*

Having

with
in
of
without

with often occurs with physical attributes:

a red haired girl = a girl with red hair.
a blue-eyed baby = a baby with blue eyes.
a grey-bearded man = a man with a grey beard.
a one-armed sailor = a sailor with (only) one arm.

in usually occurs with some reference to a person's clothing.

Mr Brown comes to the office in a dark suit.
Mary looks well in country clothes.

of in a partitive sense:

a kilo of sugar, a ton of coal, a slice of bread, a spoonful of jam, a member of the committee, a litre of oil.

of in a genitive sense:

a friend of mine, the author of the book, the price of freedom, the cost of living.

of descriptively:

a courageous man = a man of courage.
a religious matter = a matter of religion.

without = not having.

Eggs without salt aren't very nice.
It's too cold to go out without a coat.
Without money you can buy nothing.

with + **no** = not having

a dog $\begin{cases} without\ a\ tail \\ with\ no\ tail \end{cases}$

a cup $\begin{cases} without\ a\ handle \\ with\ no\ handle \end{cases}$

Reactions

> with
> about
> at

(a) *I was very angry with John.*
(b) *We were all angry about the new taxes.*
(c) *She was angry* $\left\{ \begin{matrix} at \\ about \end{matrix} \right\}$ *not being invited*

Three different stimuli have caused anger:

(a) John (a person)
(b) the new taxes and
(c) not being invited.

Generally, when the stimulus or provocation for the reaction comes from a person we use *with*:

> $I'm \left\{ \begin{matrix} pleased\ with\ Mary. \\ furious\ with\ Peter. \\ annoyed\ with\ the\ grocer. \end{matrix} \right.$

at is commonly used when the stimulus comes from a non-personal source. *At* may usually be replaced by *about*.

NOTE: *alarmed at, amused at, laugh at someone, be glad at;*
delighted with (at):

> *delighted with the flowers.* (not *at*)
> *delighted at what you said.*

disappointed with (in):

> *disappointed with the result.*
> *disappointed in you.*

Start, stop and adjust (mechanical)

on
off
out
up
down

on = in the working position

It's getting dark. Please $\left\{ \begin{array}{l} turn \\ switch \end{array} \right\}$ *the light on.*

Please turn the hot water tap on.

off = in the not working position.

Turn the radio off after the news, please.
Switch the electric fire off if you feel too warm.
Switch the engine off when you park the car.

out = extinguish (light and fire).

Turn out all the lamps except one.
Please put out your cigarettes.
Turn out the gas in the kitchen.

cut off = discontinue supplies of electricity, water, oil etc.

If we don't pay the bill today, they will cut off the telephone.

up = increase volume, power and speed of mechanical and other processes.

Turn up the sound a little, I can hardly hear the music.
Turn the heat up – this room's freezing!
You must speed up the work.
Speak up, I can hardly hear you.

down = reduce volume, power, speed and so on.
Opposite of *up*.

It's past midnight. Turn down the record player and keep the noise down.

Agents, ways and means

> *by*
> *with*
> *through*
> *with*
> *without*

by = the passive agent.

The picture was painted by Reynolds.

by after verb of movement

travel
come   } *by car, by bus, by train, by taxi, by plane* (but *on*
go   *foot, on my bicycle, in John's car*).

by = the way we do it.

He makes a whistle by cutting holes in a cane.
You can cure a headache by taking an aspirin.
Send a message by cable, at once.

through = as a result of:

She caught cold through sitting in a draught.

through = because of:

Tom succeeded through hard work.

with = tools and instruments:

You can chop wood with an axe.
She took his temperature with a thermometer.

NOTE:

The policeman wrote it down with a pencil. but *Write in pencil.*
He thought he should write with a pen. but *Write in ink.*

without = with negation:

You can't make tea without water.
He suddenly left without saying goodbye.

NOTE: *of, die of.* }
He died of cancer. } but *He suffers from heart trouble.*

Accompaniment and participation

with, in, at;
between, among, along with, without;
good at, good with

with = accompanied by:

> *I'll have a sandwich with my beer, please.*
> *Mrs Green came to see us with her husband yesterday.*
> *John works with his father.*

in = participate in an event:

> *play in a concert*
> *act in a play (film)*
> *play in the match*
> *march in the parade*
> *be injured in an accident*
> *be involved in scandal*
> *speak in a debate*

be good with = know how to handle (someone).

> *Dr Brown is very good with children.*
> *Old George is wonderful with horses. He really understands them.*

at: Nowadays we seldom hear:

> *We played at tennis, chess, football,* and so on.

At is usually dropped:

> *We played football, backgammon, draughts, dominoes,* etc.
> *We often play a game of chess with them.*
> *I like to watch a game of football,* and so on.
> *John is good at games.*
> *Mary is good at French.*
> *I'm not very good at mathematics.*

between = involves two persons or sides.

It's a secret between us two.

among = involves more than two persons or sides.

The two sons divided the old man's property between them and then shared it among their children.
Share the chocolate among all the children.

along with = together and at the same time.

Please bring my books along with your own when you come.
Along with our hotel bill the manager sent some roses.

without: This is used in connection with common pairs such as:

bacon and eggs
strawberries and cream
bread and butter
fish and chips
steak and chips
gin and tonic
whisky and soda

for negation:

strawberries without cream
bread without butter and so on.

Concession

despite, in spite of = heedless of, against, contrary to.

> *In spite of everyone's opposition, I am going to try to walk to
> London.*
> *None of these boys wears a coat despite the cold weather.*
> *The prisoners were forced to work outside in spite of the
> danger from wild animals and snakes.*

notwithstanding = despite, in spite of. It is formal and
legalistic.

for all = notwithstanding, even if.

> *He doesn't seem to read much for all his fine library.* (even if
> he has a fine library, notwithstanding his fine library.)
> *The price of gold is still rising for all the government says to
> the contrary.* (even if the government says otherwise,
> notwithstanding what the government says.)

with all = when everything has been admitted.

> *With all his failings, he has always been a good father to us.*
> *With all your advantages, you ought to get a very good job.*
> *With all its drawbacks, country life suits me.*

for = considering that.

> *It's a fine day for mid-December.*
> *A hundred metres in twelve seconds – very fast for a boy!*
> *Grandmother has just sold her first painting – not bad for a
> seventy-year old.*
> *Fifty pounds! Very good for her first try.*

though, although = given that, even if.

> *Although it is long past midnight Peter is still at his desk.*
> *Mary refuses to help him although she is his sister.*
> *I won't ask for more money although I'm sure I'd get it.*

NOTE: *though* and *although* are interchangeable in the
examples given above. *Though* sometimes takes end
positions.

> *The weather was terrible. The ship sailed on time, though.*
> *I dropped my glasses. They didn't break, though.*

In the end position, *though* = however, nevertheless.

Support and opposition

against = not in agreement with; not in favour of.

> *I am against letting people drive cars through the park.*
> *We are against working on Sundays.*

NOTE: *an inoculation against yellow fever, vaccination against smallpox.* In such cases *against* is quite often replaced by *for*.

> *The dentist gave her an injection for (against) the pain.*

for = on the side of, in favour of

> *Who's for a picnic? Hands up please.*
> *Are you for the candidate or against him?*
> *My old captain has promised to speak for me to the factory manager.*
> *We want to hear both sides of your disagreement – the points for you and against you.*

with introduces the other party in the affair after verbs such as *quarrel, fight, argue, dispute, fall out (with), disagree.*

> *We quarrelled with the landlord about our dog.*
> *John and Mary have fallen out with each other.*
> *She argues with him about everything.*

It is also used after other verbs that imply reciprocal attitudes such as *agree, discuss, converse.*

Notice however, talk *to* someone (British), talk *with* someone (American). The latter form is nowadays heard in British speech too.

> *My brother fought with the Fifty-first in the desert.*
> *He was a member of the Fifty-first and fought as one of them.*
> but *David fought with his attackers for almost an hour.*

Here *with* = against. Compare:

> *She argued with David.* = She expressed disagreement with what David said = She argued against David.

Exception and absence

except	*instead of*	*but for*
without	*but*	*apart (from)*
instead		

instead (of) = as a substitute (for) in place (of):

> *I don't like fish! May I have an omelette instead?*
> *Mr Green is here instead of Mr Smith, who has a bad cold today.*
> *Can you come on Tuesday, instead of Monday as we had arranged?*

except shows incompleteness.

> *Everyone is present today except Mr Smith, who has gone to London.*
> *The bad news surprised all of us except Bob who had already heard it.*

but = except

> *Nobody but me has a key to the drawer.*
> *All but two of these pictures were painted in Greece.*
> *Everyone but David has accepted our invitation.*

but for = gives a kind of negative condition (see conditions on p. 315ff).

> *I would have left long ago but for Mary's kindness.* (If Mary were not so kind).
> *He would come to see you at once but for the difficulty of the return journey.* (If the return journey were not so difficult)

without = excluding, not including.

> *The work will cost £500 without extras.*
> *There are six of us, without the children. They make it ten.*

apart from = extra to, further to, not including.

> *We shall need three building workers apart from the engineer.*
> *Apart from a little trouble at first, we have no complaints about the flat.*

exercise 69

Restate these sentences, using a pronoun in place of the
noun or noun phrase in italic type. You may need to
re-order the sentence.

NOTE: articles and adjectives cannot occur with pronouns.

1 You must put your *coat* on at once.
2 She gave away *ten thousand pounds*.
3 The wireless operator sent off *an S.O.S.*
4 A merchant ship picked up *the signal* at once.
5 She slipped off *her shoes* while sitting in the cinema.
6 Father filled up *his pipe* and lit it.
7 Switch off *the light* and go to sleep.
8 He took off *his jacket* because he felt hot.
9 I'd like to talk over *some business matters* with you.
10 John was trying out *a new motorcycle* when it caught fire.
11 A policeman came and took down *our particulars*.
12 He had already put out *the fire*.
13 Please write down *everything* very carefully.
14 Captain Brown took over *command* from Captain Black.
15 They turned out the *battalion* for the occasion.
16 David has taken on *some extra work*.
17 We looked out *some old clothes* to give to the poor old man.
18 They broke off *their engagement* only two weeks before the
wedding date.
19 I don't like breaking in *new shoes*.
20 Peter broke up *some wood* and began to lay the fire.

● Expressions of place are often made by means of a prepositional phrase. *At, on, in, by, beside, above, below, under, underneath, over, between, among, behind, in front of,* are commonly used in place expressions.

exercise 70

Put in suitable preposition
NOTE: *At* a small place. *In* a larger place.

1 I will meet you . . . the office tomorrow.
2 John and I sit . . . each other at the same desk.
3 There is a dog sleeping . . . the table.
4 Please put your homework . . . my desk.
5 There was a good picture . . . the fireplace.
6 Mary, come and sit . . . me on this chair.
7 Our village lies . . . two high mountains.
8 A horse usually pulls a cart . . . it.
9 Peter lives . . . 19, Black Street.
10 His flat is . . . the second floor.
11 He has lived . . . that street for many years.
12 Black Street runs . . . Main Street and Green Avenue.
13 There is nothing new . . . the sun.
14 At noon the sun shone directly . . . the town.
15 I write with my back to the window to have the light . . . me.
16 She was born . . . a little village . . . Greece.
17 He used to swim . . . the sea and sunbathe . . . the sand.
18 He learned to stay . . . water for quite a long time.
19 The village was almost . . . the top of the mountain and the river was . . . the valley . . . .
20 Mother likes to sit . . . the window and watch the people passing . . . the street outside.

● Prepositions often indicate direction of movement:

> *To, from, by, into, out of, up, down, forwards, round, in,*
> *out, along, across, back, through, around, about, for,*
> *towards.*

exercise 71

Put in the correct prepositions or adverbial particles.

1 The distance . . . London . . . Edinburgh is four hundred miles.
2 In Britain we drive . . . the left and pass . . . the right.
3 A man must take off his hat when he goes . . . a church.
4 We stepped . . . the house . . . the garden.
5 The new bridge . . . the river measures five hundred yards . . . one side . . . the other.
6 It will take five minutes to walk . . . the bridge.
7 The pendulum of a clock goes . . . and . . . all the time.
8 It is not always easy to pass thread . . . the eye of a needle.
9 Walk . . . the street, turn . . . the right, cross . . . and take the second . . . your left.
10 Send a letter . . . Peter's home and ask them to send it . . . to his new address.
11 May I take this book . . . your bookcase? I'll bring it . . . tomorrow.
12 I don't want to drive . . . the town if I can go . . . it to rejoin the main road.
13 The price of gold always goes . . .; it never comes . . . again.
14 As my friend came . . . me I walked . . . to meet him.
15 The fire engine rushed . . . the streets . . . the blaze.
16 The doctor knocked and went . . . the room and asked the patient to sit . . . in bed.
17 It is often easy to climb . . . a tree but more difficult to come . . . again.

● Prepositions are often used in forming expressions of time. *At, in, by, on, within, up to, about, under, over, after, past, before, until,* commonly form part of time expressions. These words are really adverbial in sense. Notice where reasonable changes of meaning may be obtained by replacing one preposition or adverbial particle with another.

exercise 72

1 At this time of the year the sun sets . . . nine o'clock.
2 My cousin is staying with us . . . next Wednesday.
3 A cat nearly always goes to sleep . . . a meal.
4 Please be there . . . four o'clock precisely.
5 Peter is . . . his last year at school.
6 You will be able to speak good English . . . this time next year.
7 Please pay this account . . . seven days.
8 We shall all remain in this room . . . it is time to go home.
9 A number of people have run the hundred yards in . . . ten seconds.
10 I've been waiting here for . . . an hour! Peter ought to have come . . . this time.
11 Would you like to wait? The doctor will be out . . . eight o'clock.
12 If you are sure he will be back . . . then, I'll wait, thank you.
13 I shall need . . . three days to finish the work.
14 Peter hasn't written to us for . . . three months.
15 I suppose we shall hear from him . . . the next few days.
16 . . . the concert we went to a restaurant for a late supper.
17 I'm afraid I wasn't home . . . midnight as I had promised.
18 In fact, I didn't go to bed . . . one o'clock in the morning.
19 It was long . . . time for school when I woke this morning.
20 Mary's little brother was born . . . Christmas Day.

● Prepositions and adverbial particles sometimes indicate
changes in the nature, form, shape or appearance of
persons or materials: *of, from, into, out of,* and *up* are often
used to show change.

> *A table is made of wood*   (and is still a wooden table).
> *Paper is made from wood*   (but cannot ever be wood
> again).

exercise 73

Put in prepositions or adverbial particles. Notice where
changes in appearance, etc. are indicated by the
preposition.

1 Houses are built . . . bricks or stone.
2 Nylon is made . . . many different things.
3 A great many articles are made . . . nylon.
4 The large house was made . . . two flats.
5 The little boy's toys were made . . . boxes and cotton reels.
6 Make some flour . . . a paste with water.
7 Take some beef and cut it . . . small pieces.
8 Let's make . . . our quarrel and be friends again.
9 It was only a small shop but my father worked it . . . into a
fine business.
10 The angry customer was working himself . . . into a rage.
11 Your son is a good boy. He'll grow . . . a fine young man.
12 The discussion degenerated . . . a noisy argument.
13 The argument developed . . . a quarrel.
14 The quarrel ended . . . a fight, followed . . . a night . . . jail.
15 We still don't know how to turn base metal . . . gold.
16 Divide sixteen . . . four. Four is the square root . . . sixteen.
17 We shall divide the cake . . . six large pieces.
18 We shall share it . . . us.
19 These unfortunate people will try to create a new life . . .
the ruins of the old.

exercise 74

Supply the missing prepositions or adverbial particles.
(See notes to exercises 70–73)

1 Peter travels . . . and . . . his work by bus.
2 He gets . . . at the corner and gets . . . at the fifth stop.
3 Some boy kicked a football . . . the window . . . the room.
4 Our teacher gave me eighteen marks . . . twenty for history.
5 Don't hurry. I shall wait . . . home . . . you arrive.
6 Who is the girl . . . blue . . . dark brown hair?
7 I'll meet you . . . King's Cross . . . seven o'clock.
8 She sat . . . her arm . . . his waist.
9 Shall we go . . . foot or . . . bus?
10 He lives . . . Redwater, a village . . . Surrey.
11 This playground is for children . . . six and ten years old.
12 You will pay . . . your room . . . the month . . . advance.
13 The rider fell . . . his horse as it was jumping . . . a stream.
14 Close the door . . . you when you come . . . or go . . . the room.
15 I can see you hiding . . . me . . . that large tree.
16 John took some money . . . his pocket and put it . . . the table.
17 I'm afraid I've come . . . the house . . . any money . . . my pocket.
18 There's a jug full . . . milk . . . the shelf . . . the larder.
19 You may write . . . a pencil or . . . a pen.
20 Write these exercises either . . . ink or . . . pencil.

exercise 75

Fill in the missing prepositions and adverbial particles.

1 Mt. Everest is a little . . . 29,000 feet high.
2 Children . . . sixteen years . . . age are not admitted . . .
  their parents.
3 Boxers must not punch each other . . . the belt.
4 We sat . . . the shade . . . the branches . . . a huge, old tree.
5 Fish were jumping . . . the water as the boys stood . . . the
  stream.
6 Wait . . . nine o'clock. If John hasn't arrived . . . then, come
  . . . here.
7 There is a beautiful valley . . . two mountains which shelter
  it . . . the weather.
8 You won't be late . . . your train today. You are . . . plenty
  . . . time.
9 If we leave . . . the station . . . once we shall arrive . . . ten
  minutes . . . hand.
10 Subtract two . . . ten and you are left . . . eight.
11 Our football went . . . the air and . . . the garden . . . the
  street.
12 It came . . . right . . . front . . . John's sister who threw it . . .
  . . . us.
13 Go . . . this street, take the first . . . the left, and cross . . .
  . . . the other side.
14 You can't get . . . the river . . . a boat to take you there
  and . . . .
15 Isn't there a bridge . . . the river . . . the vicinity?
16 No, but there is a tunnel . . . it that goes straight . . . the
  other side.
17 Lean your bicycle . . . the fence and climb . . . our garden.
18 Mary was looking . . . some old snapshots when she found
  one . . . me.
19 I can't come . . . a decision . . . consulting my partners . . .
  the matter.
20 Mr Brown speaks well . . . almost any subject . . . the sun.

exercise 76

Supply the missing prepositions and adverbial particles to complete the sense of these sentences.

1 The car went . . . a bend . . . the road and disappeared . . . sight.
2 Peter's home is . . . a little village . . . Sussex.
3 . . . my surprise there was a five pound note . . . the envelope.
4 Because . . . the bad weather we had to stay . . . home.
5 We want to live our lives . . . prosperity, . . . peace . . . our neighbours.
6 I prefer driving . . . daylight to travelling . . . night.
7 Mary thinks that John is . . . love . . . Jane.
8 Mother doesn't care . . . the cinema unless there is a good film . . . .
9 Who takes care . . . the office when the manager is . . . . . . business?
10 Drive straight . . . five miles then turn . . . the main road . . . the left.
11 Many animals hunt . . . night and sleep . . . the day.
12 I'm going . . . the corner . . . the post office . . . some stamps.
13 Mary prefers the blue dress . . . the green one . . . the shop window.
14 Mr Brown was . . . work when thieves broke . . . his house.
15 Professor Smith gave a lecture . . . philosophy . . . the college hall.
16 I was feeling a little . . . the weather so I took a day . . . work.
17 What's the matter . . . the old gentleman . . . that stretcher?
18 There was no discussion . . . anything . . . importance . . . the meeting.
19 Let me tell you once and . . . all that I want nothing to do . . . you.
20 David is getting . . . very well . . . business. He's quite well . . . now.
21 Break this chocolate . . . pieces and share it . . . all the children.

exercise 77

Supply the missing prepositions and adverbial particles to complete the following sentences.

1 I'm afraid we can't agree . . . each other . . . anything.
2 If you are . . . trouble you ought to confide . . . someone and ask . . . advice.
3 Peter is acting . . . behalf . . . his ageing father who has confided his affairs . . . him.
4 Naturally, we shall agree . . . any reasonable proposal, to have done . . . the matter.
5 The firm's agents abroad act . . . instructions . . . London . . . letter.
6 Our solicitors will get . . . touch . . . you . . . a few days.
7 Thank you, I should like to settle . . . with the bankers.
8 It's no use complaining. You must adapt yourself . . . your new surroundings.
9 The value of the coins in the box amounted . . . three pounds or . . . .
10 Nobody came in answer . . . the call . . . help.
11 Apply your mind . . . the problem . . . hand and find the answer . . . it.
12 'Madam, I'm Adam' is the same if you read it . . . to . . . .
13 Common politeness is all I ask . . . you . . . return . . . mine.
14 Doctors turned . . . to attend . . . the people who were hurt . . . the crash.
15 I hear that George has applied . . . the position . . . manager . . . our new branch.
16 The judge has come . . . certain conclusions based . . . the evidence . . . the court.
17 The accused man benefited . . . the extent . . . ten thousand pounds . . . his uncle's death.
18 He was charged . . . murder and brought . . . . . . trial . . . jury.
19 The wires . . . the radio set must be connected . . . to an electrical circuit.
20 How much will you charge . . . doing that . . . me?

exercise 78

Supply suitable prepositions and adverbial particles.

1　We insist . . . prompt attention . . . correspondence . . . this office.

2　According . . . the newspapers fighting had broken . . . again . . . the tribesmen.

3　If you persist . . . telling lies . . . me I shall sue you . . . slander.

4　The judge sentenced him . . . death . . . accordance . . . the law.

5　Peter Brown aims . . . make a million pounds . . . the time he is thirty.

6　Students must not absent themselves . . . class . . . good reason.

7　Troops soon become acclimatised . . . conditions . . . the tropics.

8　The delay was due . . . negligence . . . the part . . . a secretary.

9　His Majesty graciously acceded . . . our request . . . an audience . . . him.

10　The lion came . . . Mr Brown who climbed . . . a tree.

11　Although I assured him . . . the lion's friendly intentions he stayed . . . there all night.

12　The bank manager was quite indifferent . . . our plea . . . a loan and turned a deaf ear . . . us.

13　He became addicted . . . drugs and went . . . bad . . . worse.

14　You can't class me . . . the average man in the street, I'm different . . . him.

15　John's brother is co-operating . . . him . . . writing a book . . . butterflies.

16　. . . the course . . . our conversation Peter alluded . . . certain personal matters.

17　Five pounds, sir! Don't try to bargain . . . me . . . the price . . . the goods.

18　I adhere . . . my first opinion . . . the absence . . . fresh evidence.

Phrasal verbs

Introductory notes

● **1** Many English verbs are composed of two or more words the first of which is the stem while the others are particles:

> *bring on, take over, turn off, switch on,* for example.

● **2** Very often the meaning of the phrasal verb is quite different from the usual meanings of its words taken separately.

> *The grocer has brought the butter.*
> *They have <u>brought</u> up a large family.*
> *She can make a cake.*
> *I can't <u>make out</u> what you say.*

● **3** With verbs expressing physical movement the following adverbial particles are commonly used:

> *about, above, across, along, around, away, backwards, before, behind, below, between, beyond, by, down, downward, forwards, in, inside, off, on, out, outside, over, past, round, through, under, up, upwards.*

Generally their meanings as adverbials are the same as their corresponding prepositional forms.

● There is seldom any difficulty with the meanings of phrasal verbs of movement when the usual meanings of the particles are already understood.

No object   **With object**

They	come go hurry run rush	away back down along off	We	send carry take push turn	something	away back in out off

● **4(a)** The adverbial particle of a phrasal verb follows it immediately when there is no object:

> *She <u>went away</u> to London.*
> *The boys <u>came out</u> to play.*

● **4(b)**   When there is a pronoun object, the adverbial particle must follow it immediately:

> *He put them <u>back</u>.*
> *We took him <u>along</u>.*

● **4(c)**   The adverbial particle may come before or after a noun object.

> *He put <u>down</u> some money.*
> *He put some money <u>down</u>.*
>
> *Take <u>off</u> your coat.*
> *Take your coat <u>off</u>.*

NOTE: When the object is long so that the verb and adverbial particle would be far apart, we prefer to place the particle immediately after the verb.

> *She brought <u>back</u> the book with the red cover and coloured illustrations.*

Idiomatic phrasal verbs

● As we have seen phrasal verbs are often idiomatic in their meanings. Here I shall set out the most common of these idiomatic phrasal verbs. Throughout this and the following pages prepositional and adverbial particles will be called *particles*. Essential differences between them can be seen on page 108.

break out = erupt

> *Fire broke out in the basement of the house.*
> *Cholera has broken out again in the city.*
> *War broke out on 3 September 1939.*

break into = enter by force

> *A thief broke into the house while we were away.*

break off = terminate before the expected time

> *The two governments could not agree and broke off their discussions.*
> *John and Mary have broken off their engagement.*

break down = lose control of one's emotions and weep
On hearing the sad news the poor woman broke down.

break down = have engine trouble, mechanical trouble
Water got into the cylinders and the car broke down.

break down = arrange into smaller parts
I can't understand this mass of statistics. Please break it down.

break up = break into small pieces
The workmen were breaking up stones with heavy hammers.

bring about = cause to happen
The new medicine brought about an improvement.

bring up = mention, refer to, introduce into a discussion
Mr Brown brought up the cost of living again.

bring up = raise children at home
Our grandmothers brought up their families with very little help (NOTE: Children are *educated* at school.)

bring on = cause an (unwelcome) development
Reading in bad light brings on a headache.

bring out = show by contrast, emphasise
A dark background brings out the colours of the subject of a photograph.

bring off = to manage, succeed in spite of seeming improbability
He said he'd sail right round the world and he brought it off.

bring round = revive someone
The old lady had fainted. We brought her round with some cold water.

call at = pay a short passing visit
I'll call at the office during the morning.
The ship calls at Alexandria, Piraeus and Naples on the way to London.

call on = pay a short visit to a person
Mr Brown will call on you to show you our new products.

call off = cancel an event
The football match was called off because of the snow.

call back = telephone again later
Thank you for ringing. I'll call you back as soon as I have the information you want.

call up (Am.) = ring up, telephone
John called up to invite us out.

call up = conscript

 Men over eighteen years of age were called up to fight the enemy.

catch up = reach, come abreast of

 They've just left – if you hurry you'll catch them up.

carry on = continue, do not stop

 I hope you will carry on doing these exercises.
 They are very good for you.

carry on with + NOUN (as above)

 Please carry on with your discussions.
 I am too tired to carry on with this tonight.

carry out = obey, execute

 Soldiers must carry out their orders.
 It will be difficult, but we shall carry out your instructions.

carry over = transfer (to the next page)

 Take the last figure on this page and carry it over to the top of the next page.

come about = happen

 How has it come about that everybody is present today?

come across = find by chance, meet by chance

 If you come across the book I lost please send it to me.

come back = return

come in = enter.

come by = acquire, become the possessor of

 (By dishonest means, perhaps?)

come off = take place, succeed

 His plans did not come off.

come round = recover from unconsciousness or visit (someone in the neighbourhood)

come upon = unexpectedly discover something

cut down = reduce, lessen

 We must cut down our production costs to the minimum.

cut out = reduce to nothing

 You must cut out your nasty habit of chewing gum in class

cut off = discontinue, interrupt

 They cut off the electricity, because we hadn't paid the bill.
 We were cut off in the middle of our telephone conversation.

cut back = prune, reduce in order to avoid expense

> *Most firms have cut back production programmes. They have also cut back plans for expansion.*

die down = lessen in intensity

> *The building burnt fiercely all night but slowly the flames died down towards morning.*
> *Don't talk to him now – wait till his anger dies down.*

die away = lessen in volume of sound

> *The sound of the military band died away in the distance.*

die out = become extinct

> *Many kinds of animals, birds and fish have died out within the last two hundred years.*

do away with = abolish

> *They have done away with trams in most cities in England.*

do up = fasten, button, zip, tie

> *Do up your overcoat. (But undo = unfasten, unbutton, unzip, untie.)*

do without = manage without

> *You must do without my help tomorrow as I shan't be here.*

do with (often with *could*)

> *I could do with a drink.* = I wouldn't say 'no' if you offered me a drink, I would be glad of a drink.

do a room up = paint, decorate walls, ceiling

do a room out = clean it thoroughly

do someone in = kill him, murder him

> (See also 'make and do' pages 212 ff)

draw up = prepare a document, an account

> *I must draw up a report on the business and ask the bank to draw up our account.*

draw up = come to a halt, bring to a stop

> *A large car drew up outside the hotel.*
> *I asked the taxi-driver to draw up near the house.*

draw on = approach

> *The days become shorter as winter draws on.*

drop in = pay a short, very informal visit

> *Drop in for a cup of tea and a chat one day.*
> *I'll drop in to see you one day next week.*

drop out = withdraw

> *One of the runners hurt his leg and dropped out of the race.*

drop off = become less, diminish, decrease

We were very keen on television at first but our interest has dropped off lately.

fall off

The club started with a hundred members but attendance has fallen off.

fall out = quarrel

Let's not fall out over such a little thing!

fall through = fail to reach desired end

I had dreamed of going to India but my plans fell through. I'm still here.

fall in with = meet by chance

Yesterday I fell in with a man who was at school with my father.

fall in with = coincide by chance, agree

Luckily, Mary's plans for the evening fell in with mine so we went out together.
If you decide to fall in with our proposal, please send your cheque.

find out = bring to light, discover

What have you found out about the robbery?

give in = admit defeat, yield

Everyone said I was wrong so I gave in to their opinions.
The problem was too difficult for me. I had to give in.

give up = cease, stop

I gave up cigarettes six months ago.
It is hard to give up an old habit.

give up = surrender, abandon

The wanted man gave himself up to the police.
Our old house was too far away from town so we gave up living in it.

give off = emit, exude (of smells)

The liquid in the bottle gave off a strong smell of almonds.
When water is heated it gives off steam.

give away = betray

The criminal's friend gave him away to the police.
He pretended to be angry but his eyes gave him away – he was laughing inside.

give out = become exhausted

The gold in the mine gave out eventually.
He struggled against the bear until his strength gave out.

give out = distribute

> *At the new hospital they give out free medicine to everybody.*
> *A boy stood at the door giving out programmes to the visitors.*

go off = explode (by itself), fire (by itself) like a gun

go off = become stale, begin to rot

> *This egg has gone off* (it has gone bad and it smells.)

go off = take place successfully

> *The celebrations went off very well.*

go on = don't stop, continue

> *Please go on with your game.*

go in = enter

go out = stop shining, stop burning

> *The fire has gone out and I'm cold.*
> *We saw a sudden flash and the lights went out.*

go in for = Take part in, participate

> *Are you going in for the 500 metres race this year?*
> *No, I'm going in for swimming.*

hold on = wait

> Operator: *Mr Brown's line is engaged – will you hold on please?*

hold out = resist, survive

> *Although they hadn't eaten or slept for a week the regiment held out for three more days.*

hold up = delay

> *I'm sorry to be late. I was held up in a traffic jam.*
> *Important matters have been held up during the Minister's absence.*

hold up = rob (using weapons)

> *Three masked men with pistols held up a bank yesterday.*

keep off = abstain from

> *The doctor says I must keep off cigarettes.*

keep up = to maintain in good order

> *I've sold my car. It cost too much to keep up.*

keep up with = go at the same (fast) pace

> *You've such long legs I can't keep up with you.*

keep up with = live at the same (higher) standards

> *It takes a lot of money to keep up with the people in this neighbourhood.*

keep up with = be up to date with

> *There are so many new books I can't keep up with my reading.*
> *The situation changes so often and so fast I can't keep up (with it).*

leave off = discontinue, stop

> *Leave off making that noise!*

let on = reveal (a secret)

> *Don't let on to anyone that we are going out.*

let off = discharge (guns and fireworks)

> *It was New Year's Eve and people were letting off fireworks in the street.*

let off = allow someone to go unpunished

> *As he had never been in trouble before the judge let him off with a warning.*
> *You have apologized for breaking the window so I'll let you off this time.*

let in for = cause

> *I'm afraid your absence let me in for a lot of extra work.*
> *Be careful! Don't let yourself in for anything unpleasant.*

let up = relent, relax

> *The storm started this morning and hasn't let up all day.*
> *We have almost finished, don't let up yet.*

let down = break a promise, cause disappointment

> *He promised to meet me here at ten, but he has let me down again.*
> *We have been partners for thirty years and have never let each other down.*

look after = take care of

> *Who looks after the baby while you are away?*

look for = try to find

> *I've lost my ball. I must look for it.*

look into = investigate

> *The police look into all kinds of crime.*

look like = resemble

> *Little Mary looks like her mother.*

look on = watch without taking part

> *Help me! Don't just look on while I'm trying to lift this sack.*

look out = mind, be careful

> *Look out for holes in the road surface.*

look to = expect from

> *I am the head so naturally the staff look to me for help and advice.*

make for = go (or come) towards

> *This ship is making for Liverpool.*
> *The mad dog made for me so I made off.*

make up = use cosmetics

> *Television actors have to make up very carefully.*

make up = fabricate, compose

> *She knew she would be late so began making up her excuse.*
> *Do you like the song? I made it up myself.*

make up into = We buy sugar in bulk and make it up into kilo packets
> *before selling it.*

make up for = compensate for

> *A few days holiday will make up for the extra work you did last week.*

make up to = flatter, try to find favour (with)

> *The cat is making up to me, hoping to get more milk.*

make off with = run away (with)

> *The thief made off with my wallet.*

make out = discern, (by sight, by hearing, understanding)

> *He speaks so fast I can't make out what he says.*
> *Can you make out this word? – it is badly written.*

make out = prepare an account, bill, cheque

> *Make your cheque out to 'The Express Co. Ltd.' please.*

make over = transfer property

> *When father retired he made the firm over to John and me.*

make do (with) = manage as well as one can (with)

> *There are no means of cooking anything today so please make do with a*
> *sandwich for lunch.*

make up one's mind = decide, form a firm opinion

> *I can't give you an answer immediately, – I need a few days to make up my*
> *mind whether to say 'yes' or 'no'.*

put by = save, not spend

> *I have put by a little money for my old age.*

put out = extinguish

> *Please put out the light before you go to sleep.*

put out = embarrass, put (someone) in an awkward position

> *The young man's tactless questions put me out.*

put off = postpone

> *We are very busy at the office, I must put off my holiday for a while.*

put up = lodge, find a bed

> *When I am in London I usually put up at my uncle's house*
> *My sister puts us up in Edinburgh.*

put up with = bear, stand, endure, suffer

> *He's very rude. I can't put up with his bad manners.*
> *Can you put up with the pain? the dentist asked.*

put off = mislead

> *I don't often make mistakes but your bad handwriting put me off.*

put off = cause to dislike, repel

> *It's the smell that puts me off beer.*
> *The title of the film put me off and I never went to see it.*

run out of = have no more

> *We've run out of sugar so we can't have coffee, today.*

be run down = weak, not well

> *The doctor says I'm run down and need a holiday.*

run down = speak ill of someone

> *She's always running someone down but never to anyone's face.*

stand by (see look on) = be present but take no action

> *Would you stand by while someone set fire to your house?*

stand by = support someone

> *Don't be afraid to speak to the boss . . . we'll all stand by you.*

stand by = be present in case one is needed. Act as reserve

> *We shall need six men to sail the boat and two to stand by.*
> *Miss Green stands by every morning in case one of our colleagues doesn't come in.*

stand for = signify, represent

> *The letters U.N.O. stand for United Nations Organisation.*

stand for = offer oneself as a candidate

> *Is Mr Brown standing for chairman? I shall stand for parliament next year.*

set about = make a start

> *John would like to join a club but doesn't know how to set about it.*

set off = ornament, embellish

> *She wore a plain black hat set off with a little bunch of violets.*

set out = start on a journey (see set off)

set out = display, arrange in good order

> *A shopkeeper sets out his goods to attract customers.*
> *Public speakers and writers should set out their points in logical sequence.*

set up = establish, form

> *The government has set up a committee.*
> *I should like to set up my own business.*

take after = be like, resemble

> *John takes after his father in character.*

take in = cheat, deceive

> *You can't take me in with your stories of green horses and castles in Spain.*

take on = engage

> *Tell the champion I'll take him on for 50,000 dollars.*

take off = leave the ground

> *Aeroplanes take off and land all day at this busy airport.*

take off = imitate in order to ridicule

> *Have you heard Peter taking off the Prime Minister? He's really funny.*

take to = feel a liking for

> *I took to this country on my very first day here.*

take up = begin to occupy oneself with

> *I must take up tennis again.*

take over = replace, act in place of

> *At ten o'clock John takes over from the captain.*
> *The captain takes over again from John in the morning.*

turn out = result

> *I've never made a cake before but this one has turned out very well.*
> *Don't worry, everything will turn out all right.*

turn out = produce

> *Our factory turns out five hundred cars every day.*

turn out = clothe, dress

> *Mrs Smith always turns her children out very clean and tidy.*
> *Her husband is well turned out too.*

turn down = reject

> The manager turned down my request for a day off.
> His application for the chief clerk's job was turned down.

turn up = appear when not expected

> We were surprised! John turned up at the party last night.

wear out = wear until useless

> These old shoes are still very good.
> Perhaps I'll never wear them out.
> I must buy some socks – how quickly they wear out!

work out = reckon (by arithmetic)

> How much is $3\frac{1}{4}$% of £268? Work out the answer in your head.

work out = prepare (programme, timetable)

> Have you worked out a timetable for the gymnasium yet?

write off = declare it valueless

> John's car was so badly damaged that the insurance company simply wrote it off.
> Business houses usually write off (cancel) bad debts after five years.

Idiomatic uses of *be* + particle

be about $\left.\right\}$ = to be somewhere in the immediate
be around $\left.\right\}$ neighbourhood

be at (something) = engaged in doing something

be back = have returned

be behind with = be in arrears with

be off = leave; start on a journey

be off = cancelled; not to take place

be on = take place (used for performances of all sorts)

> What's on at the local cinema?

be out = not to be considered

> I won't lend you £500 – that's out.

be out = not at home

be out for = trying hard to win or get

> He's out for the manager's job.

be over = finished (used for performances of all sorts)

be through with = have finished with

> *I'm not through with my work yet.*

be up = finished (used only for time)

be up = not in bed

be up = happening, usually something bad

> *What's up?*

be up to = engaged in some activity, usually mischievous or illegal

be up to = capable of

> *She's well up to her job as supervisor.*

Notice the following slogans, exclamations and the emphatic use of the particle at the beginning of some of these phrases.

Up with the workers!	*Be off!*
Get along with you!	*Get on!*
It's all over!	*Wake up!*
Carry on!	*Hands up!*
Out with your books!	*Down tools!*
Get out!	*Down with them all!*
Look out!	*On with the next number!*
Go away!	*Off with his head!*
Hands off!	*Away with them!*
Put it down!	
Out with it!	*I'm off!*
	Turn over!
Shut up!	*Sit up!*
Run along!	*Turn it off!*
Come along!	*Lights out!*
Throw it away!	
Eat up!	*Time's up!*
	Hand it over!
	Give it me back!

exercise 79

Fill in each blank space with a suitable particle.

1 Good afternoon, won't you come . . . and sit . . . ?
2 Don't sit with your head on the table! Sit . . . at once!
3 It is very hot. I could do . . . a cool drink.
4 John lost his books yesterday. He has been looking . . . them all day.
5 You go . . . to the station. I'll catch . . . with you in a few minutes.
6 These old shoes are worn . . . I can't wear them any longer.
7 Jack looks like his mother but he takes . . . his father.
8 I hope you are taking . . . these notes on the blackboard.
9 Let's not quarrel. I don't want to fall . . . with you.
10 I'm sorry we fell . . . . Let's make it . . . .
11 They hadn't paid the bill so the company cut . . . the electricity.
12 What time do you get . . . in the morning?
13 We get . . . at seven because we have to set . . . for the office at eight.
14 Mary sat . . . in front of the mirror to make . . . her face.
15 We are running . . . of oil. We must buy some before it runs . . . altogether.
16 The aeroplane for Rome takes . . . at six o'clock tomorrow morning.
17 Take two pounds of beef and cut it . . . into small pieces.
18 It is a difficult problem but John won't give . . . until he has worked it . . . .

exercise 80

Supply the verb particles to complete the sense of the verbs in the following sentences.

1 Peter never gets . . . before eight o'clock.
2 Will you wait . . . me if I am a little late?
3 Good-bye John! Look . . . yourself!
4 Please take your hat . . . when you enter the room.
5 George's wife waits . . . him, hand and foot.
6 Look . . . this picture carefully and try to make . . . the details.
7 As soon as the aircraft takes . . . you may smoke.
8 Mary's boys are growing . . . into fine young men.
9 Will you put the radio . . . please?
10 We generally wake . . . when the alarm clock goes . . . .
11 I'm afraid I've made a mistake in counting . . . these figures.
12 Behave yourself Jack! Don't carry . . . like a madman.
13 Mr Brown is so busy that he will have to give . . . some of his activities.
14 Thank you for speaking . . . for me when everybody was against me.
15 The poor dog was tied . . . to a post, without food or water.
16 When water boils the liquid changes . . . steam.
17 One must always keep . . . appearances.
18 Mr Black is looking . . . a nice little house with a garden.
19 She's so wrapped . . . in her work that she sometimes forgets to eat.
20 My car broke . . . a few miles from town.

Some idiomatic phrasal verbs with *up, down, on* and *out*

up as adverbial particle with verbs expressing attachment:
tie, link, connect

> Tie up a boat, a ship etc. to the quay.
> Tie your horse up to a tree.
> Our new radio-telephone system links up all the islands of
> the east coast.
> When they connect the cables up the village will have
> electricity.

up with verbs expressing consumption: *eat, drink, use,
burn, swallow* The addition of *up* conveys the idea of
complete consumption.

> Eat up your spinach = eat every bit of it.
> The men drank up their beer and left the bar.
> I've used up all my stamps; can you lend me one?
> Every tree for miles around was burnt up in the forest fire.
> The shark swallowed up a large fish in two seconds.

up is added to verbs such as: *break, cut, tear, mix, grind,
smash.* We obtain the idea of repetition.

> They have broken up all the firewood (into small pieces).
> Cut up some onions for the salad (into small pieces).
> He was tearing up old papers when I saw him.
> Please grind (up) these coffee beans.

up also goes with many other verbs to show thoroughness
and completeness of action: *close, shut, open, fasten, wrap,
pack, lock, sew, stitch, seal,* are among the more common
verbs with *up.*

> He locked the door.
> We always lock up before we go to bed.
> Open the windows a little, please.
> Don't open it right up!

up with verbs of movement: *walk, run, creep, sail, rush,
drive, come* etc. = approach

> The stranger came up to me and asked my name.
> I saw Peter coming and rushed up to him.

down often implies reduction in strength, volume of sound, intensity of light, or a reduction of activity. The following verbs are frequently found with *down*: *cut, calm, die, play something down, switch, turn, water, tone.*

> We must cut down our expenses.
> Turn down the radio, please. It's too loud.
> We water down our wine. It's too strong.

on frequently gives a sense of continuity, of non-interruption when it is used as a particle with idiomatic phrasal verbs: *go, keep, walk, write, read, speak, sleep, carry* are some of the more common verbs that take the particle *on*.

> The thunder roared but father slept on.
> Don't stop, read on to the end of the chapter.
> Shall we carry on doing these exercises?

NOTE:

> What's on at the cinema tonight?
> If I've nothing else on, I'll call on you this evening.

out with a 'sound' verb such as: *speak, shout, call, roar, yell, howl, blare,* and so on, indicates loudness and absence of restraint in the person or instrument producing the sound.

> The prisoner spoke out strongly against his accusers.
> A juke-box blared out the latest hits, making conversation impossible.

out with verbs of writing and drawing such as: *write, copy, type, draw, draft,* and *set,* often indicates extended writing or drawing; the item is written or drawn in full.

> Don't use abbreviations, write the words out.
> I've made some notes in shorthand. I'll type them out, now.

out with some verbs indicates erasure or extinction: *rub, blot, fade, phase, die, stamp, burn, cancel, cross, rule* are commonly found with *out*.

> Either cross out or rub out your mistakes and correct them.
> The radio programme faded out just before the news came on.
> Clouds of smoke blotted out the burning oil wells.
> The judge said that reckless driving must be stamped out.

exercise 81

Add suitable particles to complete the meaning of the verbs.

1 Our strength began to give . . . as we had not eaten for three days.
2 The stranger gave . . . that he was a teacher on holiday but in fact he was a detective.
3 The robbers held . . . the cashier at the point of a gun.
4 An epidemic of influenza has broken . . . in Paris.
5 We breathe . . . through our noses, generally.
6 When I swim I breathe . . . through my mouth.
7 The doctor told him to cut . . . alcohol completely.
8 Some children are more difficult to bring . . . than others.
9 I won't punish you this time. I'll let you . . . with a warning.
10 I'm sorry I am late again. I was held . . . by the heavy traffic in town.
11 It isn't pleasant to hear a man running . . . his friends in their absence.
12 Don't try to tell a lie to me. I am sure to catch you . . . .
13 The letters MP stand . . . Member of Parliament.
14 John's brother sold . . . everything before he went to Australia.
15 I'm afraid I've lost my way. Can you put me . . . for the night, please?
16 I must cut . . . my smoking to ten cigarettes a day.
17 Mind that dog! It will go . . . you.
18 Please speak . . . I can't make . . . what you are saying.
19 When George finishes his studies his father will set him . . . in business.
20 A big business company bought . . . all the property in the district.

exercise 82

Supply particles to complete the sense of the following sentences.

1 A black car drew . . . at the kerb and three masked men got . . . .
2 I hope you will succeed . . . your attempt to climb Mt Everest.
3 Our income is small so we must lay it . . . very carefully.
4 Expenses have been heavy and we have been drawing . . . our savings.
5 The eldest son of a lord generally succeeds . . . the title.
6 Don't be so catty! It's disloyal to run him . . . behind his back.
7 We met on business and soon struck . . . a lasting friendship.
8 Don't forget to draw . . . a list of their names before pay-day!
9 Go straight on for a mile then strike . . . to the left, across the moors.
10 Then make . . . the wood beside the lake.
11 He is still quite new to the work so we must not expect too much . . . him.
12 Your salary will depend . . . the quality of your work.
13 We shan't fall . . . over a trivial difference of opinion.
14 There was a rush to buy houses at first but it has fallen . . . lately.
15 It's a foreign coin that someone has passed . . . on me as a penny.
16 At sixty-five he wound . . . all his business affairs and went . . . on a world tour.
17 He's so vain! He is always showing . . . and boasting to us.
18 The authorities are inquiring . . . the unusual circumstances of the accident.
19 Don't be so impudent, young man! I shan't stand . . . it.
20 It was impossible to obtain payment of the debt so the creditor wrote it . . . .

exercise 83

Supply particles to complete the meaning of the verb.
Notice that two particles are occasionally required.

1 We discovered that burglars had broken . . . and made . . .
with all our valuables.
2 The couple couldn't agree . . . each other so they broke . . .
their engagement.
3 We shall pay . . . all we have borrowed and settle . . . with
everybody next month.
4 Mr Black will look . . . the office when he has taken . . .
from the old manager next Monday.
5 We all look . . . to seeing you when you come . . . from your
holiday next month.
6 The other side would not agree . . . our terms so we broke
. . . negotiations.
7 Although she wasn't looking . . . them, Mary came . . .
some old photographs in my drawer.
8 Peter didn't care . . . boxing very much and soon gave
it . . . .
9 There will be enough food to go . . . if we eke it . . . with
more potatoes.
10 Young George fell . . . bad company and took . . . bad
habits.
11 We all look . . . Dr Schweitzer, whose name stands . . . even
among great names.
12 He's such a boastful fellow, always showing . . . and
putting . . . airs.
13 My watch had run . . . as I had forgotten to wind it . . . the
night before.
14 Books on every subject were all mixed . . . together. It took
a week to sort them . . . .
15 The cyclist set . . . along the main road then turned . . . to
the right.
16 If you think I have wronged you, let's have it . . ., and then
make it . . . .
17 The police are looking . . . the matter but they haven't
found . . . who did it yet.

exercise 84

Complete these sentences by supplying the missing particles to the verbs.

1 His enthusiasm soon died . . . when he learnt that he had to get . . . at six every morning.
2 Peter is going to take . . . boxing so that he can look . . . himself if necessary.
3 The old Cornish language has quite died . . . now.
4 I'm afraid strong coffee doesn't agree . . . . me.
5 The sound of the departing train died . . . in the distance.
6 The angry man took . . . a fighting attitude.
7 When you make a promise you must carry it . . . .
8 Do you think Peter would agree . . . your suggestion?
9 Stick . . . your work and don't give . . . at the first sign of difficulty.
10 The bride stepped forward and took . . . her position by the bridegroom's side.
11 John's imitations are wonderful! He takes . . . famous people to the life!
12 Although he gave . . . that he was an earl's brother he was really an ordinary man.
13 We shan't be able to cut . . . our expenses until the winter is over.
14 These two were bitter enemies for years but they have made . . . their quarrel now.
15 The dress rehearsal of our play went . . . like clockwork.
16 This is very good work. Keep it . . . in the future.
17 Our teacher asked us to make . . . a story about a dog, a cat and a tree.
18 We shall have to cut . . . on luxuries if we are to afford a longer holiday.
19 David walks so fast that I can't keep . . . . . . him.
20 We ought not to look . . . . . . people simply because they are poor.

exercise 85

Supply the particles to complete these sentences.

1 We shall set . . . on our journey at nine o'clock tomorrow.
2 We can't have any coffee I'm afraid as we've run . . . of sugar.
3 We broke . . . negotiations when we found it impossible to agree . . . their demands.
4 He tells lies so plausibly it is difficult to see . . . him.
5 John lived in Africa where he picked . . . the native dialect.
6 An epidemic of influenza has broken . . . in the north.
7 Mary has gone shopping for a hat to go . . . her new coat.
8 He's so narrow-minded that we can't break . . . his prejudice against new ideas.
9 Father brought us a new carpet as our old one was wearing . . . in patches.
10 I like this journalist's articles because he sets . . . his facts so clearly.
11 Mr Smith's feelings were hurt because his wife had taken him . . . in public.
12 As we walked through the town our host pointed . . . its landmarks.
13 Although the firm is insolvent they will pay . . . their debts in two years.
14 Will you run . . . this column of figures and check the total, please?
15 My total doesn't agree . . . your figures.
16 The journey takes two hours by car if it doesn't break . . . on the way.
17 We shall now call . . . the chairman to close the meeting.
18 The government has called . . . all men between twenty and thirty to the army.
19 I'm calling . . . Mary to take her to a party.
20 His father cut him . . . with a pound and disowned him.

exercise 86

Supply the missing particles.

1 We must try to find . . . as much as we can about the world we live . . . .
2 Nobody can do . . . food and drink for very long.
3 Last night I came . . . an old friend I hadn't seen for years.
4 Good-bye Peter! I hope you get . . . well at the university.
5 We're saving . . . to buy a car so we do . . . other luxuries.
6 Boil the milk, Mary. It goes . . . quickly in this thundery weather.
7 There's only a little sugar left so we must eke it . . . until the grocer comes on Friday.
8 A witness said that the prisoner had sworn . . . him very rudely.
9 We always share . . . all of our profit among the members of the club.
10 John bought . . . his business partners, then began to buy . . . all the shares.
11 The family is poor now. They have sold . . . all their valuables, piece by piece.
12 The asking price was twenty pounds but he knocked it . . . to me for twelve.
13 Good-bye, I must ring . . . now. I'll ring . . . again tomorrow.
14 Peter has gone to the park to try . . . his new model aeroplane.
15 My enthusiasm for adventure began to wear . . . after a few months in the desert.
16 Loneliness and hardship began to wear me . . . , physically and mentally.
17 Our local radio station closes . . . at midnight.
18 Mary is going to dress . . . as Columbine at the fancy dress ball.
19 That soldier was very untidy. Captain Black dressed him . . . in good, round terms.
20 David is annoying, he always turns . . . late for his appointments.

Auxiliary verbs and special finites

do, does: Simple Present auxiliary

did: Simple Past auxiliary

be: Passive voice auxiliary

am, are, is: Present Continuous Form and Present (Passive voice) auxiliaries.

was, were: Past Continuous and Past Passive auxiliaries.

were: Present Conditional of *be (If I were you)*

have, has: Present Perfect and Future *(He has gone, I shall have gone)*

had: Past Perfect and Past Conditional

shall, will: Future Perfect auxiliary

should, would: Future Conditional

* *have + object + past participle:* Causative (use *do, did* etc. for questions and negatives)

used to: This is a past time form. There is no present form.

to be to: Future by Command

* *to have to:* Circumstantial obligation (use *do, did,* etc. for questions and negatives).

ought to, should: Advice, opinion, recommendation

must, need: Compulsion and obligation

can: Ability, permission, opportunity

may: Permission, probability

might: Permission, probability

needn't: Removal of compulsion

- Only the verbs marked with an asterisk make their negative and interrogative forms in the same way as principal finite verbs. *Didn't use to* is often heard but *used not to* is considered better style.

- *Dare:* This verb forms its negative and interrogative as an auxiliary verb when it is followed by an infinitive (always without *to*)

> *Dare we disobey our orders?*
> *They dared <u>not</u> attack in daylight.*

Colloquially, *didn't dare* is often used as a negative past form.

> *He didn't dare to <u>go</u> near such a savage dog.*

Also *wouldn't dare* and *won't dare* are quite usual.

Compulsion

Direct obligation or necessity

Must (Pres.)
Had to (Past)
Must (Fut.)

Circumstantial necessity

Have to (Pres.)
Had to (Past)
Shall/will have to (Fut.)

By command or authority

Am/are/is to (Pres.)
Was/were to (Past)
Am/are/is to (Fut.)

Prohibition

Must not (Pres.)
Was/were not to (Past)
Must not (Fut.)
Had not to (Past)

Negative (Removal of compulsion)

Don't have to (Pres.)
Didn't have to (Past)
Shan't (won't) have to (Fut.)
Needn't (Pres.)
Need
Needn't
Haven't got to (Pres.)
Hadn't got (Past)
Shan't/won't have to (Fut.)

By command or authority

Am not/are not/is not to (Pres. & Fut.)
Was not/were not to (Past)

Unnecessary past actions

Didn't need to (so probably didn't)
Needn't have (but did)

● The form *hadn't to* is falling into disuse, probably because it resembles the colloquial *hadn't got to* form and causes confusion of meaning. For the same reason I have not elaborated the *haven't to forms of prohibition in the present*.

> *I haven't to tell you* = I am not to tell you.

Must is a word with which we cannot argue, which we cannot refuse to obey. It is imperative in sense. We use *must* when we give orders and when we exercise direct authority over other people and wish to make them obey without question. We use *must* when we wish to make people understand the absolute necessity of compliance with someone's wishes either for their own good, the general good or the speaker's satisfaction. Consider the following sentences:

> 1 *Students must be in class by 9 a.m.*
> 2 *People must pay taxes to the Government.*
> 3 *You may go to the dance but you must be home by midnight.*
> 4 *Good whisky must mature for five years.*
> 5 *You must keep photographic film away from light.*
> 6 *John must study for three hours every evening.*

● In the first three sentences we can easily picture

> 1 a head-master speaking with authority,
> 2 a civil servant in a high position (or a magistrate)
> 3 a parent.

Each of these three persons *imposes his inescapable will on his audience*. In the remaining sentences the persons who are talking state *what is absolutely necessary if success is desired*.

● *Must* expresses a direct command from a person or body to a person or body, or it expresses a necessary, unavoidable procedure. If we fail to do what we *must* do the consequences are usually undesirable ones. Notice that *must* often implies strong recommendation.

> *You must read Galbraith's latest book.*
> *You really must visit Edinburgh next summer.*

Direct prohibition:
must not

● Grammatically *must not* is the negative form of *must*. However in sense it is not the negative. *Must not* expresses commands also. The commands are that it is important *not* to do this or that. Let us examine some examples.

> 1 *Students must not smoke in classrooms.*
> 2 *Members of the public must not get on the bus before it stops.*
> 3 *Women and girls must not wear lipstick in church.*
> 4 *The children must not eat any more chocolate today.*
> 5 *Carpets must not stay in the sunlight.*
> 6 *You must not pour boiling water into a thick glass.*

● Clearly these first four sentences are all commands from a person or body in authority;

> 1 the headmaster
> 2 the transport company
> 3 a priest
> 4 a parent

Each of those four persons gives a command which forbids the action. They command by prohibition. In numbers **5** and **6** the sentences tell us what it is essential to avoid.

exercise 87

Express (a) absolute commands or (b) absolute necessity in the following sentences by inserting *must*. State whether the sentence expresses (a) or (b)

1 A man . . . eat to live.
2 People . . . send their children to school.
3 We . . . obey the law.
4 John . . . be in bed by ten o'clock.
5 We . . . speak English in school.

exercise 88 exercise 89

Express (a) prohibition or (b) absolute necessity to refrain from doing something by adding *must not*.

1 Car drivers . . . pass a red traffic signal.
2 Students . . . smoke during lessons.
3 People . . . obstruct a policeman.
4 The milkman . . . put water in the milk.
5 You . . . use naked lights near petrol.

Express direct compulsion or prohibition by putting *must* or *must not* in the following sentences.

1 We are late. We . . . hurry up.
2 You . . . strike a match near petrol.
3 People . . . have clean water to drink.
4 The children . . . go to bed at eight o'clock.
5 They . . . read in bed.
6 I . . . pay the electricity bill today.
7 Students . . . smoke in class.
8 Soldiers . . . obey their officers.
9 Boys . . . address their teachers as 'Sir'
10 You . . . steal from my trees.
11 People . . . keep their dogs on a lead in the street.
12 You . . . speak only in English in class.
13 Men . . . take their hats off in church.
14 He is ill. We . . . call a doctor.
15 . . . you make such a terrible noise?
16 A man . . . work or starve.
17 I . . . stay out very late, father says.
18 We . . . all be home before nine o'clock.
19 Boys . . . wear their caps in the building.
20 Everyone . . . come to school every day.

Circumstantial compulsion

- *Have to*: We use this form when we wish to indicate that indirect circumstances, which have no connection with direct commands and prohibitions, influence our actions. It is absolutely necessary to conform to circumstances. Consider the following sentences:

  1 *The last bus leaves in ten minutes so, I have to say good-night now.*
  2 *In his position in the firm he has to travel very often.*
  3 *They can't afford to buy a house so they have to rent a flat.*
  4 *Father is better now but we still have to help him to walk.*

- We can see that the necessity does not come from any direct command or prohibition. It is a product of the circumstances, e.g. if I don't catch the last bus I shall *have to* walk home or take a taxi, perhaps; but I shall not be breaking any rule or regulation or disobeying any order or prohibition. Consider the following pair of sentences:

  (a) *John has to shave every morning.*
  (b) *Soldiers must shave every morning.*

- In (a) John has a strong dark beard and this circumstance obliges him to shave every morning. In (b) soldiers obey an order to shave every morning. Of course, a soldier may say,

  We have to shave every morning,

  but then he is thinking of the general circumstances of army life and not the orders that create them.

  NOTE: The expression *have got to* is frequently used in conversation to indicate circumstantial compulsion, in the present. (*has got to* third person singular).

- The future forms are *shall have to* and *will have to*, (*got* is not used) and the past forms are *had to* or sometimes *had got to*.

  NOTE: *Do not*, *does not* and *did not* + *have to* are the negative forms:

  I don't have to be home before ten o'clock.

COLCHESTER INSTITUTE
SHEEPEN ROAD
TELE 761660 COLCHESTER

CIRCUMSTANTIAL
COMPULSION

exercise 90

Express (a) direct compulsion or (b) circumstantial
necessity in each of the following sentences. Notice where
either is possible, with any changes in emphasis and tone.

1 Most people . . . work hard to make a living.
2 Candidates . . . answer at least five examination questions.
3 Many people . . . be careful of what they eat. They get fat
   easily!
4 Some public men . . . read their speeches. They have bad
   memories.
5 Soldiers . . . obey a superior officer.
6 In winter we . . . wear heavy clothing because of the cold.
7 Everybody . . . eat and drink in order to live.
8 Many Londoners work rather far from home. They . . . take
   lunch in a canteen.
9 Mr Smith lost all his money in business and . . . sell his car.
   (past!)
10 The patient is very ill so we . . . call a doctor at once.
11 Peter's train leaves at seven in the morning so he . . . get up
   early.
12 I'm sorry I haven't enough cash on me. I'll . . . give you a
   cheque.
13 John's car has broken down so he . . . go to work by bus.
14 The cost of living has gone up again. We . . . economise a
   little.
15 I'm afraid your leg is broken and you . . . stay in bed for
   some time.
16 My husband's parents are not very well off so he . . . help
   them a little.
17 Father says we . . . all go to church next Sunday morning.
18 I will not accept a refusal, John. You . . . stay the week-end
   with us.
19 George has just telephoned to say he has missed the last
   train. He . . . to stay in town for the night.
20 All students . . . submit homework at least twice a week.

exercise 91

Insert the appropriate past forms *was, were to* + *principal verb infinitive* or *had to* + *principal verb infinitive.*

1 We ran short of money so . . . borrow some from a friend.
2 The headmaster said we . . . not to leave the classroom without permission.
3 John's doctor told him that he . . . not to smoke more than five cigarettes a day.
4 Their house was burned down and they . . . live in an hotel.
5 Peter had forgotten his book so he . . . look on with me.
6 He used to be very poor and . . . live very simply for many years.
7 One of the gentlemen felt unwell and . . . go home.
8 One of the racehorses fell and broke a leg. We . . . shoot it.
9 Peter . . . buy books with the money. However, he bought a microscope instead.
10 The train . . . leave at ten-thirty. Mary . . . leave home at half past nine to be sure of catching it.
11 Our teacher told us we . . . write three pages of composition.
12 I . . . stay in all the afternoon to finish it.
13 The telegram said that Captain Brown . . . report for duty at once.
14 He . . . go away without seeing us as he had no time.
15 Mary . . . wash the dishes and Peter . . . wipe them dry. They forgot and Mother . . . do them herself.
16 When we were in Poona we . . . lie down in the afternoon, it was so hot.
17 Father decided that they . . . attend his old school.
18 Although Mary . . . meet me at seven o'clock she didn't arrive till half past eight. I . . . wait for a very long time.
19 The cashier was dishonest so the manager . . . discharge him.
20 The old gentleman felt very tired and . . . go to bed for an hour.

Removal of compulsion

- We have already seen that we cannot remove compulsion by adding *not* to *must*. We simply convert a command into a prohibition. When we wish to remove compulsion and show that a person may do as he wishes, that he may please himself in fact, we use the *need not* construction.

  This form shows that there is neither direct nor circumstantial obligation. Let us examine some examples.

  1 *It's only seven o'clock so we needn't hurry so much.*
  2 *Father needn't wait for me this morning, I can go to town in George's car.*
  3 *We needn't get up early tomorrow as it is a holiday.*

  The above sentences all show that there is no necessity, that there is no compulsion. Father can wait if he likes but there is no necessity. We can get up early if we wish, but we may also stay in bed. There is a perfectly free choice.

- In this connection we often hear *don't have to, haven't got to* forms. The future form is *shall not/will not need to* or *shall not/will not have to*. *Needn't* is also frequently used in the future sense.

- Past form: *didn't have to* or *hadn't got to* are commonly used and *didn't need to* is also heard.

  NOTE: *Have not to* and *had not to* are direct prohibitions and do not remove compulsion or necessity.

  I haven't to leave the room = I must not leave the room.

  NOTE: the *have not to* forms to express prohibition are not commonly used nowadays, probably because they can cause confusion with other uses of *have*.

exercise 92

Remove compulsion and prohibition from these
sentences by using *need not (needn't)* or *do not have
to/doesn't have to* forms in place of must.

NOTE: *must* = compulsion, *must not* = prohibition.

1 You must begin at once.
2 She must drink all her milk.
3 We must get up before seven.
4 He must go to bed early.
5 I must pay in cash.
6 He mustn't do it again.
7 She must leave today.
8 We must work for a living.
9 They mustn't write in ink.
10 He mustn't stay later than five o'clock.
11 She must prepare this lesson for Monday.
12 You mustn't be rude!
13 They must finish the job tonight.
14 You must pronounce the 'H' in 'hotel'.
15 He mustn't sit in a draught.
16 We mustn't spend more than five pounds.
17 She must have some new clothes. (careful! some = any).
18 Peter must take his medicine before meals.
19 They mustn't come here again.
20 She must stay in bed for a fortnight.

Unnecessary
past effort

- *Need not have (needn't have)* with the past participle is the form we use when we indicate that although a certain action took place, it was unnecessary or a waste of time or effort. Consider the following examples.

    1 *John needn't have sent an expensive telegram. A letter would have arrived within two days.*
    2 *You needn't have dressed so early. The wedding is at three o'clock and it is only ten o'clock now.*
    3 *You needn't have given the waiter five pounds. Fifty pence would have been more than enough.*
    4 *You needn't have bought such a beautiful gift, dear. A big bunch of flowers would have pleased me as much.*

- After the clause which contains the *needn't have* form there is an unspoken parenthesis which may refer to any previous present or past time: In number **1** he did send a telegram; in **2** 'but I see you have dressed already' in **3** 'but you gave him five pounds' in **4** 'you have given me this beautiful gift'. All of the examples refer to actions which have happened before the present moment of speaking. In the speaker's opinion the action was unnecessary, a waste of time and effort, or otherwise undesirable, but it did happen.

NOTE: The main verb *to need* which means *to require, to be in want of, to be in need of,* is an ordinary, regular transitive verb and its forms are those we normally use for verbs like *walk, talk,* etc.

However, note the affirmative construction *need + infinitive* (without *to*):

Nobody need ever learn our secret (unless one of us tells).

Also note the transferred negative in sentences such as:

I don't suppose you need come early = I suppose you needn't come early.

NOTE: The auxiliary forms are *needn't, needn't have,* and in the interrogative, *need* ... The reply to a *need* question is either *No, you needn't,* or *Yes, you must,*

   (a) *Need I come home early?   Yes, you must*
   (b) *Need he pay all the money in cash?   No, he needn't.*

Wasted effort
(present and future)

- *Need not* or *needn't* is often used when we want to show that to make an attempt or effort now or in the future will simply invite failure. There is no hope of success. Consider the following sentences:

   1 *George <u>needn't</u> propose marriage to me. I shall refuse him.*
   2 *You <u>needn't</u> try to tell lies. We already know the truth.*
   3 *I <u>needn't</u> expect sympathy from such a hard-hearted skinflint as you.*

These sentences all show that

   1 George will waste his time.
   2 that trying to tell lies is useless.
   3 tears are useless and a waste of time, and to expect sympathy is out of the question.

The form *needn't* is used for the present and future.

Use *didn't have to, didn't need to* and *needn't have* forms appropriately to complete the sense of the following sentences.

NOTE: I *didn't have to* write (so I probably didn't) and I *needn't* have written (I did write, although it wasn't necessary).

1 We were lucky we (go) out in such bad weather.
2 Good morning, sir. You (come) all this way just to see me.
3 She (buy) so much meat. We shall never eat it all.
4 We had plenty of fruit in the house so we (buy) any last week.
5 Although she (tell) me about him, I'm glad that she did.
6 Peter (give) the waiter such a large tip. He (tip) him at all.
7 My exercise was correct so I (write) it out again.
8 He was very wealthy and (work) nearly so hard as he did.
9 Mary was very hurt. Peter (speak) to her in such a rude manner.
10 Father felt much better and (take) his medicine any more.
11 John (play) those records so loudly. You could hear them for miles.
12 We used to like going for walks, especially as we (spend) much money.
13 You (make) those foolish remarks. Everybody was very upset.
14 The boys felt very shy. Fortunately, they (say) very much.
15 David went to the cinema as he (do) any homework.
16 What beautiful flowers! You (bring) me so many, thank you.
17 I took John's bicycle. I knew that I (ask) his permission.
18 You (sell) your car. You had enough money in the bank.
19 The doctor said I was quite well so I (stay) in bed any more.
20 What an impolite man! He (slam) the door like that.

Certainty:
must, can't

- We use *must* when we wish to show that what we say is beyond doubt – at least to the speaker.

    1 *Father is not at home, he is not at the office. He must be at the club.*

    2 *My husband always comes straight home from the office. Tonight he is a little late. His train must be late.*

    3 *What! Five pounds for a hat like that! You must think I'm crazy!*

    4 *That man never works. He must get his money somewhere, he spends plenty.*

    5 *I always see Mr Smith coming home in the early morning. He must work at nights.*

    6 *You can't lose a large bunch of keys, Mary! Look in all your pockets. It must be in one of them.*

In these sentences *must* shows a deduction from the evidence that you obtain from the other sentences in the example or from the speaker's experience. The speaker has no doubt at all that what she says is the correct conclusion. The *must not* form can never be used in this way. Instead we use *can't* when we are sure of a negative deduction:

Peter can't have arrived in Australia yet. He left only last week.

Today can't be the tenth of the month: I'm sure yesterday was.

Mary can't have forgotten to telephone: she is always punctual about this.

172

Must have, can't have

- When we want to express what, we feel, certainly happened at any time in the past or at any time before the present moment of speaking we use *must have* with the past participle for all persons singular and plural. Again the speaker makes deductions from the evidence or from experience and gives an opinion which he believes to be reasonable. Thus:

  1 *The late John Brown left all his money to the Cats' Home. He <u>must have been</u> out of his mind!*
  2 *Mary's father has given her five thousand pounds. He <u>must have found</u> a gold mine.*
  3 *If the accused man bought poison of which his wife later died, he <u>must have given</u> it to her.*
  4 *The new clerk used to work for Messrs. Brown and Company. He <u>must have gained</u> good experience there.*
  5 *I can't find my ticket. I <u>must have lost</u> it!*

  The phrases with *must* express the speaker's certainty and that he feels that these are the most logical inferences to make from the facts.

- If the speaker wishes to indicate that in his opinion the action must have occupied a period of past time or a period of time before the moment of speaking he uses the form *must have been* for all persons and adds the present participle of the principal verb. Thus:

  1 *My watch had stopped but as I had covered ten miles I <u>must have been walking</u> for nearly three hours.*
  2 *Peter <u>must have been living</u> alone when his wife was in hospital. I know he didn't go to his parents' home.*
  3 *You look very tired. You <u>must have been working</u> hard.*
  4 *What a lovely sun tan! She <u>must have been sunbathing</u> all the time she was in Spain.*
  5 *My dear, if you say I was talking in my sleep last night then I <u>must have been (talking).</u>*

- We use both Certainty of the Past forms to express

  (a) before now in the present and
  (b) before then in the past.

  There are no separate forms for Present Perfect and Past Perfect.

exercise 94

Put in *must* or *must have*, *can't* and *can't have* to indicate (a) certainty in the present or (b) certainty of the past. *Can't* and *can't have* are the negative forms; they express certainty in the speaker's mind about the impossibility of the matter.

1 The alarm clock is ringing. It . . . be time to get up.
2 He ate a huge supper. He . . . been very hungry.
3 John was very late last night. He . . . missed the last bus.
4 The car won't start this morning. The battery . . . be flat.
5 The doctor's car is outside the Browns' house. Someone . . . be ill there.
6 I have no cigarettes left. I . . . smoked more than usual this morning.
7 Peter looks very brown. He . . . had wonderful weather on his holiday.
8 There wasn't any milk this morning. The milkman . . . forgotten to leave it.
9 I feel hungry. It . . . be almost dinner time.
10 Who is knocking at the door? It . . . be your father so early!
11 By Jove, it's hot today! The thermometer . . . be showing a hundred degrees.
12 Professor Jones has been here for ages. He . . . passed his seventieth birthday years ago.
13 Here's John, already. He . . . caught the earlier train.
14 I've finished my homework, sir.   You . . . finished already.
15 The streets are all white this morning. It . . . snowed during the night.
16 She has three diplomas, although she is so young. She . . . studied very hard.
17 I feel a draught. The windows . . . be open.
18 Yes, they are. Mary . . . forgotten to close them.
19 We all have good appetites. The sea air . . . made us hungry.
20 Peter missed his train this morning. He . . . arrived late at the office.

Ought to

- We must understand clearly that *ought to* and *must* have nothing in common. *Must* expresses compulsion, *ought to* does not express anything of the kind.

- We use *ought to* when the speaker wishes to show what he thinks is desirable, proper and right. The speaker gives his advice. He may remind another person of what he, the speaker, feels is right, correct, just and proper. He does not command or prohibit. Usually he is not in a position to do either or if he is in a position to command and prohibit, he does not wish to do so. More often than not he simply wishes to show that a certain action is in accordance with accepted, normal standards of behaviour, common sense or custom. He advises and recommends. The following sentences and explanations will help to clarify the matter.

Recommendation and Advice

1. *Peter is losing weight. He <u>ought to see</u> a doctor.*
2. *Forty cigarettes a day! You <u>ought not to</u> smoke so much.*
3. *You were up late last night so you <u>ought to go</u> to bed early tonight.*

The speaker in these sentences gives his advice, which the other person may take or leave as he likes. There is no compulsion.

Ought to sometimes indicates reasonable supposition or expectations:

It's nearly five o'clock. Father ought to be home soon.
He ought to arrive on the next bus, or the one after that.

Reminders of Duty or Obligation

1. *Mary <u>ought to be</u> more respectful to her parents.*
2. *John <u>ought to wipe</u> his feet before he comes into the house.*
3. *George is so well off! He <u>ought to help</u> his parents a little.*
4. *You <u>ought to raise</u> your hat to a lady when you meet her.*

Here again the speaker does not impose his wishes upon anyone. He merely points out what he thinks is right and proper. It is for the others to conform or not as they wish. The speaker indicates what he thinks would be a good thing to do.

exercise 95

Put in *must* to indicate certainty of the present and *ought to* to express an opinion of what is desirable.

1 Poor fellow! He really . . . have better luck.
2 There's nobody at home. They . . . be away on holiday.
3 It's a beautiful car. It . . . cost a lot of money.
4 Mary's a wonderful cook. She . . . come and live with us.
5 John's boxing is better than the champion's He . . . be champion.
6 There's the postman! It . . . be nine o'clock already.
7 He's so punctual he . . . have a medal.
8 Mary's so convincing! She . . . act on the stage!
9 You've been working very hard. You . . . feel rather tired now.
10 These compositions are too well written. I'm afraid John . . . be copying from a book.
11 Peter is so well informed. Really, he . . . stand for Parliament.
12 Look at the red carpet! The mayor . . . be expecting important visitors.
13 She hasn't eaten for twenty-four hours. She . . . feel very hungry.
14 Father's very late tonight. He . . . working overtime.
15 Peter has a fine tenor voice. He . . . be an opera singer.
16 English people drink a lot of tea. They . . . like it, I suppose.
17 The dog is barking. There . . . be a stranger outside the house.
18 Stop beating that donkey! Somebody . . . beat you like that.
19 In such wet weather they . . . close the school.
20 If you say that, you . . . dislike rain very much.

exercise 96

Express advice or recommendation by putting in *ought to*, *ought not to (oughtn't to)* when the negative makes sense.

1   You look tired. You . . . rest for an hour or two.
2   It's a bargain at five pounds. We . . . buy it, I think.
3   Don't you think we . . . examine it first?
4   She . . . wear her reading glasses when she's writing.
5   Peter . . . eat such heavy meals just before bedtime.
6   Boys . . . to walk about with their hands in their pockets.
7   Everybody . . . be able to go to school.
8   George . . . see his dentist about his broken tooth.
9   Mary says he . . . have it out.
10 Don't you think we . . . study more?
11 I'm getting old, I . . . retire from business.
12 Perhaps, but even retired people . . . have something to do.
13 That's true. Everybody . . . take an interest in a particular subject.
14 Of course! You . . . write a book about your career in commerce.
15 No, I can't agree that I . . . do that.
16 Are there parts of it that the public . . . to know?
17 Peter, my boy, you . . . to speak to me like that.
18 . . . we to spend so much money, John?
19 I suppose we . . . to, but you have only one birthday a year.
20 You . . . practise these exercises more often.

● Sometimes the speaker wishes to indicate an action which, in his opinion, would be very desirable. He gives opinions but, unfortunately, cannot compel or oblige anybody to act on them. Examine the following sentences. Very often they cannot be put into effect.

1 *What a fine speech! That man ought to be Prime Minister.*
2 *I love the summer! It ought to be summer all the year round.*
3 *He is such a brave soldier! They ought to give him a decoration.*
4 *Mary is a clever woman and ought to have a better job.*

Most of these sentences make recommendations that cannot be put into effect or that are unlikely to find acceptance.

exercise 97

Put in *must* or *ought* to complete these sentences. Notice the difference of meaning caused by using one of these forms in place of the other. Use *must not (mustn't)* or *ought not to (oughtn't to)* for the negative form.

1 My wife says I . . . smoke a pipe sometimes.
2 The doctor told me that I . . . rest for six months.
3 My bankers inform me that I . . . deposit some money today.
4 Really John you . . . be more careful with a bank account.
5 You are right! I . . . not to write so many cheques.
6 However, we . . . economise until Easter.
7 Business . . . be better by then, I think.
8 A soldier . . . obey his officers.
9 Don't you think Peter . . . try to become an officer?
10 Mary says that all schoolgirls . . . play hockey.
11 All children . . . play games in the open air.

Probability

- The speaker cannot say for certain what will happen but, with knowledge of what usually happens in given circumstances he can forecast with reasonable certainty. He can say what he thinks is probable. Examine these sentences:

  1 *There is a red sky tonight so we <u>ought to have</u> a fine day tomorrow.*
  2 *All my old friends will be at the party so it <u>ought to be</u> a lovely evening.*
  3 *It is the right time of year for fishing. You <u>ought to catch</u> a few good salmon.*
  4 *The soil here is heavy clay. Roses <u>ought to grow</u> very well on it.*

The speaker gives his opinion. He states what he thinks is quite probable. He says nothing about certainty. Who would state, with certainty, tomorrow's weather in England, or the number of fish he would catch? Note that *should = ought to* in all the above examples, and that it is often used,

It's almost six o'clock. Mary should be home soon.

exercise 98

Express reasonable probability or opinion by using *ought to* or *should* or give strong expression of the speaker's certainty by using *must* to make good sense.

1 There isn't much to do. I . . . finish it in half an hour.
2 John left an hour ago! He . . . arrive any minute now.
3 He made a lot of money in business. He . . . be almost a millionaire.
4 You can borrow my overcoat. It . . . fit you well enough.
5 There's frost on the ground. It . . . be freezing outside.
6 It . . . get warmer later in the morning.
7 Mary . . . speak good French after so long in Paris.
8 The light has gone out. The bulb . . . be burnt out.
9 Why do they make such expensive cars? Somebody . . . buy them, I suppose.
10 All our friends are coming so we . . . have a lovely time.
11 She has studied hard. I feel she . . . pass the examination.
12 If the roads are fairly clear we . . . do the journey in an hour.
13 You . . . intend to drive very fast indeed, then.
14 On the contrary, you . . . crawl along if it takes you much longer.
15 Our cat is lost. She . . . be somewhere in the neighbourhood.
16 Father isn't in, I'm sorry. He . . . come home from work soon, though.
17 If you walk towards the station you . . . meet him on the way.
18 George . . . be very hungry. He missed lunch today.
19 John . . . feel pleased with the result of the election.
20 Mary's cold . . . to be better now. It's a fortnight since she caught it.

Recommendations, advice, probability in the past

- When we wish to indicate
  - (a) that in the past a particular procedure would have been better or
  - (b) that it would have been better to fulfil a certain duty or obligation or
  - (c) in view of the evidence, a certain development was probable,

we use the form *ought to have* with the past participle of the principal verb. Now, sentences of the (a) and (b) types can only imply that the speaker knows that the desirable action did not take place. There is a negative sense in such statements. Frequently the speaker is being 'wise after the event.' In (c) type sentences we do not always imply a negative. The general trend of the conversation will indicate negation or otherwise. Consider these examples:

  - (a) George *ought to have saved* his money when he was young.
    The child had a low temperature. You *ought to have called* a doctor.
  - (b) I'm sorry you didn't sleep well. I *ought to have warned you* there is a ghost in that room.
    I ought to have replied to your letter earlier but I have been very busy.
    John went to the dance alone last night. He *ought to have taken* Mary.
  - (c) We haven't any milk in the refrigerator! Never mind, the milkman *ought to have left* some on the doorstep.
    John *ought to have received* our telegram by now, so he may arrive soon.

In all of these examples we either express an unconfirmed opinion as to what was probable or that people did not do what they ought to have done. The first example in (c) indicates the reasonable but so far unconfirmed opinion that the milkman has already called and left the milk. The first example in (a) may be read in either sense, according to context. (Probably he saved – I don't know) or (Although it was desirable he didn't do it). In all these examples *should have* can replace *ought to have*.

should,
should have

- These auxiliary forms are often used, especially in conversation, instead of *ought to* and *ought to have*. Do not confuse them with the conditional forms which they resemble.

NOTE: After *should* we omit *to,*

    (a) *You should have knocked before you came in.*
    (b) *You should have seen the manager's face!*

exercise 99

Express what would have been better by using *ought to have* and *should have* or what we feel certainly happened by using *must have* constructions (negative = *can't have* = very improbable or impossible).

1 She . . . told me and then I could have helped her.
2 Peter . . . left earlier. He wouldn't have been late then.
3 There's no cake left. The children . . . eaten it all, can they?
4 That's too bad of them. They . . . left a little for us.
5 No sir, this isn't the way to Cambridge. You . . . turned right two miles back.
6 Thank you, I . . . misread my road map.
7 Mary . . . gone to school yesterday instead of the cinema.
8 She . . . played truant in the afternoon!
9 Mr Black says that he . . . studied mathematics more than he did.
10 My front tyre has a puncture. I . . . ridden over some broken glass.
11 You . . . kept your eyes open and ridden round it.
12 Peter . . . asked permission before taking John's bicycle.
13 He . . . (not) taken it without asking. John was quite annoyed.
14 There's no salt in the soup. Mother . . . forgotten to put it in.
15 She . . . been dreaming while she was in the kitchen.
16 She . . . (not) said that when she wasn't sure of the facts.
17 You are right. She . . . (not) known whether it was true or not.
18 It . . . been the cheese I ate that kept me awake last night.
19 We . . . (not) eaten such a large meal. We couldn't sleep for hours.
20 The children . . . (not) spent as much as you say they did.

have to, must, ought to

● Remember that *must* expresses a direct command, which must be obeyed, or absolute necessity, while *have to* expresses the compulsion imposed by circumstances. *Ought to* is advisory and neither commands or compels. *Ought to* expresses the speaker's opinion, or what is desirable in his view.

NOTE: *should* is very often used in place of *ought to* with no change of meaning. *Would* cannot be used in this way.

exercise 100

Insert the appropriate forms of *must, have to* or *ought to* as required. Note where any of them can be used and the difference in meaning between the sentences when one form is used instead of the others.

1 It isn't wise to keep large sums of money in your pocket, John. You ... put it in the bank.
2 You are quite right Peter, but today is Friday and I ... pay my employees.
3 Of course, John. Under the law an employer ... pay wages regularly.
4 A man ... eat to live, but really Peter, you are so fat I think you ... eat a little less.
5 Yes, John. My doctor says I ... not eat chocolate, potatoes and bread.

exercise 100 (contd.)

6 If I go on getting fatter I . . . buy new clothes, soon. (Future!)

7 Mary is still too young. She . . . have her father's consent before she can marry, according to law.

8 Even when a girl is old enough, she . . . ask her parent's blessing when she marries.

9 People . . . clean their teeth at least once a day. Children especially . . . see a dentist regularly. They . . . not eat too many sweets.

10 The people of a country . . . obey the law but the law . . . be just.

11 . . . the children make such a noise? . . . n't they to be in bed?

12 I can't repair it myself so I . . . send it to the garage. (Future!)

13 I suppose I . . . try to learn a little about cars. Repairs are so expensive!

14 Every Friday John . . . stay at an hotel in town as he finishes work very late.

15 Poor fellow! He . . . look for a house nearer his office.

16 Yes, I suppose he . . . , or perhaps he . . . try to find an office nearer home.

17 The present office is too small so he . . . look for another, anyway.

18 It is very hot this afternoon. I don't think we . . . go out before five o'clock, in such heat.

19 You are quite right, but I'm afraid I . . . keep an appointment at three o'clock. My cousin is arriving by train and I . . . go to the station.

20 Students . . . do their homework regularly because it helps them.

can, could:
permission

- People often use *can* as a synonym of *may*, that is to say, when they ask or give permission. Very strict speakers still consider that *can* is a vulgarism when we use it in this way, but ninety-nine people out of a hundred do say *can* when they ask for permission or grant it. *May* of course, is also very common and most people use both forms. There is a feeling that *may* is a little more polite. Let us now look at some examples of *can* in which permission is asked or granted.

  1 *Father says I can go to the cinema on Saturday.*
  2 *The patient can have a little exercise tomorrow.*
  3 *John can come in the car with me if he is in a hurry.*
  4 *My uncle left me a fortune but I can have only £20 a month until I'm twenty-five.*
  5 *They can see the children's programme on television and then they must go to bed.*
  6 *Mary can't eat ice-cream until her cold is better.*

  In all of these sentences someone, not necessarily the speaker, gives or refuses permission. In **2** probably the doctor permits a little exercise, in **4** the terms of his uncle's will do not permit more than £20 a month, in **5** and **6** obviously mother is talking, giving and withholding permission.

- When we talk of permission to do something in the future we know about the permission now. If we did not know now, it would not be possible to speak of it. Thus, as in sentences **1** and **2** *can* indicates present permission for a future event. For permission in the past we use *could*,

  The doctor said I could get up, yesterday.
  The boys could go wherever they liked when they were on holiday last summer.

Change *can* to show past permission. Change the forms of other verbs in the sentence where necessary to express the past.

1 The children can stay up late tonight. (last night).
2 Mary can use my dictionary when she wants to.
3 You can spend up to five pounds.
4 John can wear my tie if he needs one.
5 The patient can get up today. The doctor said . . . .
6 The children can have their friends to tea on Wednesdays.
7 Jane can stay here whenever she wants to.
8 You can't have your dog in the house at night.
9 Of course, they can eat as much as they want to at meals.
10 They can't eat anything between meals.
11 She can't stay out after dark.
12 No, John, you can't have more than two pieces of cake.
13 At Aunt Mary's I can have as much as I like.
14 You can't go to the cinema without permission.
15 David can come to town with us every day, in our car.
16 Mary can pick as many flowers as she likes, in our garden.
17 Jane can't marry without her father's consent.
18 We can have pocket money every Saturday, for sweets.
19 She can have a very small glass of wine on birthdays and holidays.
20 Nobody can leave the country without a passport.

can: ability

- *Can, shall be able to, will be able to, could.*
  can is used in a number of ways. First we use it to denote physical or mental ability within persons themselves. (They are in no way dependent on any other person's permission. They exercise their own faculties and skill). When we say sentences like those that follow we show that a person is capable of performing some task or activity because of his physical, mental or intellectual ability.

  1 *John can swim like a fish.*
  2 *Mary can say her lessons backwards.*
  3 *We can all learn English if we try.*
  4 *Peter can speak English well but he can't write it so well.*
  5 *My brother can sing like a bird.*
  6 *A policeman can usually direct you if you ask him the way.*

- Let us turn these sentences into future ones with the meaning that these people will acquire some physical, mental or intellectual ability or skill. Then we do not use any form of the verb *can* but prefer the expressions *shall be able, will be able,* So the sentences now read:

  1 *John will be able to swim like a fish (after a few more lessons).*
  2 *We shall all be able to learn English if we try.*
  3 *Peter will be able to speak English well (in a few months' time).*

- When we speak of past ability we generally use *could*. The sentences,

  Mary could say her lesson backwards,
  My brother could sing like a bird,
  Peter couldn't write English very well,

  are examples of skill and ability in the past.

exercise 102

Convert the following sentences from present to (a) past
and (b) future time. Add the phrase given in the brackets
to show that ability is or was still to be acquired. Use the
shall/will be able and *was/were able* forms throughout the
exercise.

1   He can swim like a fish. (soon)
2   She can sing beautifully. (after months of training)
3   I can do it. (by trying very hard)
4   They can win the game. (by playing good football)
5   He can understand the lesson. (by paying careful
    attention)
6   She can cook a good dinner. (after a fortnight of married
    life)
7   He can drive a car. (soon)
8   She can walk without a stick. (in a few weeks time)
9   We can dance quite well. (after the tenth lesson)
10 I can eat anything. (after my operation)
11 You can write with your left hand. (with practice)
12 He can play tennis. (when his broken arm heals)
13 We can lift heavy weights. (by developing our muscles)
14 They can remember everything. (by repeating it to
    themselves twice)
15 She can knit anything. (after a few minutes' study of the
    pattern)
16 I can advise you. (when I have more information)
17 He can take his examination. (at the next sitting)
18 You can speak good English too. (in time)
19 She can keep house very well. (with a little more
    experience)
20 They can leave hospital. (before long)

exercise 103

Express the following sentences (a) in the past, and (b) in the future. Take care to notice whether they refer to permission or to ability and whether the *could* or *able to* forms apply.

1 Doctors can cure nearly everything.
2 They can't prevent the common cold, though.
3 You can put your car in our garage for the night.
4 Children under sixteen can't see that film.
5 You can't come in here without knocking.
6 Children can't know so much as their parents.
7 Peter can't speak Spanish very well.
8 Mary can practise on our piano if she wants to.
9 You can always have dinner at the club.
10 He says that he can't come till next week.
11 The children can have some chocolate if they are good.
12 I am so tired I can't keep my eyes open.
13 David's new car can do eighty miles an hour.
14 Are you sure he can drive safely at that speed?
15 Nobody can do more than thirty miles an hour in town.
16 Mother says we can have a party at Christmas.
17 I can't remember her name.
18 She can make the best apple pie in England.
19 You can't stay here all night in this cold weather.
20 I can't give you his address without his permission.

can: physical circumstance and achievement

● Again, personal permission does not play any part in our condition. We think, this time, of a person's health, his physical or mental capacity, and consider his abilities with regard to them and how they limit or permit certain activities. Let us examine the following examples.

1 *I feel a little better and <u>can</u> (am able to) take light food.*
2 *Mother is very old now but she <u>can</u> (is able to) look after the house.*
3 *The poor old fellow is so surprised that he <u>cannot</u> (is unable to) speak.*
4 *John suffers from rheumatism but he <u>can</u> (is able to) earn a living in the summer months.*

Future forms are *shall/will be able to.* The past forms are usually *was/were able to* although *could* is sometimes heard.

● When we speak of what someone really managed to do, what someone really achieved, the *was/were able to* forms are always used.

1 *M. Poirot <u>was able to</u> solve the Mystery of the Haunted House.*
2 *The dying man <u>was able</u> to call for a priest.*
3 *Mary <u>was able</u> to answer every question at the examination.*
4 *The young boxer <u>was able</u> to beat the champion on points.*

All these examples show that someone managed to achieve his objective.

● *Can* is also used to show that a person is free, that is, not engaged, either at present or at some future time.

(a) *The doctor can see you now.*
(b) *We can meet you next Friday evening.*

The sentences show (a) that the doctor is now free to see us and (b) that we have no other engagement to prevent our meeting on Friday.

● *Shall be able to* and *will be able to* are often used for the future although *can* is also very common. Both *could* and *was/were able to* forms are used to express the past.

exercise 104

Show (a) past opportunity and (b) future opportunity in each of the following sentences by using the correct *able to* form in place of *can*. Change the times of other verbs where it is necessary.

1 The shop isn't busy. I can make a cup of coffee quickly.
2 The rain has stopped at last. We can take a walk in the park.
3 School doesn't break up for another month. We can spend a few weeks at the seaside.
4 It's my day off work so I can do as I please.
5 Mary's new dress is ready. She can wear it at the birthday party.
6 Mr Brown is working in France. He can polish up his French while he's there.
7 As I am free for the moment I can glance through the newspaper.
8 When you go to the Palace you can see the Queen.
9 He sells his pictures so he can buy a fine house.
10 David has a small boat. We can go fishing when we want to.
11 When the light is good we can take wonderful snapshots.
12 John is very busy. He can't come out with you.
13 Mary has to go to school. She can't go to the country for the day.
14 We don't have to get up early. We can have breakfast in bed.
15 Mary sees the Prime Minister every day but she can't speak to him.
16 Peter has to study very hard. He can't spend his time on amusements.
17 David's car has just broken down. He can't use it for the next few days.
18 Jane lives in town so she can go to the theatre almost any evening.
19 As you aren't driving you can sleep in the back of the car.

can: have the opportunity

● Sometimes we use *can* in this sense. A few examples will illustrate the definition more clearly.

   1 *While John is in London he can learn English.*
   2 *I like to play a game of tennis occasionally but I can't play today. I'm busy.*
   3 *It is my day off so I can spend a few hours with my friends.*
   4 *Mary can call on mother while she is in Putney. Mother lives near there.*
   5 *Studying is easier when one can use the big public libraries.*
   6 *The rain has stopped so we can go home without an umbrella.*

● In these examples physical, mental or personal ability and permission have nothing to do with the circumstances.

   1 John is in London. Therefore the *opportunities* for learning English are all around him. We do not mention his ability or anybody's permission.
   2 The speaker has *no opportunity* to play today.
   3 The circumstances of my employment are responsible. Personal ability or permission do not play a part in this *opportunity*.
   4 Again the circumstances that Mary is going to Putney and mother lives near there, make the *opportunity*.
   5 In London there are big public libraries. This circumstance helps students who use them. The students' ability is not discussed, they have the *opportunity* to use these libraries.
   6 The rain has nothing to do with anybody's ability or with permission. It has stopped and the circumstance is quite independent (so far) of mortal skill or permission. We have the *opportunity* to go home in dry weather.

● We express past opportunities with *was/were able to* and future opportunities with *shall/will be able to,*

   I was able to finish writing my letters while you were out.
   Mary will be able to practise her English when she goes to London.

193

may:
permission

We have already discussed *can* and have seen that although *can* is often used in asking and granting permission, people often use *may* instead of *can*. The following examples will show this usage:

1 *May I go to the zoo on Sunday?*
2 *I'm sorry to disturb you. May I come in?*
3 *Mother says we may invite our friends to tea on Saturday.*
4 *The boys may stay up late tonight as they have no lessons tomorrow.*
5 *You may not smoke in this room.*

Most people feel that *may* and *may not (mayn't)* are more formal and polite than *can* and *can't*. Certainly, *may*, and *may not (mayn't)* forms are better when politeness is essential to the sense of the sentence:

May I smoke?
May I ask you for the next dance?
May we help you?

● *May* serves for the present and future time forms while *might* is used when speaking of the past. *Might* often indicates the speaker's fear of receiving a negative answer or that he feels that he is asking a little too much. We use *might* when we ask permission with more than usual deference:

Might my friend stay with you over the weekend?
Might I borrow your razor?

Complete the sense of the following sentences by using
may or *might* to replace *can* in asking or granting
permission.

1   Can I speak to you for a moment?
2   Of course you can. What is it?
3   They can't spend more than five pounds.
4   Can I have another cup of coffee, please?
5   You certainly can, sir. Black or white?
6   Can't we stay up a little later this evening?
7   Yes, you can, if you are good boys.
8   Can my friend sit near the door, please?
9   Can I ask you a favour?
10 Naturally, you can ask anything within reason.
11 Thank you. Can I say that you will recommend me?
12 Yes, you can, at all times.
13 Can't I spend my own money as I like?
14 No, you can't. You must pay your taxes first.
15 Can I ring you up shortly after ten o'clock?
16 I'm afraid I can't receive telephone calls at work.
17 She can't go out until her cold is quite better.
18 Can she get up and sit by the fire?
19 Can John borrow your book, Peter?
20 I'm sorry, I need mine. He can have it tomorrow if he likes.

may, might:
possibility and probability

● We sometimes wish to indicate the mere possibility of truth or correctness of a statement or deduction without being definite about it. We do not go so far as to suggest strong probability, however. The following examples will help to show how we use this form:

1 *Father hasn't come home yet. He may be working late at the office.*
2 *If John is free on Saturday he might go to the football match.*
3 *Peter might go to Australia next year.*
4 *This is a very bad cut. It may need several stitches.*
5 *Don't say such things! Somebody might hear you.*

We use *might* when we stress that the possibility is very slight:

My nephew might become Prime Minister when he grows up. Yes, he might, and pigs might fly!

● When *might* is used to express bare possibility without much probability there is no difference in timing between *may* and *might*. Both forms are used to express the present and future equally, except for the difference in the degree of probability.

exercise 106

Put in *may* or *might* to express probability or bare possibility.

1 Take your coat! It . . . turn cold in the evening.
2 Some of these old papers . . . be quite valuable.
3 They . . . have some historical importance.
4 Don't wait up for me. I . . . have to stay in town tonight.
5 The newspapers say the railwaymen . . . go on strike today.
6 Father is late tonight. He . . . have extra work at the office.
7 He usually rings up. The office 'phone . . . be out of order, of course.
8 The doctor is very busy at present. He . . . have to ask for an assistant.
9 Don't drink that water. It . . . be infected although it looks clean.
10 David says that Peter . . . come round this afternoon.
11 John . . . write a book about his experiences.
12 It . . . make very interesting reading.
13 He . . . earn a lot of money with it.
14 On the other hand, people . . . not buy it.
15 . . . not Mr Brown write poetry just to amuse himself?
16 Buy a lottery ticket. You . . . win a large prize.
17 Mrs Brown . . . have to go out this afternoon.
18 I don't know much about mathematics but I . . . be able to help you.
19 You never can tell! Peter . . . become Prime Minister one day.
20 He . . . become nothing at all, if he doesn't begin to work soon.

Unrealised possibility

- Sometimes we think of the past and remember all the things that were possible then although, for one reason or another, these past opportunities and possibilities were not realised but remained unfulfilled. We build our 'castles in the air' as we imagine the circumstances that would, possibly, exist now if we had done this or if we hadn't done that. We remember our past mistakes of omission and commission, and imagine what *might have been* the result if we had not made these mistakes. We also remember past actions that, if they had taken place, *might have had* pleasant results, or *might have developed* differently. Consider:

  1 *If Napoleon had not gone to Moscow he <u>might</u> have become master of the world.*
  2 *If John had set the alarm clock, he <u>might</u> have wakened in time for his train.*
  3 *The firm <u>might</u> have lost all its money if it had followed Mr Black's advice.*

  Notice the conditional parts of these sentences are what is contradictory to fact: *If I had* (but I did not) and *if I hadn't* (but I did).

- The same form *might have* is also used when we suggest, without definite knowledge, that a particular action took place, since it was possible. Consider the following sentences:

  1 *How did Peter get to school so quickly?*
  He <u>might have</u> come on his bicycle. (Perhaps he came on his bicycle).
  2 *What makes the soup taste so funny?*
  The cook <u>might have</u> used sugar instead of salt. (Perhaps the cook used sugar instead of salt).

exercise 107

Put in *may, might, might have* to express permission, probability or bare possibility, and unrealised past possibility.

1 ... we have a party tomorrow, please? Yes, you ....
2 Mother said we ... invite six friends to tea.
3 I can't find my pocket book. It ... be in my other jacket.
4 I ... left it there when I changed my suit.
5 ... David stay the night, please?
6 I thought he ... want to, so his room is ready for him.
7 Why did you take such a risk? You ... died!
8 That was a silly thing to do. She ... hurt herself badly.
9 Peter rang up to say that he ... n't be able to come tomorrow.
10 My father advised me that my plans ... n't be successful.
11 If I had listened I ... lost less time and money.
12 We ... n't use the car without asking permission.
13 If we ask we ... n't get permission.
14 ... I ask you a very personal question?
15 If John had gone to Australia he ... become a sheep farmer.
16 When I go to London I ... spend a few days seeing the sights.
17 Mr Brown comes from your home town, so you ... have friends in common.
18 It's a very large town, you know. He ... n't even know our district.
19 If she has any money she ... go abroad next summer.
20 Do you think Peter ... make a success of his new job?

Causative:
have, get

- Sometimes another person or organisation provides services for individual members of the public. The individual himself may pay for these services or not according to the particular circumstances. To indicate that another person provides the service, we use the forms *have*, and *has* followed by the direct object of the sentence followed by the past participle of the principal verb, e.g.

    I have my car washed.   (have + object + participle)

  I shall not wash my car. Somebody else will wash the car for me. I shall ask someone at the garage to wash the car. I shall cause him to perform a service for me. Consider:

    1 *Jane has her hair done at an expensive hairdresser's.*
    2 *They always have their garden looked after by a professional gardener.*

  In **1** Jane does not look after her own hair by herself; she pays an expensive hairdresser to do it. The family are not amateur gardeners in the second example; they pay a man to look after the garden.

- The form *get* is often used instead of *have*. The future forms are *shall/will have* or *shall/will get*. Causative *have* and *get* are both constructed as finite verbs, that is, the auxiliary verbs (do, be, have, will, shall, etc.) are used to form the various forms.

  NOTE: In the imperative *have* and *get* do not mean quite the same thing. Very often *get* seems much more imperative than *have*, or much less polite. Look at these examples.

    1(a) *Have your shoes cleaned by the boot boy.*
     (b) *Get your shoes cleaned!*
    2(a) *Please have my evening suit pressed. I'm dining out.*
     (b) *Get my trousers pressed! I'm dining out.*

- The remark in **1**(a) could come from a hotel manager to a guest and **2**(a) from a polite guest to the manager. The remark in **1**(b) is what we might hear from an angry corporal or parent. In **2**(b) we see a rather impolite demand for a service. It is peremptory in tone.

exercise 108

Rewrite these sentences, using the *have/get* causative
construction. The causative subject is in italic type to help
you. Convert it to the subject form where necessary.

1   *Peter* takes his car to the garage for cleaning.
2   *Mary*'s clothes are made for her in Paris.
3   *I* go to the barber's at the corner for my haircut.
4   *The Smiths'* new house will be built on the hill.
5   *George* gives his suits out for pressing to the shop in the
    High Street.
6   *Mrs Black* always asks shopkeepers to send the shopping
    home.
7   *Our* shoes are mended at Last's.
8   A man comes to clean *their* windows once a week.
9   A daily woman does the heavy work for *Jane*.
10 *Our* teeth are inspected every six months.
11 *The manager*'s letters are typed for him.
12 Somebody posts them for *him*, too.
13 A maid cleans *my* room every morning.
14 *I* always request them to bring coffee to my room.
15 *David*'s newspapers are delivered before breakfast.
16 An old man looks after *my mother*'s garden.
17 Somebody does *my* laundry for me.
18 A carpenter is making a new front door for *us*.
19 *We* are going to ask someone to translate this.
20 *They* asked the baker to bake a cake for them.

Personal causative: *have*

- We sometimes use a form of words to emphasise that a person will be caused to do something and the interest and emphasis are not so much in the action to be performed as in the person who will do it. Let us discuss some examples.

  1 *We have heard the previous speakers. Now <u>we shall have</u> the chairman give his opinion.*
  2 *You have broken my window with your football. <u>I'll have</u> you pay for it.*
  3 *Don't be impudent young man! <u>I'll have</u> you know that I'm manager here.*
  4 *My wife and I would like to <u>have you</u> come to dinner one evening, soon.*
  5 *What a woman! <u>She had me</u> show her every hat in the shop!*

- In these examples people are caused to act by invitation, request, demand or even force, according to circumstances. **1** clearly shows that he shall request the chairman's opinion. **3** implies that I'll make you understand in no gentle manner!

- Notice that interrogative and negative constructions take the auxiliaries (*do, does, did, shall, will*, etc.) and that the particle *to* is not used before the infinitive.

  NOTE: Confusion sometimes arises between these causative forms and forms that retain the particle *to* with the infinitive,

  We shall have Mr Smith <u>to help</u> us.

In sentences of this kind *have* is not causative and the infinitive introduces clauses of purpose or reason: Mr Smith will be with us for the purpose of helping us (in order to help us).

exercise 109

Rewrite these sentences using the Personal (have) Causative forms.

1 She asked them to show her dozens of pairs of shoes.
2 We told the taxi driver to call at seven o'clock.
3 The manager asked me to copy it out again.
4 He made me write it all in my best handwriting!
5 Will you ask the doctor to come, please?
6 Mrs Brown told the maid to wash everything in the house.
7 She made me polish all the furniture, too.
8 Our teacher made us learn the poem by heart.
9 Please ask my secretary to come here at once. (imperative)
10 They invited him to come for the weekend.
11 The doctor ordered us to keep all the windows open.
12 That customer caused me to run up and down the ladder twenty times.
13 The bank manager will ask the police to keep an eye on the bank.
14 Sergeant Smith ordered the platoon to double march for two miles.
15 Tell Miss Brown to write this letter with three copies. (imperative)
16 A policeman requested me to accompany him to the police station.
17 His mother made him apologise for his rudeness.
18 Tell someone to mend that broken window. (imperative)
19 Ask the porter to bring my luggage, please. (imperative)
20 Father made John go back upstairs to turn his bedroom light off.

NOTE: *She'll have him eating out of her hand in a week.*

This construction is often used when the intention is to show a continuous situation which will be created by training, teaching, persuading, coaxing, etc.

Personal causative: *get*

- The person who uses this form of speech intends to cause someone to act, usually by persuasion or careful 'management.' There is not, generally, any suggestion of authority or command. Kind words, flattery, gentle persuasion, coaxing and suggestion may all be used to get somebody to do something. Let us examine some examples:

  1 *Mrs Smith can get her husband to do anything she likes.*
  2 *Mary has spent all her pocket money. She'll get her father to give her some more.*
  3 *Peter has been trying to get Mary to marry him for years.*
  4 *The directors hope to get the bank to advance sufficient capital.*
  5 *I couldn't get the camel to kneel down so I had to use a ladder.*

- All of these examples are concerned with persuading, managing or manoeuvring people or animals so that they do what others want them to do. Firmness may be used **5**, although the other methods described above are more usual, especially when we are dealing with people.

- It is clear the *get* forms can only replace *have* forms in the Personal Causative (*have*) sense very rarely since the ideas in the speaker's mind are not the same when he uses one or other of these forms.

- Notice that in the *get* form the infinitive particle *to* is not dropped and that the interrogative and negative forms take the auxiliaries (*do, does, did, shall, will*, etc.).

exercise 110

Rewrite these sentences using the *have* and *get* Personal Causative forms according to the sense required.

1   I'll persuade John to help me carry my bags.
2   Mary will ask her father to clean her bicycle.
3   Try to coax the baby to eat his breakfast.
4   Our teacher made us all speak English only, in class.
5   You can't make the milkman walk up six flights of stairs every day.
6   The proprietor ordered us to repair the damage at once.
7   He tried to force Peter to pay for it out of his pocket money.
8   In the end we persuaded him to take a few pence from each of us.
9   I'll ask my brother to look after the house while we are away.
10 She made me repeat everything three times over.
11 Mary is going to ask her husband to plant a cherry tree.
12 Mary's husband obliges her to account for every penny she spends.
13 Do you think we can persuade the mayor to come to our party?
14 Captain Brown ordered his men to paint the flag pole.
15 She's so charming that she can make anybody do anything for her.
16 Shall we request Mr White to play the piano for us?
17 Let's ask the orchestra to play some gipsy music, shall we?
18 The minister ordered everybody to come to his room at once.
19 I wish I could make my birthday come a little sooner.
20 She coaxed the strange dog to eat a little meat.

Get

● *Get* is often described as the lazy man's verb because
English-speaking people tend to overwork it by using it
unnecessarily as a substitute, rather vague in meaning, for
many other verbs,

> He can't *get* (reach) home before seven o'clock.
> She can't *get* away (leave) until tomorrow.

However, *get* has its proper place in our idiomatic
language as you will see below.

get + adjective/participial adjective

1 You *are getting* fat, John! ⎫
2 Grandfather's *getting* too old to work. ⎬ *get = become*
3 John *got* hurt in an accident. ⎭
4 His *watch got broken* too.

Get in the last two sentences gives a passive or reflexive
sense to the verbs, consider:

> John *hurt himself* in an accident
> His *watch was broken* too.

NOTE:

> 1 She *gets* tired quickly.   (She isn't very strong.)
> 2 She *tired herself* quickly.   (She worked too fast and
>   too hard.)

In **1** we do not hold her responsible for getting tired, while
in **2** we do place the responsibility on the subject.

NOTE ALSO:

> He *got himself dressed*.
> They *got themselves washed*.
> I'll *get myself ready*.

exercise 111

Restate the sentences by using *get* to replace the verbs in italic type.

1 Little John's *growing* taller every day.
2 You'll *become* quite brown if you lie in the sun.
3 Grandfather is *growing* very forgetful nowadays.
4 Well, he isn't *becoming* any younger, you know.
5 Iron *goes* white when it *becomes* very hot.
6 Peter's watch *was* lost in the fire.
7 We shan't *reach* (to) London before ten o'clock tonight.
8 I'm sorry, I can't *catch* the earlier train.
9 Will you *book* sleeping berths for us?
10 I'm sorry the toast *was* burnt this morning.
11 The shopkeeper *turned* nasty when I asked for my money back.
12 Butter *goes* soft in a warm room.
13 You'll *become* dirty if you play with that mud!
14 His shoes *were* worn out with walking so much.
15 We *were* tired of waiting for a bus so we walked home.
16 Do you think you can *arrive* home a little earlier tonight.
17 The days *grow* longer before midsummer.
18 I'm *becoming* bored with having nothing to do.
19 Mr Green *was* wounded in the war.
20 Milk *turns* sour in hot weather.

● *Get* is frequently used colloquially and vaguely, as a synonym of *obtain, acquire*. People often use *get* when they cannot be or do not wish to be specific about the method of obtaining or acquiring goods, an advantage, a characteristic etc.

> *Where did you get such a valuable diamond?*
> *The enemy got secret information about our movements.*

NOTE: *Get/got* forms replace the whole passive: *I was given = I got.*

● NOTE: *Got* frequently accompanies *have* when *have* means *own* or *possess*.

> *What have you got for lunch?*
> *We haven't got much money.*
> *John has got a new car.*

Many people consider that *got* is an unnecessary and therefore undesirable word in this sense. However, the idiom is very widespread and therefore cannot be ignored.

exercise 112

Restate the sentences by using *get* to replace the verbs in italics.

1 Where did you *buy* this wonderful coffee?
2 I didn't buy it. I *borrowed* some from our neighbour.
3 Burglars *stole* a lot of money at the bank.
4 We *received* your letter this morning.
5 Will you *fetch* me a glass of water, please?
6 Mr Brown's son *gained* good marks in the examination.
7 The police sometimes *obtain* information in the underworld.
8 Jane *acquired* a perfect French accent on her holiday in Paris.
9 David has *won* first prize in the competition.
10 George *earns* more than ten thousand pounds a year.
11 We can *have* lunch on the train, if we want it.
12 How did you *come by* such a valuable ring?
13 We can't *procure* the books we need until next week.
14 You must arrange to *purchase* them as soon as possible.
15 We *obtain* everything we need from the local shops.
16 The firm *was paid* ten thousand pounds in advance.
17 Did John *find* what he was looking for?
18 She *is given* two weeks' holiday every year.
19 Mary *was presented with* a large bouquet of roses.
20 Messrs Smith and Brown *purchased* the property for a song.

let

- *Let* frequently introduces a suggestion or a proposition:

  Let's go to the theatre tonight.   That's a good idea, let's do that, shall we?

Notice carefully that the tag question form of *let* in this sense is *shall we? (shall I?* in the singular). The negative form is *let's not.*

  Let's not quarrel over a little thing like that.

We sometimes use *let* with the first and third persons singular and plural to convey indifference or that the speaker abandons all interest and responsibility in the matter under discussion:

  If John refuses to see a dentist, let him suffer toothache.
  If a man will not work let him go hungry.
  When a man is guilty of a crime let him be punished.

In the third example the speaker gives his considered opinion, having taken all the circumstances into consideration.

- The verb *let* is always followed by the infinitive of the principal verb without the particle *to*,

  He let me see his stamp collection

- *Let* very often means permit or allow:

  Father never lets anybody else drive the car.
  We never let our dog go out of the garden.
  Please let me help you to carry that heavy suitcase.

- When *let* means permit or allow we use the auxiliary verbs (*do, does,* etc.) to make the past, present and future forms.

- *Let* (imperative)

  Let me alone!   (Stop annoying me! Leave me in peace!)
  Open the door and let me in.
  Let me go!   (Take your hands off me! Release me!)

- The tag question form in a *let* sentence in the imperative takes the auxiliary *will*:

  Let me speak, will you?

exercise 113

Use *let, let's not* forms to complete these sentences. When *let* means *permit* or *allow* the usual *auxiliary verb* + *let* constructions are used to form the negative and interrogative.

He didn't let me speak.

1 ... me go, you're breaking my arm!
2 ... anyone know what I've just told you. (negative)
3 ... 's invite some friends in tomorrow, shall we?
4 The manager ... anybody have the key to the safe. (negative)
5 I asked him to ... me stay a little longer.
6 ... that dog come near me! (negative)
7 ... 's not go tonight. It's so cold outside.
8 Peter shouldn't ... gossip upset him so much.
9 ... me sleep in peace. Stop that noise, will you!
10 Will you ... me use your telephone, please?
11 ... grandfather walk too far. (negative)
12 Don't interrupt! Please ... me speak my mind.
13 ... 's go to the seaside for the weekend.
14 ... 's not stay at that dreadful hotel again.
15 They ... people have keys to their room, did they? (negative)
16 ... that little girl alone or I'll box your ears!
17 Does your elder brother ... you borrow his books?
18 ... 's have lunch out today, shall we?
19 My short lunch break ... me go very far from the office. (negative)
20 This special glass ... us see out but other people can't see in.

make
and do

- **make**

  We use this verb to express a number of different actions. Its general meanings are: *manufacture, produce* and *create*. Very often, work with the hands is indicated or some other activity which produces a visible or otherwise observable result, that is to say when we *make* something (an appointment, a cake, a noise, an impression) we *bring it into existence* so that people can see, hear, feel or understand it. Consider the following examples:

  1 *Mother is making a cake.*
  2 *They make aeroplanes in that factory.*
  3 *John made a noise like a cat in class today.*
  4 *My brother has made a model ship.*
  5 *He went abroad when he was young and made a fortune.*
  6 *God made man.*
  7 *Snipps, the tailor, makes my clothes.*

- **do**

  This verb refers to movement or physical activity not necessarily connected with production, manufacture or creation. Its basic sense implies performance, execution, completion and the carrying out of the usual daily tasks, duties and routines. Let us compare a pair of sentences:

  (a) *Mother does all the work in the house.*
  (b) *Untidy children make work in the house.*

  In the sentence (a) we see that Mother performs all the usual household tasks. She carries out all the housekeeping duties. She *does* the cooking and *makes* good meals. In (b) untidy children are the creators of work. They *make* work for Mother *to do*. Consider the following:

  Hello Peter, what are you making? I'm making a table.
  (and a little later) *What are you doing Peter?   I'm bandaging my finger.*

exercise 114

Supply *make* or *do* to complete these sentences.

1 I'm sorry, I've . . . a mistake.
2 He worked hard and . . . a fortune.
3 We started early and . . . a lot of work before noon.
4 Our firm . . . business with South America.
5 I can't . . . a decision without speaking to my partners.
6 Peter could never . . . geometry at school.
7 Mary is still in her room. She's . . . her hair.
8 It . . . no difference whether you pay in cash or by cheque.
9 The sinking ship tried to . . . contact with London by radio.
10 We always . . . the crossword puzzles in the newspapers.
11 Can you . . . the tango?
12 Don't . . . such a fuss about nothing!
13 Mary . . . an appointment to see the doctor the next day.
14 Don't forget to . . . your teeth before you go to bed.
15 That silly fellow is always . . . a nuisance of himself.
16 I'm afraid I can't . . . such difficult problems in algebra.
17 If you don't mend your ways somebody will . . . trouble for you.
18 Why are you laughing like that? Are you . . . a fool of me?
19 My father always . . . exercises at the open window.
20 The engine of the car was . . . a very strange noise.

make

In many contexts *make* means: *force, compel* or *cause*. The following examples will demonstrate these usages. Note that in ordinary conversational English *make* is better than *cause* which is less idiomatic.

1 *A heavy meal makes one sleepy.*
2 *Travelling on a ship makes Mary sick.*
3 *The burglar made me open the safe.*
4 *He made me promise not to tell the police.*

The first two examples show *make* as *cause* (to become sleepy, or sick). The other two show *make* as *force, compel*).

do

A sense of completion or of achievement is often understood when *do* is used. The verb *to be* with the past participle *done* nearly always gives this sense of completeness or finality, or achievement. The examples will show you more clearly how to use this construction.

1 *What is done cannot be undone.*
2 *You may go out when your homework is done.*
3 *The roast beef was done to a turn.*
4 *For twenty years we have tried to solve this problem and now we have done it!*

exercise 115

Supply *make* or *do* to complete the sense of these sentences.

NOTE:

(active) *make* + *noun or pronoun* + infinitive without
to: *He made us work hard.*
(passive) *be made* + *to* + infinitive:
We were made to work hard.
The dog was made to stop barking.

1   The rolling of a ship . . . one sick.
2   The thief . . . me hand over all my valuables.
3   My wife . . . her shopping in the afternoon.
4   So much hard work has . . . me tired.
5   Our teachers . . . us study every evening.
6   John likes . . . the cooking on Sundays.
7   We shouted to the boys but couldn't . . . them hear.
8   Perhaps a good sleep will . . . him feel better.
9   Mary's new dress . . . her look slimmer.
10 These horrid paintings would . . . Rembrandt turn in his
    grave.
11 Joan always . . . the ironing in the evenings.
12 You can take a horse to water but you can't . . . him drink.
13 Will you . . . the carpet in my room, please? It is dirty.
14 They say that a red rag . . . a bull angry.
15 The sight of a bull . . . me run.
16 Elizabeth is . . . her homework in the other room.
17 She hasn't enough to . . . so she tries to . . . work to pass the
    time.
18 A loud explosion . . . him quite deaf.
19 Will you . . . me a favour?
20 I'll do anything to . . . you happy.

Gerund or verbal noun

- Many of the names of activities, sports and pastimes are gerunds: *Swimming* is good exercise. Mrs Brown likes *dancing*. *Eating* makes me fat. *Seeing* is *believing*. The words in *italic* type are either the subject or object of their verbs. The subject or object of a verb is clearly a noun and does the work of a noun in the sentence, although it is verbal in form. This type of verbal noun (-*ing*) is called a gerund. We use the gerund after a preposition:

  1 *He went to prison for stealing.*
  2 *She was tired of waiting for his return.*
  3 *She suffered for years without complaining.*
  4 *They made money by buying and selling wool.*

  In these examples the gerund is really the object of the preposition and does the work of a noun. Consider:

  He went to prison for theft (stealing).

  The two words can be freely used, one for the other, only because they perform the same function, that of a noun. However, many people prefer to use the name *Verbal Noun* since very often the gerund has a double sense: the deed and the doing of it.

- We have already seen that the gerund is a noun and that it may, therefore, be modified by adjectives or represented by a pronoun in the same way as any other noun. A gerund may also be qualified by a noun in the possessive case.

  Mary's swimming is excellent but her driving is bad.

  When we use a gerund we sometimes feel that its verbal part is stronger than the noun, even though a gerund is grammatically a noun:

  Driving a bus through busy streets is hard work.

  However these are just as truly nouns in the grammatical sense and may carry adjectives and so on just the same as all other nouns.

Supply gerunds to replace the noun objects of the
prepositions and note any change in meaning. Omit
redundant articles and prepositions.

EXAMPLE:

> They earned a living by the sale of old cars.
> *They earned a living by selling old cars.*

1　She spent an hour in the purchase of a hat.
2　The firm is engaged in the manufacture of radio sets.
3　I can't understand Peter's way of thought sometimes.
4　Peter gives great attention to the preparation of his work.
5　We never discussed politics, by agreement to avoid such
　topics.
6　The general formed his plans after consultation with his
　officers.
7　Our only hope lay in escape at the first opportunity.
8　He is tired out through overwork.
9　John's wife says she's tired of life in the country.
10　Can't we have some fresh food? I'm sick of the sight of
　tinned meat.
11　Electricity provides us with light and heat.
12　After the sight of such a wonderful picture, she wanted to
　buy it.
13　A life of work without any play becomes very dull.
14　We communicate our thoughts chiefly by speech.
15　Dogs can find their way home by the smell of the ground.
16　The soldiers had a ten minute rest for a smoke and a chat.
17　Then they had to get ready for the fight.
18　Many farmers lost their crops during the recent floods in
　the valley.
19　She caught cold through the wait in the rain in the theatre
　queue.

The —*ing* form after temporal prepositions

- Temporal prepositions are often called Adverbial Particles of Time because they indicate the chronology of an action:

    1 *On entering the house, he took off his hat.*
    2 *On seeing the cat, the dog ran after it.*
    3 *After walking for three hours, he felt tired.*
    4 *She looked in the mirror before going downstairs.*

In these sentences the —*ing* form has a definite verbal sense. The sentences might be re-stated by exchanging the —*ing* form for a time form of the verb

    1 *As he entered the house he took off his hat.*
    2 *As soon as the dog saw the cat, it ran after it.*
    3 *When he had been walking for three hours, he felt tired.*

Verbs
(infinitive and —*ing*)

- Some verbs are followed either by the infinitive or by —*ing* and often there is little or no change in meaning:

    (a) *I like to drive a fast car.*
    (b) *I like driving a fast car.*

    In the pair of sentences above the only possible difference is that (b) might apply to the present moment while I am driving a fast car, and (a) might apply either to the present moment or more generally to the speaker's liking for fast cars at any time.

- Sometimes we deliberately choose the infinitive to show the active personal participation of the subject of the main verb:

    (a) *Mary likes to dance occasionally.*
    (b) *Mary likes dancing.*
    (c) *Grandmother likes dancing for little girls.*

    In (a) it is clear that Mary takes part in dancing; in (c) it is clear that grandmother approves of, or recommends dancing (it is improbable that a grandmother herself takes part in a dance). In (b) as the sentence stands, we do not know exactly what it means; whether Mary likes to dance, as in (a) or whether she approves of it as in (c). The context in which the sentence occurs will generally clarify the meaning of the gerund.

● The following verbs may be followed either by a gerund or by an infinitive: a different meaning will be produced in each case.

remember

> *I remember answering your letter* (. . . that I answered)
> *I always remember to answer letters.* (I never forget, I never neglect them).

stop

> *They stopped to talk to us* (. . . stopped in order to talk, to have a chat with us).
> *They stopped talking* (They became silent, they broke off their conversation).

forget

> *They forgot to visit us.* (They didn't come to us)
> *They had forgotten visiting us.* (They had forgotten that they had visited).

try

> *Try sleeping without a pillow* (as an experiment)
> *Try to work without making too much noise* (try = make the necessary effort)

need

> *We need to earn more money* (we require . . . it is necessary to earn more money)
> *My hands need washing* (they are dirty and in need of a wash).

exercise 117

Express the word in brackets either as a gerund or as an
infinitive to make the most probable sense and notice
carefully whether a real change in meaning results.

1 Mary likes (go) to the seaside in summer.
2 We simply hate (wait) in the rain for a bus.
3 Peter simply loves (walk) in the mountains.
4 His wife prefers (sit) quietly in the shade of a tree.
5 The Government intends (build) a new hospital here.
6 Margaret has begun (write) a historical novel.
7 Don't attempt (cross) the road until the traffic stops.
8 We never neglect (wash) our hands before a meal.
9 Mr Brown has omitted (sign) this letter.
10 I don't like (travel) by night if I can avoid it.
11 Most people prefer (sleep) in a real bed.
12 I'm sorry, I forgot (post) your letters.
13 Does that child never stop (talk)?
14 Do you remember (see) that film at the Granada last year?
15 Before she began (take) regular exercise she was very
stout.
16 John didn't start (smoke) until he was twenty-five.
17 Professor Brown will start (teach) next Monday.
18 Peter never remembers (put) the light out before he goes to
sleep.
19 We shall never forget (hear) Gigli in the Opera House that
night.
20 Will you stop (make) such a noise down there?

Main verbs + gerund:

Case of the pronoun

- Generally speaking the case of the pronoun before the —*ing* or gerund is objective since the pronoun is often the object of the main verb:

    (a) *She doesn't like me wearing this old suit.*
    (b) *I don't mind him smoking in the office.*

- Often we use the possessive to qualify the gerund which is the object of the main verb.

    (a) *I appreciate his playing that music, just for me.*
    (b) *We prefer his writing to telephoning about important matters.*

- The objective pronoun is used more commonly than the possessive adjective, even when the latter would be correct, and frequently there is little or no change in meaning:

    Do you mind us eating chicken with our fingers?
    Do you mind our eating chicken with our fingers?

- Sometimes, however, a certain change is caused, especially when the possessive adjective or objective pronoun is stressed:

    (a) *Do you remember him (as he was) singing that comical song?*
    (b) *Do you remember his singing that comical song?*

In (a), do you remember *him*, how amusing he was when he sang the song? In (b), do you remember *that he sang* that comical song? What we see in (a) is that the objective pronoun can be quite correctly used as the object:

I can just see him agreeing to that!
We all heard them saying she would come.

Compare:

I didn't feel the dentist (him) drilling my tooth.
I can't imagine $\begin{cases} \textit{him hurting anybody.} \\ \textit{his} \end{cases}$

A useful difference in meaning results from stressing the objective. I can't imagine him – that he could hurt anybody. This places the focus of meaning on the doer.

● Many verbs control the —*ing* form of the verb that follows them. Either a gerund or another —*ing* form follows the verbs in the following lists. The —*ing* form is sometimes preceded by a possessive adjective when the —*ing* form is the object of the verb. Otherwise, an objective pronoun follows the verb.

> (a) *dislike*
> *admire*
> *excuse*
> *pardon*
> *forgive*
> *regret*
> *watch*
> *finish*
> *detest*
> *understand*
> *enjoy*
> *fancy*
> *comprehend*
> *recollect*
> *bear* (= suffer, endure)
> *stand* (= put up with)
> *can't help.*

These verbs all require —*ing* in the following verb. Both possessive adjectives and objective pronouns are used. (But: *I can't bear to see you so unhappy;* and *I regret to say . . .* are also used)

> (b) *see*
> *hear*
> *feel*
> *smell*
> *notice*
> *observe*
> *perceive*
> *start* (a machine working)
> *catch* (him doing something)
> *keep* (somebody waiting)

The pronoun after these verbs and before the —*ing* form is usually objective Cf. List (b) p.229

(c) *appreciate*
    avoid
    delay
    deny
    defer
    fear
    impede
    suggest
    postpone
    propose
    risk

The —*ing* form after these verbs usually takes the possessive adjective.

NOTE: *propose* may = *intend*. *I propose to do it myself.*

(d) *like*
    love
    hate
    begin
    permit
    prefer
    intend
    attempt
    neglect
    omit
    cause
    advise

These verbs take either —*ing* or the infinitive after them, according to the sense of the sentence.

NOTE: The phrasal constructions *look forward to, used to, averse to, agreeable to,* and some others are followed by —*ing* forms. *To* is a preposition in these expressions.

NOTE: *to be used to + gerund:*

I am used to living in a hot climate.

exercise 118

Replace the nouns in italic with a possessive adjective or objective pronoun and convert the verbs in brackets into —ing forms.

1 We enjoyed *John's* (play) the piano and (sing) comic songs.
2 He regrets *Peter's* (hurt) your feelings by (insult) you at the party.
3 I excuse *Peter's* (mistake) me for someone else through (mis-hear) my name.
4 Everybody remembers *Mr Brown's* (leave) immediately after (give) his speech.
5 Do you approve of the *children* (wake up) the whole street with their (shout)?
6 Everybody appreciates *David's* (want) to help with (lay) the table.
7 I generally see *Mary* (walk) towards the school after (get) off the bus at the corner.
8 The policeman watched the *criminal* (try) to enter the bank by (break) a window.
9 I remember *George* (take) out his cheque book but I didn't notice him (write) in it.
10 Do you mind my *brother's* (smoke) a cigar?
11 I deny (tell) you anything about *Mary's* (be) in love with Tom.
12 The authorities deferred *David's* (serve) in the army by (allow) him to complete his studies first.
13 I can't bear *our friends* (think) of our (leave) the party without even (say) good-night.
14 When she hears *her husband's* (whistle) she accompanies it with (sing).
15 The driver started *the engine* running by (press) a button.

● Some examples of reduced relative clauses may be useful:

> *I met your father (who was) going to the market.*
> *There were four boys (who were) all swimming in the river.*
> *We watched the stranger* $\left.\begin{array}{l}\textit{(who was)} \\ \textit{(as he was)}\end{array}\right\}$ *walking up the hill.*
>
> *Look at those birds* $\left.\begin{array}{l}\textit{(that are)} \\ \textit{(which are)} \\ \textit{(as they are)}\end{array}\right\}$ *catching fish.*

● The —*ing* forms in the sentences are present participles, they indicate continuous tenses and do not accept possessive adjectives before them. Objective pronouns do occur:

> *Look at them catching fish.*

● **1** The —*ing* form often combines with a following noun:

> *A walking-stick; a swimming suit; a sailing-boat; a washing-machine.*

The two words combine and in fact form a compound noun, with or without a hyphen. Stress falls on the first syllable: a wàlkǐng-stǐck; a a swìmmǐng-suǐt; an ìronǐng-bǒard; a sìngǐng lěsson; a frỳǐng-pǎn. In these compound words, the -*ing* part describes the use or purpose of its following part: a frying-pan is for frying food in; a singing lesson is for teaching and learning singing at, a sewing-machine is for sewing clothes on.

● **2** The —*ing* form often precedes a noun as a participial adjective:

> *a sleèpǐng dòg* = a dog that is sleeping;
> *a breàkǐng heàrt* = a heart that is breaking;
> *a gròwǐng bòy* = a boy who is (still) growing.

The —*ing* form in such examples does not compound with the following noun but stands as an adjective with it.

Notice that the stress is not only on the root syllable of the
—*ing* but also on the noun: *an increàsing dìfficulty; a tìring
dày; an ìnteresting lècture.* Compare:

sìngĭng tĕachĕrs = teachers of singing.

sìngĭng tèachĕrs = teachers who $\left\{ \begin{array}{l} \text{are} \\ \text{were} \\ \text{will be} \\ \text{etc.} \end{array} \right\}$ singing

a hùntĭng dŏg = a dog for hunting, a hunter's dog

a hùntĭng dòg = a dog $\left\{ \begin{array}{l} \text{that is} \\ \text{was} \\ \text{will be} \end{array} \right\}$ hunting

Twenty fìghtĭng shĭps = ships of war, warships

Twenty fìghtĭng shìps = ships that $\left\{ \begin{array}{l} \text{are} \\ \text{were} \\ \text{will be} \end{array} \right\}$ fighting

From these few examples you can see that correct stress is
essential to the meaning of the —*ing* + *noun* constructions.

NOTE:

He wrote a letter saying how well he felt after his holiday =
in which he said.
*I signed a document stating (which stated) that the accident
had been my own fault.*

In these examples the —*ing* form, which is a present
participle, is used adjectivally.

Infinitive

- When a following clause has the same subject as the principal clause in the sentence, an infinitive construction restates the former more briefly and idiomatically and is, therefore, often better English. Consider the following examples:

    I'm pleased that I'm home again = I'm pleased to be home again.

    The infinitive often replaces the relative clause after a superlative expression:

    She was the youngest woman that (who) ever sat in Parliament. = She was the youngest woman ever to sit in Parliament.

- When a sentence expresses a desire, request or command the infinitive form is used for that part of the sentence which follows the desire, request or command. Consider these examples:

    1 *I want to see a doctor.*
    2 *He asked me to lend him five pounds.*
    3 *He ordered them to leave the room.*
    4 *The manager wishes to speak to Mr Smith privately.*

    In each of these examples a desire, request or command is expressed by the first verb. The second part of the sentence tells us exactly what the command, request or desire is, and the infinitive form of the verb is used for this.

Infinitive to express purpose or reason

● A clause of Purpose or Reason is often stated by using an infinitive verb. Students must take care to avoid the use of *for* before the infinitive in these clauses. In the following examples the clauses underlined will indicate either purpose or reason.

　　1 *We have come to pay you a visit.*
　　2 *He works hard to earn a living.*
　　3 *Eat to live, do not live to eat.*
　　4 *He has gone out to see a man about a dog.*

NOTE: *For* must always be omitted before the infinitive.

● Many verbs are followed by an infinitive construction. Most of the common ones can be found in the following lists.

　　(a) Verb + object + infinitive　　*I expect you to be honest.*

　　　　expect
　　　　believe
　　　　think
　　　　suppose
　　　　know
　　　　find
　　　　acknowledge
　　　　understand
　　　　consider

　　(b) Verb + infinitive (without *to*).　　*I watched him jump.*

　　　　watch
　　　　observe
　　　　see
　　　　hear
　　　　notice
　　　　let
　　　　help
　　　　feel
　　　　make
　　　　smell

See List (b), p.223

(c) Verb + infinitive (with *to*).   *She will try to help.*

try	*want*
agree	*desire*
arrange	*wish*
care	*learn*
consent	*refuse*
condescend	*swear*
endeavour	*hesitate*
attempt	*offer*
decide	*prefer*
determine	

NOTE: *want, wish, prefer, like + noun + infinitive.*

$$I\ saw\ him \left\{ \begin{array}{c} come \\ coming \end{array} \right\} out\ of\ the\ house.$$

The bare infinitive indicates interest simply in the fact that he came out of the house. The —*ing* form implies that the event continued for some time.

I heard someone   shout   (perhaps just one shout)
                  shouting   (for some time)

(d) Verb + object + infinitive (+ object of infinitive)
     I helped him to change the wheel.

help	*oblige*
advise	*force*
tell	*compel*
teach	*press*
instruct	*ask*
order	*request*
command	*cause*
encourage	*warn*
permit	*tempt*
allow	*leave*
invite	

(e) Verb + how to + infinitive   *We learnt how to make a cake.*

ask
advise
decide
explain
forget
know
learn
hear
think
teach
understand
observe
see
consider
wonder
tell
remember

Some of these verbs can have an objective noun or pronoun before *how*.

I told him how to find the way.

(f) Verbs of Process   *She seemed to recognise him.*

commence
begin
start
come
grow
appear
seem
get
happen

Infinitive with *too* and *enough*

● *Too* indicates an excessive quantity or degree in adjectives and adverbs and has a negative sense:

> *It is <u>too</u> hot today. I can't play football.*

The two sentences can be joined by using the infinitive to replace the negative verb:

> (a) *It is too hot <u>to play</u> football,* or
> (b) *It is too hot <u>for me</u> to play football.*

For me, you, him, her, it, us, them and so forth always come into the sentence when we want to show clearly that we refer to particular people:

> *Mary is too young to marry yet* = She is too young. She can't marry at all yet.
> *Mary is too young for John to marry.* = John is much older than Mary and their marriage would be unsuitable.

It is a question of whether or not the subject of the infinitive is also the subject of the sentence. Compare:

> *I'd like to talk to him about it* and
> *I'd like you to talk to him about it.*

● *Enough* indicates sufficiency or adequacy when used with adjectives, adverbs and nouns. *Enough* comes before a noun and follows adjectives and adverbs:

> *He has enough money for his needs.*

Consider the following:

> *John is strong. He can carry two suitcases*
> = John is strong enough to carry two suitcases.

We combine the two sentences by using *enough* followed by the infinitive when *enough* qualifies an adjective or adverb. When *enough* refers to a noun we construct the combined sentence quite easily:

> *I have some money. I can go by taxi* = I have enough money to go by taxi.

NOTE: *Enough* sometimes follows the noun when the speaker's meaning is: *More than enough* or *plenty.*

> *There is time enough to catch the train. We still have an hour to spare.*
> *The poor woman has had trouble enough (and to spare).*

exercise 119

Put *enough* into its correct place in the sentence. The word it qualifies or modifies is in italic type.

1 Have you *money* on you?
2 Yes, the cinema is *cheap*, isn't it?
3 I'm afraid you haven't come *early*. The doctor is out.
4 Peter isn't *old* for the manager's job.
5 Hurry up! You haven't *time* to read the paper after breakfast.
6 There isn't *sugar* in my coffee.
7 Otherwise you've made it *well*.
8 I'm sorry it isn't *sweet* for you, sir.
9 Was your coffee *strong* this morning?
10 I'm afraid I never have *leisure* to read very much.
11 Peter certainly works *hard* to earn his salary.
12 Farmers are complaining that there isn't *sunshine* this summer.
13 The sun is shining *brightly* today for a change.
14 Have we *food* in the house for tomorrow as well?
15 I don't think there's *bread* for two days.
16 It won't be *fresh* for sandwiches in any case.
17 I shan't have *time* to finish this exercise.
18 Yes, you will, if you work *fast*.
19 After all it's *easy*, when you know how to do it.
20 I'm sorry, I haven't put *salt* in the soup.

exercise 120

Rewrite each pair of sentences with *too* and *enough* using the infinitive to form one complete sentence from the two.

1 This parcel is too large. I can't carry it.
2 There is enough food. It will last a week.
3 I saw him clearly enough. I should know him again.
4 These cups are too small. They won't hold half a pint of milk.
5 They have enough money. They can live comfortably.
6 She spoke too softly. He didn't hear.
7 There is enough time. We can have a cup of tea.
8 I'm afraid I haven't enough patience. I can't do embroidery.
9 These goods are too cheap. They can't be very good.
10 This cup of coffee is too sweet. Father won't drink it.
11 Everything happened too quickly. We couldn't do anything.
12 It rained too often. We couldn't go out every day.
13 We hadn't got enough flour. We couldn't make a cake.
14 A large car is too dear. Peter can't buy one.
15 A little donkey isn't strong enough. It can't pull such a heavy load.
16 Joan isn't well enough. She can't go to school today.
17 Tap water is hot enough. I can shave with it.
18 She's had enough trouble of her own. She will understand yours.
19 There's too much work. One man can't do it all.
20 She's too young. She can't stay out late at night.

Infinitive particle *to*

● We often leave *to* standing by itself as the last word in a phrase or sentence to express the whole infinitive clause:

> *Have you invited John? Not yet, but I'm going to.*
> (invite John).
> *I'll help you if you want me to.* (help you).

Instead of saying the whole infinitive clause we stop the sentence at *to* leaving the rest of the clause to be understood, when a previous sentence or clause contains the essential sense of the unspoken infinitive clause. We do this especially after *want, desire, hope, propose, intend, like, promise, deserve* and others of the *verb + infinitive* type, and *used to, have to, ought to, be able to, going to,* etc.:

> *I didn't come because I didn't have to.* (come)

exercise 121

Complete these sentences. The final *to* stands for the whole infinitive clause.

> *I didn't invite him to the party because I didn't want to.*
> *Mary wrote to her friends as often as she was able to.*

1 The boys in this school can play football if . . . .
2 John goes to the theatre whenever . . . .
3 I won't tell anybody if you don't . . . .
4 You needn't answer this question unless . . . .
5 Our students may take books from the library whenever . . . .
6 I'll go to the cinema with you if . . . .
7 Is John coming tomorrow? He hopes . . . .
8 Don't promise to help if you . . . .
9 Shall I help you? Yes, if you . . . .
10 She eats a lot of chocolate although she . . . .
11 We don't go to the cinema nowadays although we . . . .
12 Will you pass the examination? Well, I . . . .
13 Have you finished your work? No, I'm just . . . .

exercise 122

Supply the infinitive or the *-ing* form correctly to replace the verbs in brackets. Notice *to* is omitted sometimes. (See list b, page 229, and see note, page 223, (b).)

1   Everybody knows him (be) a good man at (repair) clocks.
2   We warn you (have) nothing to do with (help) these lawbreakers.
3   How do you expect me (know) whether John intends (marry) soon?
4   We can't force you (tell) us but we are interested in (know) about our friends.
5   If you begin (cook) supper I'll get on with (lay) the table.
6   Will you see to (heat) some bath water for me (use) later?
7   Friends have invited us (stay) next weekend, after (hear) of John's recent illness.
8   I watched carefully (see) what he would do next, but he went on (look) in the shop window.
9   The chairman decided (close) the meeting on (hear) that one of the members was ill.
10 On (learn) of our difficulties a friend immediately offered (help) us out.
11 If you happen (meet) Mr Brown, tell him I should like (see) him soon.
12 A business matter compels me. (stay) overnight, but I shall try (be) back tomorrow.
13 (Drive) very fast on this bad road, might result in an accident.
14 In (try) (overtake) at a high speed he crashed into an oncoming car.
15 Nobody noticed us (leave) the house on our way (look for) a policeman.
16 One can't learn (do) anything without (make) mistakes.
17 I wish (see) an architect (ask) about (re-build) my old house.
18 Do you know how (put) a ship into a bottle without (break) it.

Perfect Infinitive

● The perfect infinitive form *to have arrived, to have finished* is very often used in English. Let us consider some examples:

   (a) *The manager expects me to have finished the job by next Saturday.*

   (b) *I want to have read the whole report before I answer questions about it.*

   (c) *I want to have travelled right round the world by the time I am thirty years old.*

   (d) *Peter is to have arrived in New York before the conference opens.*

These four examples each have a clause which expresses future time (underlined). The perfect infinitive forms

   (a) *to have finished*   (c) *to have travelled*
   (b) *to have read*   (d) *to have arrived,*

indicate actions which will be completed before that certain future time. The speaker, when that specific future moment arrives, will be able to look back and say

   (a) *I have done the work.*

   (b) *I have read the report.*

   (c) *I have travelled round the world.*

   (d) *Peter has arrived, he is there.*

● NOTE: Some people would say that there is little or no difference in meaning, in these sentences, between the simple infinitives (*to finish, to read* etc.) and the perfect infinitive forms. However, the perfect infinitive implies very strongly that *completion* of the action is to take place *before the specified future time.* The simple infinitive extends the time limit since it usually means that the action may become complete *before* or *at* the future moment although not after it. Compare:

   (a) *We are to leave the house on 30 June.*

   (b) *We are to have left on 1 July.*

In (b) we shall have left before 1 July. On the morning of that date our old house will be vacant, perhaps from the day before (a) or even before then. The order at (b) is to be completed before the given time.

We are to leave by 30 June = We are to have left on 1 July.

Perfect Infinitive (Unrealised past)

● The past forms of *be* followed by the perfect infinitive nearly always indicate that although a certain arrangement, order, command, intention or agreement existed, it was not fulfilled.

> 1 *Peter was to have arrived on the ten o'clock train.* (However he arrived earlier, later or not at all.)
> 2 *He was to have gone to bed early.* (But didn't.)
> 3 *Father was to have bought fish for dinner.*(But forgot.)
> 4 *Mary was to have telephoned the theatre to book seats.* (She didn't do so – so we went to the cinema.)
> 5 *The headmaster was to have presented the prizes.* (He couldn't come on that day as he had a bad cold.)

Many people would use the simple infinitive (*was to arrive*) but to keep the feeling of non-fulfilment at a previous time the perfect infinitive is necessary.

exercise 123

Rewrite the following sentences changing the infinitive verb forms into the perfect infinitive forms. Remember that after *was/were* the perfect infinitive often shows non-fulfilment of the action, or doubt about whether it was realised.

1 I want to learn Spanish by next summer.
2 She imagines herself to be a great lady.
3 He wishes to speak to his partners before giving a final decision.
4 The doctor expected him to die before morning.
5 He intends to make a fortune before he is forty.
6 We were to finish by twelve o'clock.
7 The firm undertakes to complete the job on 30 June.
8 She plans to do her shopping before the rush begins.
9 Peter was to take up his new post at once.
10 We are sorry to give you so much trouble.
11 They think it wiser to buy a house before they get married.
12 We are sad to lose such a good friend as he was.
13 She understood him to say that he was a police officer.
14 Mr Brown expects to pay his debts in two years' time.
15 He was to leave on the four o'clock train.
16 Peter ought to ring me up every day.
17 I know Peter Smith to be an honest man at all times.
18 John hopes to master mathematics before he is much older.
19 He wants to live in every capital in Europe before he settles down.
20 Everybody wants to do some good with his life.

exercise 124

Restate these sentences expressing the parts in italics as infinitive or perfect infinitive clauses as required.

1 He was the first man *who flew* across the Atlantic.
2 The captain was the last person *that left* the sinking ship.
3 Mr Brown was the only person *who saw* the accident.
4 Miss Green was the last but one *who arrived* at the party.
5 This is the finest diamond *that has come* out of India.
6 Father sent me money *so that I could buy* books.
7 She was the first woman *that sat* in Parliament.
8 Your father is the best person *that can advise you* on these matters.
9 She is the youngest girl *who ever came* to our school.
10 Peter's uncle was the oldest man *who had swum* the Channel.
11 The Queen Elizabeth is the largest ship *that has crossed* the Atlantic.
12 I am sorry *I give you* a great deal of trouble.
13 This is the coldest winter *that has occurred* within living memory.
14 Our teacher showed me the easiest way *in which one can solve* the problem.
15 I'm sorry, I have no better news *that I can give* you.
16 There is no other way *that one can do* this work.
17 His nephew was the sole relative *that survived* him.
18 Who will be the first man *that lives* on the moon?
19 He was glad *that he was able* to help you.
20 We were delighted *that we were able* to visit you.

mperative

- The imperative form of the verb states a command or request by the speaker. It is formed from the infinitive without the particle *to*. Consider:

    Go away!
    Please come in!
    Tell Mary I shall be late for dinner, please.
    Take this medicine after meals.

- Verbs which very often have two objects (*give, tell, send*), one direct and the other indirect, have these objects in either order e.g.

    Give twenty pounds to John or *Give John twenty pounds.*

    Notice that the preposition is dropped when the indirect object comes first.

    NOTE: *Explain, suggest, describe* and *propose* are always followed by the direct object:

    Explain the lesson to me, please.

- When the direct object is a personal pronoun it follows the imperative verb immediately while the indirect object with its preposition takes the second place.

    Send Peter a birthday card.   Send it to him.
    Give John a pound note.   Give it to him.
    Tell Jack the story.   Tell it to Jack.

- *Do not (don't)* makes the negative of the imperative:

    Do not smoke in this room.
    Please do not park outside my garage door.
    Don't wait more than ten minutes for me.

- Note the use of *do* with the imperative to indicate emphasis, especially in reply to a request, or offer of service.

    May I open the window?   Please do.
    Shall I make you a sandwich?   Please do. I'm quite hungry.
    May we stay till Monday?   Please do. We like your company.

- NOTE: *Do be quiet. Do sit still. Do stop talking.* These are often spoken in an impatient or irritated tone of voice.

exercise 125

Form objective pronouns from the direct and indirect objects of the imperative verb and put them in the correct order. (The correct preposition is given in brackets).

1 Give Peter a piece of cake. (to)
2 Send Mary a birthday present. (to)
3 Tell the gentleman your name. (to)
4 Offer our guests some tea. (to)
5 Write the manager a strong letter. (to)
6 Address the envelope to John Brown & Co.
7 Give the boys their pocket money, please. (to)
8 Buy mother some apricot jam, please. (for)
9 Fetch the headmaster a chair, please. (for)
10 Get Mrs Brown some coloured chalk, please (for)
11 Tell the children a story!
12 Offer your friends some sweets. (to)
13 Get the teacher a glass of cold water, please. (for)
14 Fetch your father his pipe, will you? (for)
15 Send the treasurer a cheque, will you please? (to)
16 Will you please make Grandma a nice cup of tea? (for)
17 Give the old gipsy your left hand. (to)
18 Will you please buy the boy some new shoes? (for)
19 Write your teacher a short composition. (for)
20 Take Mary a nice bunch of flowers. (to)

ummary of
resent Time

We can express present time in English in four different ways which we can sum up as follows:

- **Present Continuous**   This tense usually expresses
  - (a) what is happening at the actual moment of speaking
  - (b) what is happening over a temporary present period
  - (c) what is happening as an exception to usual custom, habit, routine

- **Present Simple**   This tense generally expresses actions
  - (a) that happen again and again
  - (b) that are normal routine actions, and habitual or customary
  - (c) that are natural truths

- **Present Perfect**   We use this tense
  - (a) whenever the chronologically undefined past has some effect on the present, that is to say, when there is present outcome, result, consequence or interest
  - (b) when an action has occupied a period which began at a previous time and includes the time of speaking. We use it to express actions which have taken place within the expired part of a period of present time and for actions which have taken place so recently that we think of them as being almost present.

- **Present Perfect Continuous**
  We use this for actions which have occupied a period of time which began in the past, includes the present and may continue after the present into the future. We also use it to direct attention to actions which have been taking place before and up to the moment of speaking, and which may have ceased by the moment of speaking. A present outcome, result, consequence or interest is not necessarily implied although there may be one. We also use this tense to express repeated actions in the chronologically undefined recent past. (*Recently, lately, during the last few days*, etc.).

Present Continuous

- Let us examine the following sentences:
  1 *The sun is shining so it is a lovely day for a picnic.*
  2 *Mother is busy just now as she is making a cake for tea.*
  3 *Please be quiet! The baby is sleeping.*
  4 *Listen! The neighbours are quarrelling again.*
  5 *Somebody is knocking at the door. Please see who it is.*
  6 *The telephone is ringing. Answer it at once.*

- **Analysis**
  1 The speaker can see the sunshine. He is not talking of yesterday's weather, nor of tomorrow's weather. He is not discussing the weather of even five minutes ago. *He is talking about what he can see now at this moment.*
  2 Mother has flour, butter, eggs, sugar, and all the things for making a cake. *She is using them at the time these words are uttered.*
  3 Please be quiet *now (at this moment.)* The baby is sleeping. Don't wake him up!
  4 The neighbours have loud, angry voices and I can hear them *now at this moment.*
  5 At the moment of speaking, someone is knocking. I can hear the rat-tat-tat *now while I am speaking.*
  6 The telephone bell *is ringing* while I *am speaking at this very moment.* Answer it *now.*

- **Conclusion**

  Clearly the sentences above refer to an action which is going on at this temporary moment of speaking. They do not say whether the actions are habitual or regular, repeated or frequent. They simply say what the speaker or writer is seeing or hearing with his own eyes or ears at the time of speaking or what he knows is happening while he is speaking. The actions themselves may, obviously, be of previous and later duration.

Present Simple

- Let us examine the following sentences:

  1 *My nephew goes to grammar school.*
  2 *Peter works at the aircraft factory.*
  3 *Cows give milk and sheep give wool.*
  4 *Birds fly and fish swim.*
  5 *We often go to the Majestic Cinema.*
  6 *We come to our English class three times a week.*

- **Analysis**

  1 The speaker wants us to understand that his
    nephew is a pupil at the grammar school and goes
    to school on every school day. That is to say, the boy
    is a regular pupil, and goes to school regularly,
    repeatedly, as a daily routine.

  2 Tells us that Peter goes to the aircraft factory
    regularly and implies that his permanent place of
    employment is the aircraft factory.

  3 and **4** The speaker mentions *natural facts*. Cows give
    milk today, they gave milk in the past and will go on
    giving milk for ever and ever. Cows are our
    permanent suppliers of milk, sheep are our *permanent*
    suppliers of wool. A *permanent* natural *characteristic*
    of birds is that they fly. Fish *always* swim.

  5 and **6** introduce the idea of repetition of the action
    in accordance with the adverb of frequency used in
    the sentence. The word *often* and the phrase *times a
    week* clearly show that the action is a repeated or
    habitual one.

- **Conclusion**

  When we wish to express an action which takes place
  regularly, repeatedly or habitually at the present time, but
  which is not necessarily happening while we are speaking
  we use the Present Simple Tense. We use this tense to
  express all natural facts or permanent truth,

  (a) *Cows give milk.*
  (b) *Money does not always bring happiness.*
  (c) *The sun rises in the east.*
  (d) *The British people speak English.*

Comparisons between Present Continuous and Simple Present

- We have seen that these are two present tense forms of the verb in English. The Present Continuous is used to indicate that the event or action is in progress at this present moment, which is temporary although it may continue for some time (I'm reading *War and Peace*) and in no way connected to any other point in time either before or after. Frequency adverbs are rarely heard with this tense, in this sense.

- The Simple Present indicates habit, regularity, repetition and permanence. The frequency adverbs are often heard with this tense.

- **Comparisons**

  Let us now consider the following pairs of sentences:

  (a) *Mr Brown works at the Blackwood Bank.*
      George is working at the Blackwood Bank.
  (b) *Mary dances beautifully.*
      Margaret is dancing very well tonight.
  (c) *Father smokes his pipe after dinner.*
      Father is smoking his after-dinner pipe.
  (d) *This train goes to London non-stop.*
      This train is going to London non-stop.

  In (a) the verb *works* implies regularity and permanence. We can safely assume that Mr Brown is a member of the bank staff (perhaps he is a cashier, a clerk or a bank messenger) while the verb *is working* conveys the idea that George is not always at the Blackwood Bank. There is a suggestion that there is something unusual about it, that he is working there for the time being only. He may be one of the many tradesmen who work in a building for a few days or a few weeks, temporarily. For example he may be a carpenter, an electrician, a plain-clothes policeman or even a bank employee from another branch who is temporarily at the Blackwood Bank. We cannot assume that George is a member of the bank staff. Rather, we take it that he is not, that he is there temporarily or that he does not mean to stay there permanently.

  In (b) Mary has a reputation as an excellent dancer: A reputation is not a thing of the moment and we can

reasonably say that a person's reputation is permanent in the present. The verb *dances* conveys to the listener that Mary is known for her dancing. She may or may not be dancing when the speaker says these words in the sentence. Margaret, on the other hand, is receiving praise for her ability on this one present occasion only. There is the suggestion that Margaret is dancing better than she usually does. The compliment is for this evening only and does not refer to her general ability in the ballroom. This is temporary as the verb *is dancing* clearly shows.

● The pair of sentences at (c) shows clearly:
1 that it is father's habit to smoke a pipe after dinner. The verb *smokes* indicates habit and regularity while:
2 the verb *is smoking* indicates what is happening now before the eyes of the speaker or otherwise indicates the speaker's knowledge of father's activity at this existing moment.

In (d) the first train *runs* according to timetable and regular railway routine. The second for some reason or another *is running* non-stop on this present journey. This is exceptional and therefore temporary.

Conclusion

● Sentence pairs (a) and (b) show us quite clearly that the Present Continuous *sometimes* indicates actions which *occupy a temporary period of time.* These actions, generally may really be happening while the speaker is talking but they are always temporary in character, or unusual, or unexpected or are *exceptions to the normal routine event.*

The first sentence in each pair indicates regularity, habit, custom, repetition, permanence and routine. The action is not neccessarily in progress at this moment.

These observations, then, make it possible to say that when an action is of this present moment or occasion, or when it is an exception to normal routine custom or habit, we generally use the Present Continuous.

When the action is repeated, or when normal routine, custom and habit are indicated, we generally use the Repeated Permanent Present (Simple Present).

exercise 126

(a) **Form the interrogative, orally.**
(b) **Form the negative, first orally, using *don't* and *doesn't*, then in writing, using *do not* and *does not*.**

EXAMPLE:

> *John doesn't go to school.* (oral),
> *John does not go to school.* (written).

1 Mary takes the dog for a walk in the evenings.
2 Peter buys a morning newspaper, usually.
3 He reads it in the bus.
4 Mr Brown teaches Spanish.
5 I come to every lesson.
6 The boys in our class write with fountain pens.
7 We use blue-black ink in them.
8 Our teacher says our handwriting is good.
9 We go to the seaside every summer.
10 I drink a cup of coffee at eleven o'clock.
11 You go shopping on Saturday mornings.
12 Peter plays the piano very well.
13 The sun rises in the west.
14 It shines every day of the year.
15 My big brother knows everything.
16 Dogs like cats.
17 Some children like chocolate.
18 A deaf person hears well.
19 It rains very often in summer.
20 Soap costs a lot of money.

exercise 127

Do, does; Am, are, is.
The questions below must be answered by using the correct pronoun and auxiliary. The full verb (*Yes, I like chocolate*) is not permitted at this stage. The exercises provide oral practice rather than written.

EXAMPLE:

(a) *Does George like reading?*
Yes, he does. or *No, he doesn't.*
(b) *Are you listening to the radio?*
Yes, we are. or *Yes, I am.*
No, we aren't. or *No, I am not.*

1 Does tea come from India?
2 Do people in China drink tea?
3 Is grass green?
4 Is the sky green?
5 Are you learning English?
6 Do donkeys work hard?
7 Does milk come from cows?
8 Do sheep give us wool?
9 Do horses give us wool?
10 Is a horse bigger than a donkey?
11 Do cats like dogs?
12 Do dogs like cats?
13 Are you sitting at a desk?
14 Is the sun shining?
15 Is it raining?
16 Is your teacher standing?
17 Is he sitting?
18 Does he write on the blackboard?
19 Is he writing on the blackboard?
20 Is China in the East?

exercise 128

> **Insert the correct form – Simple Present or Present Continuous**
>
> 1 Elephants (not eat) meat.
> 2 Men (not agree) on every subject.
> 3 He (visit) Aunt Mary for a few days at present.
> 4 He (not see) her very often.
> 5 He (go) to the pictures once a week.
> 6 He (not see) always a good film.
> 7 He usually (go) to the Majestic Cinema.
> 8 This evening he (not go) there.
> 9 He (try) the Alhambra for a change.
> 10 Uncle George always (come) to dinner on Sundays.
> 11 He (meet) an old school friend instead.
> 12 He (not work) on Sundays, of course.
> 13 Now he is old and (stay) at home.
> 14 He (have) a pension and (not need) to work.
> 15 Look! A big white bird (sit) in our garden.

exercise 129

Insert the correct form of the Simple Present or Present
Continuous.

1 The boy (go) to school every day.
2 The sun (shine) now. Let us go out!
3 Listen! The dog (bark).
4 Hush! The baby (sleep).
5 He can't come to the phone. He (have) a bath.
6 We always (travel) by air.
7 John never (come) early.
8 Look at Peter! He (ride) his bicycle with no hands.
9 Father (shave) himself every other day.
10 He (shave) himself at present.
11 They usually (go) to school on Mondays but today they
(visit) the dentist.
12 This morning I (have) coffee although I generally (take)
tea.
13 I see that Peter (smoke) a pipe today! Yes, he (prefer) cigars
but (not buy) them often because they are too dear.
14 We (go) to the theatre every Friday. This week we (go) on
Wednesday, instead.
15 Maria (live) with her aunt in London where she (study)
English at present.
16 'Be quiet! Can't you see I (speak) on the telephone?'
17 We never (expect) many birthday presents. We always
(receive) some presents but this year Father (give) us a
cheque, instead.
18 Peter seldom (drink) wine with his meals. He (take) water
generally.
19 John often (interrupt) when another person (speak).
20 In summer he often (lie) down in the afternoon. He (rest)
now. Sometimes he (fall) asleep.

Verbs of perception and cognition

- *Smell, see, hear, taste, understand, know, recognise, love, like, hate, dislike* and some other verbs that express the *automatic* senses and emotions which we cannot consciously control are not often used in the Present Continuous. Consider:

  (a) *I know Peter very well.*
  (b) *I am knowing Peter very well.*

  The second sentence is ridiculous because I cannot know a person for the temporary present time only. If I know a man today I shall know him again and for always. (b) is not acceptable English.

- NOTE:

  I hear my neighbour's radio, usually when I am listening to a concert on my own.

  Hear is automatic. If a man has normal, healthy ears he will hear a great deal of sound, noise and conversation whether he wants to or not. He cannot stop hearing, at will. *Listen* is not automatic because, in order to listen, a person must exercise his will. He listens because he wants to hear. In the same way I *look* when I want to *see*. *See* is automatic and seldom appears in the Present Continuous while *look* is very often used in this form of the verb.

- NOTE:

  I am seeing (meeting) Mary next Thursday.

  The verb *see* in the context could be replaced by *meet*.

Present Perfect

- In discussing the Present Perfect we must first agree that *today*, *this week*, *this century* are expressions which indicate the present time.

- *The twentieth century* is a period of present time just as *the tenth century* is a period of definite past time. In the same way *this week* and *today* are periods of present time.

- We use the Present Perfect to link a past event with the present time. Compare:
    - (a) *Peter worked as an engineer for ten years.*
    - (b) *Peter has worked as an engineer for ten years.*

The simple Past *worked* in (a) indicates that Peter no longer works as an engineer. This period of his life is finished, he has changed his job. In (b) the Present Perfect indicates that he is still an engineer, as he has been for the past ten years, the past is connected to the present.

exercise 130

Put in the Present Perfect Simple form of the verbs.

1   She (do) no homework this month.
2   The firm (make) good profits this year.
3   Doctors (learn) a great deal in the last fifty years.
4   He (add) five pounds to the first prize which is now £100.
5   Our students (progress) very well this term so far.
6   Nobody (discover) a cure for the common cold yet.
7   No, but they (invent) a mechanical heart.
8   I'm afraid we must drink tea. I (forgot) to buy coffee.
9   The room is very cold. The fire (go) out.
10 Miss Brown (never see) a television programme.
11 Our salaries (rise) twice since Christmas.
12 Mary (not buy) a new dress for years.
13 The cost of living (go) up a great deal since last year.
14 He (wear) a black suit ever since his wife died.
15 The Smiths (live) here for the last five years.
16 My sister (visit) our mother every Friday for years and years.
17 Peter (be) in hospital for almost six weeks.
18 The cathedral (stand) on this spot since the fourteenth century.
19 France (be) a republic for many years.
20 Peter and Mary (attend) church ever since they were married there.

exercise 131

● Answer the following questions by using the appropriate personal pronoun and the auxiliaries *have* and *has*. Do not use the full form of the verb (*Yes, I have seen an elephant*). The exercise is for oral practice, rather than written.

EXAMPLE:

> *Have you ever seen an elephant?*
> *Yes, I have.*
> *No, I haven't.*

1 Have you lived here long?
2 Has your sister married yet?
3 Have you been out this morning?
4 Has Mr Smith telephoned this morning?
5 Has that tall student on your left ever been to England?
6 Have you been home to your village lately?
7 Has the old place changed much?
8 Have I told you the story about the Scotsman and the Irishman?
9 Have you heard that story before?
10 Has the clock struck ten yet?
11 Have you been waiting long?
12 Has Mary brought my coffee?
13 Have you had coffee this morning?
14 Have motor cars taken the place of horses?
15 Have you seen the newspapers this morning?
16 Has Mary heard the news?
17 Has she understood its importance?
18 Have you been learning English very long?
19 Have you been sleeping?
20 Have you ever tried to learn a foreign language?

since, for

- Phrases of time are often introduced by one of these
  words. Let us study the following sentences:
  - (a) *Peter has been living in Germany since 1952.*
  - (b) *The children have been going to school since they were
    five years old.*
  - (c) *The church bells have been ringing since early this
    morning.*

Since

- **1** *Since* introduces a phrase which contains a past time
  expression which marks the beginning of a period of time
  which has come to an end now. *Since* phrases are used to
  connect the past moment to the present moment and to
  show a repetition of the action expressed in the Present
  Perfect Continuous form clause or to express an unbroken
  continuous action, between then and now. Note that the
  Present Perfect Continuous is used in these sentences to
  give the idea of continuity up to the present moment of
  speaking and perhaps beyond now, into the future, while
  the Simple Present Perfect suggests that both the period
  and the action stop now.

  > *I've been waiting since six o'clock and still my turn hasn't
  > come.* (I shall go on waiting for my turn.)
  > *I have waited for half an hour – I'm going home.*

- **2** *Since* sometimes introduces a phrase which contains a
  past time expression which marks a definite beginning to a
  period of time which ends with the present moment of
  speaking. However the idea of continuity or repetition is
  not always intended. The speaker may wish to state that
  on at least one (possibly more than one) occasion a certain
  action or event has taken place between then and now (in
  the meantime). Consider these sentences:
  - (a) *I have not seen Peter since last Saturday.*
  - (b) *The doctor has visited the patient twice since midnight.*
  - (c) *Since we last met I have changed my address.*
  - (d) *I have been living in the same house for some time.*

These sentences all refer to occurrences between then and now. Notice that (d) implies continuity and that the others state that an occurrence has taken place in the meantime, between then and now, although no definite chronology is expressed. Notice, too, that the Simple Present Perfect is used to convey this sense of the verb, which has occurred between then and now.

For

● The word *for* also introduces expressions of time periods but, instead of giving the beginning of the period, expressions with *for* give the total duration of the time until now. Consider these examples:

(a) *The weather has been very warm for a week now.*
(b) *This class has been studying English for two years.*
(c) *I have been expecting a letter from you for a long time.*
(d) *Peter has been working in the bank for ten years.*

These expressions (underlined) tells us of the total duration of the period up to now, the moment of speaking. If we wish to know when the period began in (a) we can calculate by subtracting seven days from today's date thus:

The weather has been fine since last Monday (presuming that today is also Monday)

or in (b) presuming that the present year is 1985 we would have:

This class has been studying since 1983.

● Notice that the Present Perfect Continuous often suggests that the action will go on into the future while the Simple Past Perfect brings us up to the present moment. Consider:

(a) *I have waited for an hour exactly.*
(b) *I have been waiting for an hour exactly.*

In the first sentence (a) the speaker probably does not intend to wait any longer. He is going home! In the second sentence (b) the speaker is complaining but is not expressing an intention to stop waiting. Rather, he is unhappy at the thought that he must continue to wait.

exercise 132

Put in *since* or *for*, whichever is appropriate. Remember
that *since* mentions a point of previous time and that *for*
mentions the total period up to now.

1   I have been awake . . . three hours – . . . six o'clock.
2   We have been working . . . nine o'clock – . . . five hours.
3   That old apple tree has been standing . . . fifty years – . . .
    Grandfather's wedding day.
4   The weather has been very cold . . . Christmas – . . . a
    month now.
5   The baby has been sleeping . . . two o'clock – . . . two
    hours.
6   The aerodrome has been out of use . . . ten years – . . . the
    new one was opened.
7   I haven't worn a top hat . . . 1948– . . . over thirty-five
    years.
8   Mary hasn't seen Peter . . . a week – . . . last Friday
    morning.
9   We haven't had a swim . . . last summer – . . . almost a
    year.
10 Mary's husband hasn't been ill . . . the day they were
    married – . . . about twelve years.
11 Peter hasn't travelled by train . . . about six months – . . . he
    bought his new car.
12 Mother hasn't had a headache . . . she began to wear her
    new glasses – . . . about three months.
13 My brother has been working abroad . . . the last five
    years – . . . his twenty-first birthday.
14 I've been standing here in the rain . . . half an hour – . . .
    half past four.
15 How long have you been smoking a pipe? . . . about six
    months, . . . New Year's Day.
16 How long has John been learning English? . . . quite a long
    time, . . . last summer.
17 How long have you been married? . . . last Easter – . . .
    twelve months.

exercise 133

Complete these sentences by using

    (a) *for* and

    (b) *since* expressions,

EXAMPLE:

    Mary has been in England (a) *for six months,* (b)
    since Christmas.

NOTE:

    Ever since + time phrase = always, every time, all
                          the time, since I was
                          born.

1 Father has smoked a pipe.
2 He has worked in the same office.
3 Our family has lived here.
4 My uncle has been in America.
5 He hasn't been home.
6 He has written to us regularly.
7 Our tenants have paid the rent promptly.
8 You have given me a birthday present every year.
9 The children have always helped in the house.
10 The Pyramids have stood there.
11 We have been home on a visit every summer.
12 My brother hasn't been home.
13 Dr Smith has been our family doctor.
14 John and Mary have been married.
15 The bad weather has lasted.
16 Captain Smith has been serving in the infantry.
17 John has been writing letters in his room.
18 My sister has been knitting a pullover.
19 We have been looking for a new house.
20 My cousin Peter has been learning English.

Previous cause of a present result, consequence or sequel

- The Present Perfect and Present Perfect Continuous are used *when the present and previous time meet in the mind of the speaker*. When a person speaks of a previous action but thinks of its present value, usefulness, interest, result or consequence, he creates in his mind a period of time which begins with the previous action and ends with the present thought about the present value, usefulness, interest, result or consequence of that past action.

- Now a period of time which began at a previous moment and includes the present moment is in the same category as periods like *this week, this year, today* and so on. Just as they began before the present moment, and also include it, so does the period in the speaker's mind in which he connects the past to the present.

- Quite logically then, we use the Perfect Present to express actions which happened in the *undefined past* when these actions are notionally connected (in the mind of the speaker) with any present value, usefulness, interest, result or consequence. Some examples follow. Please notice that the present value, interest, etc., is very often not spoken but takes the form of an unspoken parenthesis.

Present outcome of the undefined past

1 (a) *John has eaten all the cake.*
  (b) Now there *is* no cake for Robert.
2 (a) *The manager has gone out.*
  (b) You *cannot meet* him, he is not here.

● The (a) sentences indicate what has already taken place at an undefined time before the time of speaking. The (b) sentences show some of the present implications of previous actions.

● Notice particularly that in the (a) sentences there is no adverb or phrase to show that the action took place at a fixed, defined, past time. If such a fixed time expression existed, the Present Perfect could not be used.

● The Present Perfect indicates that the present outcome of the past action is of more importance than the chronology of that past action. Past time adverbs cannot be used since it is not necessary to define the time of the action but to relate the previous occurrence to its present result, outcome, consequence or interest.

● We use the Present Perfect when we wish to show that an action has happened so recently that we think of it as a present action, almost. The word *just* often indicates that the action in the sentence is a very recent one. The following sentences make this use of the Present Perfect clear.

  1 *Will you have a cigarette?*
    No, thank you, I have just put one out.
  2 *Why is John not at school today?*
    He has just got out of bed after a bad cold. I shall send him tomorrow.

● All the verbs underlined express actions which happened so recently in the past that we tend to think of them as present – within these recent few days, hours, minutes or even seconds according to the nature of the action. The Present Perfect is normal usage in such cases.

exercise 134

> Supply a present consequence or result of the previous causes given in the exercise.
>
> EXAMPLE:
>
> > 1 *I have corrected the mistakes in my homework –
> > now I am free to go out.* or *It is ready for the teacher.*
> > or *I can now prepare for tomorrow.*
>
> Students must try to give as many reasonable consequences as possible to each example.

1 I have corrected the mistakes in my homework.
2 I'm sorry the doctor has gone away.
3 My uncle has lived in Spain for ten years.
4 John has never seen a lemon tree.
5 Anne has forgotten to buy a pencil.
6 Mr Brown has taught in this school for forty years.
7 His brother has been very successful in business.
8 Mary has lost her keys.
9 I'm afraid I haven't seen them anywhere.
10 Today we have been very busy indeed.
11 It has stopped raining.
12 Mr Brown has worked here for forty years.
13 I haven't had breakfast yet.
14 Our guests have arrived, at last.
15 I have forgotten to bring my watch to school.
16 Mary has broken her pencil.
17 Poor Mr Smith has broken his leg.
18 Peter has just come back from Timbuktu.
19 I have never seen a dromedary.
20 John hasn't shaved for three days.

exercise 135

Supply a previous cause for the present consequences given in the exercise.

EXAMPLE:

> Consequence: *I feel sleepy,*
> Previous cause: *I have eaten too much for lunch.* or *I have been sleeping badly, recently.*

Students should try to supply more than one reasonably probable previous cause for each exercise. In some of them *for* and *since* expressions should be used.

1 The streets are still wet.
2 Yes, that man is wet through.
3 Peter is beautifully tanned.
4 My grandfather is very wise.
5 Why aren't you at work today?
6 Can you explain this problem in algebra, please? Yes, ...
7 Do you speak English very well yet? No, ...
8 I see you are happy today.
9 No, she doesn't write to me any more.
10 Your children are very polite, Mrs Brown.
11 This class knows its lessons very well.
12 I can't smoke my pipe today.
13 I'm sorry sir, I can't repeat the lesson today.
14 No, I don't understand Spanish.
15 Yes, I can tell you the way to Oxford Circus.
16 Do you know where John lives now?
17 Do you feel better this morning? (Yes, . . . or No, ...)
18 Why won't you take a cup of coffee.
19 May I borrow your newspaper? Certainly, ...
20 I'm sorry, I don't know the result of the football match.

Present Perfect Continuous

- When we wish to express an action which began at some undefined previous time, includes the present moment and goes beyond it we use the Present Perfect Continuous. For example:

  John has been serving in the Navy for 25 years.
  Mary has been practising the piano for an hour.
  I have been wearing this old dress for three summers.
  Your mother has been telling me about your new job.

- The Present Perfect Continuous is generally used to reckon only the time from the beginning of the action up to the present moment of speaking, but does not necessarily complete the action. It permits the action to continue beyond the present moment into the future.

  1 *John has been mending the car.*
  2 *Robert and Betty have been going to get married for the last five years.*
  3 *I've been eating black bread for years.*
  4 *I've been trying to win a prize all my life.*
  5 *I've been learning to dance recently.*
  6 *Peter has been breaking things ever since he was a little boy.*

It is the events before the present moment of speaking that interest us. They tell us somebody has spent quite a long time in the various activities that the speaker mentions. They do not tell us whether he has completed the action or achieved a result. There may, of course, be present consequences as well, e.g. in **1** dirty hands, in **2** nobody is excited at their announcements any more, and in **6** we call him 'butter fingers'.

exercise 136, exercise 137

Put the verb in brackets in the Present Perfect Continuous.

1 Will that gramophone never stop? It (play) the same tune for two hours.
2 Sergeant Black is a real old soldier. He (serve) for nearly twenty years.
3 Turn the television set off. The children (watch) for too long a time.
4 Mary is learning the piano. She (practise) since breakfast time.
5 He (live) in this country for many years but he still can't speak our language.
6 The new students (behave) very well so far.
7 John needs a holiday. He (work) too hard.
8 Please wake Peter soon. He (sleep) for ten hours.
9 We (travel) for three days and we are still only half way to London.
10 We must economise next month. We (spend) far too much money lately.

Put in the correct Present form of the verb. Present Simple, Present Continuous, Present Perfect or Present Perfect Continuous.

1 We never (smoke) cigarettes at any time. John always (smoke) a pipe but we (prefer) cigars.
2 My wife's mother (live) with us for the last six months.
3 She (go) away today. My wife (help) her with her packing now.
4 The boys (eat) green apples all day. Now they (be) ill and their mother (talk) to the doctor on the phone.
5 The boys (go) to bed because they are ill. The doctor (prescribe) some medicine. Their mother (give) them some now.
6 My brother usually (visit) his business friends two or three times a year. He (travel) in Germany at present.
7 She (read) many books on astronomy and so she really (know) the subject.

exercise 137 (contd.)

8   I (listen) to you for twenty minutes but I (not understand) anything. People usually (think) first and (speak) afterwards.

9   Peter (drive) a car for years but he (never drive) at night before.

10 John (go) out. He just (put) his coat on.

11 Peter (read) in bad light and now he (have) a headache.

12 Our train usually (leave) at two o'clock. Father (travel) by that train every Friday for five years.

13 Look out of the window . . . it (rain)? I hope not as I (not bring) a raincoat today.

14 Hello, John. Where . . . you (be)? I (look) for you all morning.

15 I can see Mr Brown through the open window. He (sit) at his desk. He (write) on a piece of paper. He always (sit) with his face to the window.

16 . . . you (finish) dinner yet? No, I still (prepare) the dessert.

17 This fine old tree (stand) here for two hundred years. People (say) it is a danger to traffic. The (want) it cut down.

18 My uncle's gardener (know) everything about roses. He (grow) them for the last fifty years and he still (try) to produce a blue one.

19 What's the time? I'm sorry, I (not know). My watch (stop).

20 Mr Brown (not go) home for lunch very often. The office is always busy. People (come) and (go) all the time, so he usually (take) a sandwich whenever he (find) a free moment.

21 Mrs Smith generally (do) all the housework by herself. She (cook) and (clean), (knit) and (sew). She's in the kitchen now. She (bake) a cake for tea.

22 . . . you ever (heard) a recording of your own voice? Listen! . . . you (recognise) yourself? I (play) a recording of your voice now!

23 Mr Brown usually goes to the theatre on Fridays. He (do) that for more than twenty years. Tonight, for a change, he (stay) a home.

24 Mary (not have) her summer holiday yet. At the moment she (work) in London. She (live) there for the past few weeks.

Past time

Simple past

We use this form of the verb when we wish to show

(a) that an action occurred *once* at a stated time in the past,

(b) that it occurred *generally, repeatedly or continually* during a period in past time.

Let us examine the following sentences:

1 *We went to Blackpool last summer. We caught the 9.20 train.*
2 *Yesterday the postman brought me three letters.*
3 *Ten years ago, I asked my wife to marry me.*
4 *William Shakespeare attended the Grammar School at Stratford.*
5 *King James I reigned from 1603-25.*
6 *He served in the R.A.F. during the war.*
7 *John and Peter went to school together (when they were boys).*
8 *In his younger days father always walked to the office.*
9 *They spent their early married life in a boarding house.*
10 *Grandfather drank nothing but milk for the last five years (of his life).*

● In numbers **1, 2** and **3** the words represent a fixed point or moment in the past. The words define the past moment at which the action or event took place. In number **4** the past time is not mentioned. However I think we can agree that to talk of William Shakespeare's habitual actions is to talk of the past. In numbers **5, 6, 7, 8, 9** and **10** the phrases underlined represent not a moment in time but a period of time. They represent a period during which the actions occurred repeatedly, habitually, continually or generally during the whole of the past time within the limits of the period in the sentence. The sentences describe the permanent routine during the past period.

- In sentences **7** and **10** the words in brackets are not really necessary. The form of the verb shows clearly that the speaker's words refer to a time which is past and finished. Compare:

  1 (a) *Grandfather drank nothing but milk for the last five years.*

  (b) *Grandfather has drunk nothing but milk for the last five years.*

  2 (a) *John and Mary lived here all their lives.*

  (b) *John and Mary have lived here all their lives.*

- In **1**(a) and **2**(a) the verb forms *drank* and *lived* refer to a time that is past and finished. It finished some time ago in the past. It has no connection with the present moment. Therefore in **1**(a) Grandfather's last five years are a time of the past. Grandfather died some time ago.

- In **2**(a) the same logic applies; since *lived* is a form of the verb we use to show what is definitely past and finished then the time phrase *all their lives* must indicate past lives. In **1**(b) and **2**(b) however the Present Perfect form of the verb brings the previous time up to the present moment. The five year period includes today, their lives include today. Therefore we are referring to persons who are still alive, now.

- So at the time of speaking, in **1**(b) Grandfather is still with us, and in **2**(b) John and Mary still live here.

- NOTE: The Present Perfect can never be used with an adverb of fixed past time or with a phrase that indicates a period of time which expired in the past. The Past Simple is then correct.

exercise 138

Express the following sentences (a) in the interrogative, and (b) in the negative. Use the auxiliary verbs *did* and *did not*.

1 He went out early.
2 He came back for lunch.
3 They gave him a present.
4 Father took us to the theatre.
5 We sat in the fourth row.
6 You saw everything very well.
7 They bought some chocolate.
8 We ate it during the interval.
9 Some of the ladies drank tea.
10 We spoke to some of the actors after the show.
11 One of them wrote something on Mary's programme.
12 She kept it as a souvenir.
13 She lost it in the end.
14 A friend found it for her.
15 You spent too much money last month.
16 The grocer forgot to send sugar.
17 You rang him up to order it.
18 He hurt himself when he fell.
19 His head struck the table.
20 You cut yourself while you were shaving.

exercise 139

Supply the Simple Past Form.

1 We (go) swimming yesterday. It (be) a lovely day and we (stay) in the water for hours.

2 John (buy) a second-hand car last week. He (pay) ninety pounds for it. It (run) well enough on the first day but on the second day he (cannot) start it.

3 Our neighbours (keep) a very fierce dog until one day it (bite) the postman who generally (come) to the front door.

4 For breakfast last Tuesday my sister (make) coffee in a new kind of machine. It (taste) horrible and everyone (spit) it out.

5 The lecturer (speak) very clearly and simply so everybody (understand) him although his subject (be) quite difficult.

6 They (have) more horses than cars when I (be) young.

7 In the country, boys (ride) to school on ponies then. Teachers always (come) on foot. The headmaster sometimes (take) a cab.

8 Lessons always (begin) at nine o'clock. Every morning the headmaster (say) prayers with us and (read) the lesson for the day. Then our teachers (lead) us to the classroom.

9 In my grandfather's youth few people (know) how to read and write. Every evening they (meet) at the village inn where someone (tell) them the news and (write) short letters for them. Sometimes they (drink) quite a lot of beer.

10 In olden times sailors always (eat) salt beef because nobody (know) how to keep food fresh for long periods.

exercise 140

Restate the following sentences in the Simple Past using the past time expressions given in brackets.

1 I think you are right (yesterday).
2 Peter runs like a deer (at the school sports).
3 Joan sews all her own clothes (until last year).
4 Our children always drink milk (when they were little).
5 He always rings the bell twice for his secretary (in our old office).
6 We grow roses in my garden (when we lived in the country).
7 The boy brings my newspapers (before seven o'clock yesterday).
8 The Prime Minister often flies to New York (in those days).
9 I know Peter Smith (before he got married).
10 English people sing carols (last Christmas).
11 We often buy a chicken for dinner (when they were cheap).
12 A policeman stands at the corner (every day last week).
13 Bees sometimes sting me (when I removed the honeycomb).
14 My brother has a small car (in 1979).
15 It isn't quite large enough (after the children were born).
16 He can't afford to buy a new one (at that time).
17 Many garages sell good second-hand cars (in those days).
18 Mary cuts out all the pictures in the newspapers (before she learnt to read).
19 She gets a lot of information from them (then).
20 Our clock strikes every hour (before we broke it).

exercise 141

Supply the Simple Past Form to show (a) cause and (b) the immediate effect of the cause in the past time.

1 The work (be) very difficult so we (get) tired.
2 The film (interest) me so much that I (see) it a second time.
3 The exercise (do) him so much good that he (feel) much better in a week.
4 The naughty children (eat) green apples and (become) ill at once.
5 The light (go) out so we (cannot) do our homework last night.
6 She (not know) the answer so she (look) it up at the back of the book.
7 She (see) a mouse under the bed and (scream) for help.
8 The old king (die) and the prince (take) his place on the throne.
9 The ball (strike) the window and (break) it.
10 They always (bring) flowers which (please) mother very much.

exercise 142

Complete the following sentences by adding a phrase in
the Simple Past.

EXAMPLE:

> *In 1492 . . . Columbus discovered America.*

1 A hundred years ago . . . .
2 In 1815 . . . .
3 On our wedding day . . . .
4 In his youth . . . .
5 . . . when I was a little girl (boy).
6 . . . the day before yesterday.
7 . . . in the Middle Ages.
8 In the reign of King Charles I . . . .
9 Only last week . . . .
10 . . . a few days ago.
11 . . . before you were born.
12 . . . just after you were born.
13 In the Stone Age . . . .
14 Before the Flood . . . .
15 . . . between 1920 and 1930.
16 . . . in the days of Alexander the Great.
17 . . . during the Golden Age of Greece.
18 After the First World War . . . .
19 . . . half an hour ago.
20 When Grandpapa met Grandmama . . . .

Past Continuous

● When we wish to speak of an action which was in progress at a particular point or which occupied a temporary period of past time we use the Past Continuous. Note that we do not use this form to denote that the action was complete. We use it simply to show that the action was progressing. Let us examine the following examples.

NOTE: We do not use this form for *repeated* actions, nor to express habit, custom or routine events.

1 *I was having a bath when the telephone rang.*
2 *When the teacher came in the children were sitting like little angels.*
3 *The old lady fell as she was getting off the bus.*
4 *As Mary was walking down the street she saw a lovely cat.*
5 *While father was listening to the radio the children began to shout.*
6 *Peter caught the train just as it was leaving.*

In sentence 1 the poor fellow was in the warm bath water when the telephone rang. The telephone bell interrupted him in his bath. We do not know what happened after that. We leave him in the middle of his bath. At that past moment 2 when the teacher came in, the class was sitting quietly. What happened after or before the teacher's entry we do not know. We only know that she entered during the time when the children were sitting like little angels. 3 shows us the old lady was in the act of getting off the bus when suddenly she fell. 4 Mary's walk was interrupted. We do not know whether she went on or not. What we do know is that she met a lovely cat during her walk. Father's enjoyment of the radio programme was interrupted by the shouting in 5, while, in 6, the train was in motion. Peter got on the train while it was moving. Note that the examples *I was having a bath*, etc., all express actions that usually occupy a shorter or longer period of time (not a single moment), and that the action which interrupts that period is always expressed in the Simple Past Form.

● Now let us examine some more sentences:

1 *At this time yesterday I was playing football*
2 *Five years ago I was working in Scotland*
3 *Half an hour ago he was singing. Now he is crying.*
4 *Mary was learning French last year. Now she is learning German.*

The key is in sentences **3** and **4**. The speaker is usually comparing what was happening then at that temporary moment or period in the past with what is happening now at this temporary moment or period in the present. The phrase underlined in **1** represents a point of past time which occurred during the game which was in progress at this time yesterday. When the game began and when it ended we do not know and in **2** we do not know when the man began to work in Scotland nor do we know when he stopped work there. In **3** we do not know when he began to sing; we do not know if he sang for an hour or a whole afternoon. We only know that at a certain moment of past time he was singing. In **4** whether Mary finally learned French or not is still a mystery. We do not know when she began or, when she finished. The Past Continuous does not express achievement or completion. Compare:

(a) *I went out when Peter came.*
(b) *I was going out when Peter came.*

In sentence (a) when Peter came I opened the door and left the house or the room, either with Peter or to avoid him! Perhaps I was free to go out because he came to take over my work. In (b) I was ready to go out, I was wearing my coat and hat perhaps. What is sure is that Peter arrived during my preparations for going out. Whether I eventually went out or not is not mentioned.

The sentence at (a) is in fact a *cause and effect* sentence. *Peter came* is the cause and *I went out* is the effect. A past cause and its immediate effect are always expressed in the same tense, the Simple Past.

exercise 143, exercise 144

Put in the Past Continuous Form and the Simple Past Form.
NOTE: **Cause and immediate effect take the same Simple Past Form.**

1 Peter (stay) at a seaside hotel on holiday when he first (meet) his wife.
2 The sun (shine) when I (set) out on my walk.
3 It (rain) when I (arrive) at my destination.
4 While I (have) lunch the sun (come) out again.
5 Peter (serve) in the artillery when a mule (kick) him.
6 It (kick) him as he (pass) behind it.
7 Where . . . you (live) before you moved house to come here?
8 Who . . . you (talk) to on the telephone just now?
9 As Mary (type) the letter she (notice) many spelling mistakes.
10 While Peter (carve) the chicken his wife (lay) the table.

Put in the Past Continuous for the interrupted action and the Simple Past for the action which interrupts it.

1 She (go) to bed when suddenly she (see) a mouse.
2 We (sit) down to dinner when someone (ring) the door bell.
3 Columbus (try) to reach India when he (find) America.
4 The family (watch) a television programme when the burglar (break) into the house.
5 Peter (meet) with an accident as he (cross) the street.
6 He (suffer) from shock when I (see) him in hospital.
7 He made a good recovery and when I last (see) him he (work) as hard as ever.
8 While he (lie) in bed his firm (pay) his wages every week.
9 Mary's grandfather (hurt) his back while he (dig) in the vegetable garden yesterday.
10 They put him to bed at once. Just as he (fall) asleep the doctor (arrive).

exercise 145

Supply the correct past forms of the verbs, Simple Past or Past Continuous.

1 She (clean) her teeth when one of them (come) out.
2 Who . . . you (speak) to on the telephone when I (bring) your coffee?
3 The doctor (ask) whether I always (take) my medicine.
4 The maid (polish) the silver once a week, on Fridays.
5 What . . . she (wear) when you (see) her at the party?
6 . . . John (work) at the time you (call) on him yesterday?
7 Yes, he (try) to make a new garden gate. It (not look) very strong.
8 Hush! I (hear) a sound. Perhaps my brother (talk) in his sleep.
9 We (go) swimming nearly every day while we (be) on holiday.
10 My father sometimes (drink) a glass of milk before he (go) to bed.
11 What . . . she (want) when she (visit) you yesterday?
12 Somebody (knock) on the front door as I (have) breakfast.
13 How much money . . . you (spend) last Christmas?
14 My father (give) me a cheque and I (spend) it all in one day.
15 Peter (not feel) very well so he (consult) his doctor.
16 Where . . . you (live) this time last year?
17 We (stay) at the Bristol Hotel and (work) in an office.
18 Peter (not look) at me as he (speak).
19 When the ambulance (arrive) the patient (sleep) like a child.
20 Our friends always (drop) in when they (pass) this way.

Past Perfect

● The Past Perfect is used to indicate what had already happened before or by a certain moment of time past. The action at that certain moment was the result, consequence or outcome of what had already taken place. The previous action is of no particular interest to the speaker by itself. There must be a result, consequence or outcome, either spoken or understood, to complete the significance.

NOTE: Exact chronology can be mentioned with the Past Perfect. See notes on the Present Perfect and compare the Past and Present Perfect forms.

1 *We had finished our work so we went home.*
2 *I had broken my leg the previous day so I couldn't go to school.*
3 *Mary gave us some flowers, she had just picked.*
4 *Peter had not arrived by two o'clock so I did not wait.*

exercise 146

Put in the Past Perfect to show the previous cause of a later effect, result, consequence or interest.

1 Our guests (meet) before so we didn't need to introduce them to one another.
2 The old man (be) a great traveller in his youth and could tell a tale about many strange places.
3 Mary (prepare) our meals on the previous day so she was able to visit her sister in the country.
4 John had nothing to smoke because he (forget) to buy tobacco.
5 We couldn't play football that Saturday as it (rain) all the previous week.
6 The ground was under water because it (not stop) raining for six days and nights.
7 They (not eat) for twenty-four hours and were very hungry.
8 He lived quietly on a little money he (save) before his retirement.

exercise 147

Use a Simple Past form of the verb. Give a reasonable later consequence, effect, result or interest to complete these sentences. Try to find more than one probability for each. *For* and *since* expressions may be useful in some sentences.

EXAMPLE:

    1 The train had already gone ...
       (a) *so I waited for the next one.*
       (b) *therefore I couldn't leave London till next morning.*

2   We had seen the film ....
3   The sun had gone down ....
4   We had run out of coffee ....
5   They had never seen a camel before ....
6   She had finished her book ....
7   He had invited us to dinner ....
8   It hadn't stopped raining ....
9   We had never been in an aeroplane before ....
10 His wife had prepared an excellent meal ....
11 The postman had brought a letter from my rich uncle ....
12 He had sent me a cheque for five hundred pounds ....
13 Our teacher had explained the lesson very carefully ....
14 I hadn't finished reading the newspaper ....
15 You had just left school ....
16 I had heard stories about ghosts before ....
17 The army had marched all night ....
18 Poor Peter had had malaria very badly ....
19 John had taken driving lessons ....
20 He had given me his telephone number ....

exercise 148

Supply the Simple Past for the effect, consequence, result or interest and the Past Perfect for the previous cause.

1 They (spend) all their money and (not know) where to find any more.
2 We (finish) our work so we (sit) down to talk.
3 The sky (be) black for some time before the rain (begin) to fall.
4 I (give) you the work to do again because you (do) it badly.
5 When I (thank) my hostess I (leave) the house and (go) home.
6 Yesterday my wife (tell) me about a beautiful hat she (see) a few days earlier.
7 Dr Brown (just return) so they (give) him the message.
8 One of his patients (break) his leg and (need) a doctor at once.
9 The doctor (hope) for a quiet night. He (feel) disappointed.
10 After the children (go) to bed the house (be) very quiet.
11 They always (live) in a small village and (not understand) the city people.
12 I (can't) read because I (forget) to fetch my glasses.
13 Peter (have) dinner in town that evening as his wife (go) to visit her mother.
14 We (never be) in Athens before so we (want) to see the sights.
15 The child (lose) his money so he (cannot buy) sweets.

exercise 149

Supply reasonable previous causes in the past for these consequences, results, effects or interest. Use the Past Perfect and try to find more than one previous cause for each sentence.

EXAMPLE:

> *She knew how to bake a cake because* . . .
> (a) *her mother had taught her.*
> (b) *she had learned at school.*
> (c) *she had read about it in a book.*

Use *as* and *because* as links where necessary.

1 He gave his horse a lump of sugar . . . .
2 She asked me to repeat my name . . . .
3 We asked her to sing the song again . . . .
4 They called the boy Moses . . . .
5 Father tipped the waiter very well . . . .
6 The man was out of breath . . . .
7 I sent my watch to the watchmaker's . . . .
8 Our visitor was very tired . . . .
9 It was very cold outside in the garden . . . .
10 We gave the patient first aid . . . .
11 We didn't meet yesterday after all . . . .
12 I couldn't eat the food at lunch time . . . .
13 Peter didn't know the answer to the question . . . .
14 John looked very smart at his sister's wedding . . . .
15 The tramp had three days' beard . . . .
16 The president arrived half an hour late . . . .
17 We called a doctor . . . .
18 Peter wasn't very happy when we met him . . . .
19 The Colonel had great experience of men . . . .
20 The children were late for school . . . .

Used to (Temporary Past)

- We often prefer the form *used to* when we wish to show that an action happened repeatedly or continuously over a period of past time. The period began and finished in the past.

    1 *John used to live in London.*
    2 *We used to go to the country for our holidays.*
    3 *When they were young they used to dance the polka.*
    4 *My brother, who went to Rome last year, used to live in Paris.*

    These examples all mention periods of past time and actions which occurred repeatedly or continuously within these past periods. Both period and action began, went on and finished in the past.

    NOTE: There is no other form of this idiom. We cannot say *I use to* to express present habit or custom. We use the Simple Present verb forms for that.

- The idiomatic forms *to be used to* and *get used to* have nothing in common with the temporary past idiom *used to*; their meanings are quite different.

- **To be used to**

    1 *We are used to the climate in England now.*
    2 *Our children are used to good, plain food.*

    These two examples show that *to be used to* = *to be acclimatised* or *to be accustomed to.*

- **To get used to**

    1 *You will get used to working at night and sleeping by day.*
    2 *My friends from abroad soon get used to driving their cars on the left-hand side of the road.*

    Get used to means *become accustomed to.* Notice that the *to* in the expressions *to be used to, to get used to* is not an infinitive particle therefore the gerund is the correct form to follow these expressions: I am used to *cooking* my own meals. Of course, a noun may also follow them:

    Mary is used to life in the country.

exercise 150

Supply the Simple Past to show cause and immediate effect or the Past Perfect to show previous cause. The Simple Past expresses the later consequence.

1 He (press) the switch and the engine (start).
2 Peter (forget) to fill up with petrol so the car (stop) just outside the garage.
3 We (not eat) much for breakfast so we (feel) hungry at lunchtime.
4 John (not arrive) by seven-thirty, so Mary (go) to the cinema alone.
5 Mr Smith (misunderstand) the question because he (not hear) it well.
6 Professor Smith (heat) a metal bar and it (expand).
7 His firm (give) him a better position last year because he (earn) it.
8 As we (miss) the express from London we (travel) on a slow train.
9 Our host (introduce) me to Mrs Brown whom I (not meet) before.
10 Peter (sunbathe) too long and (get) blisters on his back.
11 Mary (not be) abroad before so everything (seem) strange to her.
12 ... he (refuse) to see me because I (not write) for an appointment?
13 She (not go) out in the rain because she (not have) an umbrella.
14 ... he (become) angry when you (accuse) him of stealing?
15 As we (not have) notice of the general's arrival, naturally we (not expect) him.
16 Something heavy (strike) me on the head and (knock) me out.
17 ... she (find out) for herself or ... someone (tell) her?
18 We (wake) up late because the alarm clock (not ring).
19 The policeman (put) up his hand and the traffic (stop).
20 Susan's dinner (go) cold so Alan (warm) it up for her.

Past Perfect Continuous

- We use this form of the verb when we wish to show that the action took place either *continuously* or *repeatedly* over a period of past time extending up to and usually including the defined moment. Some examples follow:

    1 *We had been studying for months* (so we felt confident on examination day).
    2 *John had not been sleeping well* (so he asked the doctor for some sleeping pills).
    3 *Peter had been living in Italy for five years.* (Naturally, he spoke good Italian when he came home).
    4 *The rain had been falling steadily all day* (when suddenly the sun broke through).

- The phrases in *italic* type show actions which were (a) repeated or (b) continuous over a period of previous past time.

- In numbers 1, 2 and 4 the examination, the sleeping pills and the sunshine put an end to the studying, John's sleeplessness and the rain.

- In number 3 either John returned from Italy, thus ending his residence there, or the speaker met John in Italy.

- We can see then that *the actions* in the phrases in *italic* type need not necessarily end at the past time or moments implied in the phrases between brackets. *Some of them went on and some of them stopped.* All of them are necessarily repeated or continuous actions which occurred over a period of time up to and including a certain past moment and, possibly, beyond it. Consider these sentences:

    1 *John had been living in London for ten years when the war broke out.*
    2 *We had been talking about Peter when he entered the room.*

- The phrases underlined are simple measurements of past time. The actions contained in them are not necessarily causes of subsequent events.

exercise 151

Supply the Past Perfect Continuous forms of the verb to show that the actions were (a) repeated (continual) or (b) continuous between the farther past and the later past.

1 She (read) in a bad light and her eyes were sore.
2 We (try) to solve the mystery for weeks but we hadn't succeeded.
3 Peter (ask) Mary to marry him for three years before they were engaged.
4 It (rain) for days on end and everything was soaked.
5 I (teach) for seven years when I began to write this book.
6 She still couldn't sing although she (take) lessons for years.
7 We took mother to the doctor yesterday. She (complain) of pains in her back.
8 The children went to the zoo yesterday. They (want) to go for a very long time.
9 The professor (teach) in the university for forty years on the day he retired.
10 Shakespeare (write) for a number of years before he became really well-known.
11 The firm went bankrupt. They (lose) money for quite a long time.
12 A good fire (burn) all day and the house was comfortably warm.
13 Grandfather (not take) exercise regularly. That was why he began to put on weight.
14 We (wait) for more than an hour but there was still no sign of a bus.
15 My friends advised me to take a holiday. They said I (worry) about business too much and I needed rest.

Future time

going to

Be going to + infinitive

● This idiomatic construction is used to convey a number of shades of meaning in connection with a future action. Let us first examine the *declared intention of the subject* of the verb.

1 *Peter says he is going to be a doctor when he grows up.*
2 *The orchestra is going to play a Strauss Waltz. It is number six on the programme.*
3 *Mary says that she is going to get married when she is twenty, and that she is going to have three children.*
4 *I'm not going to pay you until you finish the work.*

● These sentences all express clearly and firmly the declared intention of the subject of the verb. Whether Peter in **1** and Mary in **3** manage to carry out their intentions is irrelevant. At the time of speaking they tell us of what they mean to do in the future and as **4** shows, the intention is often emphatically stated.

● Notice that the *shall* and *will* future forms are not suitable in these sentences as they frequently indicate mere acceptance of the future and what it may bring; see note, p. 295.

Certainty of the future

● Circumstances at the moment may combine so strongly that, given time, a certain future development is the only logical outcome. Consider the following:

1 *The wind has changed and the clouds are black. I'm afraid it is going to rain.*
2 *Your son is a fine boy, Mary! He's going to be taller than his father by the look of him.*
3 *Prices have gone down and the market is quiet. Some of the merchants are going to lose money this season.*
4 *I have forgotten my umbrella, it is going to rain, and I'm going to get wet!*

● None of these examples expresses any intention for the future. They do indicate either pleasure or regret at situations which, given time, inevitably develop from present circumstances.

Certainty of the imminent future

● The *going to* forms are frequently heard when the speaker feels certain of *what is going to happen very suddenly*. Consider:

    1 *Help the old lady! She's going to fall down!*
    2 *Mind that mule! It's going to kick!*
    3 *Look out! These cars are going to crash!*
    4 *I'll have to take the tooth out. It is going to hurt a little so be brave.*
    5 *Good, it's out now. You're going to have a good night's sleep.*

exercise 152

Rewrite the verbs in brackets to show either the subject's intention for the future or certainty of the future.

1 It (be) a warm summer according to the weather experts.
2 Mind that vase! You (drop) it!
3 He's already quite tall but he (grow) a few inches taller.
4 I hope your cough (not develop) into something more serious.
5 Come off that branch! Can't you see it (break)?
6 He told me he (buy) a partnership in a small firm.
7 I'm afraid the poor man is very ill. He (die), I think.
8 We (not sell) you anything until you pay for the last order.
9 Peter says he (live) all alone on a desert island.
10 Look here! I (not put) up with any more of your nonsense.
11 We (not listen) to anything you have to say.
12 Look at the sky! The children (get) wet on the way home.
13 Life is hard at present but everything (be) different, soon.
14 We (stay) in London for a year to learn the language well.
15 We have lost our way. I (ask) a policeman to direct us.
16 I (look) for a hotel to spend the night in.
17 John says he (not work) so hard in future.
18 It (take) a lot of hard work to prepare this class for the examination.
19 Mr Brown (sit) down for a while as he feels tired.
20 Building a model cathedral out of matchsticks (need) patience and skill.

Commands or official decisions

- Governments, councils, committees, ministries, officers in the armed services and, in fact, all persons in authority find it necessary to give orders or announce official decisions.

- Very often we use the Present form of the auxiliary verb *to be* and the infinitive of the principal verb to express a present command or official decision which refers to the future. Let us study the following:

  1 *Sgt Robinson is to report to Headquarters by Friday.*
  2 *The accused is guilty and is to undergo six months' imprisonment.*
  3 *We are to spend no more than fifty pence, Father says.*
  4 *The Prime Minister is to visit Russia next year.*
  5 *The wedding of Miss Angela Smith and Mr Peter Brown is to take place in St Andrew's Church.*
  6 *I am to speak on behalf of the Collectors' Society next Friday.*

- In the first three sentences the person in authority is speaking (or writing). In **1** an officer or a superior at least, is passing on an order that he has received. In **2** the judge is speaking, and giving punishment according to law. In **3** an elder brother or sister is passing on the instructions he has received from Father. In the next three sentences the speaker is not reporting a command. He is reporting a decision which the responsible authorities have made. **4** The Prime Minister, after discussion with the Cabinet, and after reaching agreement with it, is to go to the Kremlin. This is an official announcement regarding the future. **5** The wedding is to take place, after discussion with all the interested parties. This is an official announcement. **6** The Society has agreed that I am to speak. The decision is the outcome of discussion with the interested parties. It is an official announcement.

● The first three sentences are commands. Commands very often come from a quite impersonal source. Sgt Robinson's order is from an office rather than from an officer; the accused receives his punishment from the Law and not from the judge.

● The elder child is not giving his own orders, but is passing on Father's instructions. The first three sentences are *indirect impersonal commands* since they do not come from person to person but from an impersonal authority to the person who is to obey. In **3** Father is, of course, a person but he is also an authority to his children. His word is Law.

● The speaker in **3** is passing on the instruction from the Authority. He is not originating the command.

● The other three sentences show decisions by the official or responsible bodies. The sentences show that after consultation or discussion, they have agreed that *a proposal for the future is to become fact* in the future.

Conclusion

● The forms *am, are, is* with the infinitive are used to indicate present impersonal commands from an authority to the individual(s). The command usually refers to an act of obedience which someone is to carry out at a stated future time.

NOTE: This form may also be used when immediate or present obedience is commanded.
   You are to leave my house at once!

● These forms are also used to show that the relevant authority has discussed and agreed to the future action. It may also indicate that the relevant authority has appointed the person in the sentence (see **4** and **6**) for the future activity.

exercise 153

Put in the correct form to give an impersonal command or direct official decision concerning the future: *am; are; is* + infinitive with *to*.

1 You (arrive) next Thursday at 4 p.m.
2 Captain Smith (command) the new ship.
3 Carpenters' wages (be raised) from the first of next month.
4 All passengers from the east (report) to the medical officer.
5 The battalion (spend) the night in the open.
6 Officers and men (not light) fires.
7 Students (not smoke) in lecture rooms.
8 Father says that John (pay) for the broken window.
9 The witnesses (attend) the court every day during the trial.
10 If John doesn't work harder, he (leave) the university.

Arrangements and programmes

- The future is sometimes recorded in programmes, timetables, appointments, books, etc. Thus, sometimes we may know, as far as mortal man may know, what to expect at a given time in the future. We have this knowledge now of an arrangement which already exists. We know at present what the future arrangement is. To express this we use two of the forms we have already met in the section on *The Present*.

- We use the *Present Simple* and the *Present Continuous*. These two forms keep their original characteristics of temporary and permanent time. Let us consider the following:

  1(a) *The children go back to school on the first Monday in September.*
  (b) *Our children are going back on 8th September.*
  2(a) *The train for Scotland leaves at 10 a.m. on Saturday.*
  (b) *It is leaving at 10.10 a.m. next Saturday.*
  3(a) *Peter is the eldest son so he goes into the family business.*
  (b) *Really! He tells me that he is going into the Navy soon.*
  4(a) *The office manager goes on holiday in July.*
  (b) *Mr Brown is taking his place as Smith will be away.*
  5(a) *Father retires at sixty so I take over from him next year.*
  (b) *My father is retiring in the summer. He's getting old.*

Simple Present as a future tense

- The (a) sentences show the fixed routine arrangements.

  1 The first Monday in September is the day which has been fixed by the authorities. It is the regular day.
  2 The 10 a.m. train runs every Saturday and so the speaker implies that next Saturday will be no exception.
  3 Peter is a young man whose career must follow family custom. The eldest son goes into the business in accordance with the normal routine and custom.
  4 The manager, in accordance with arrangements already in force, a programme already fixed, goes on holiday. Office routine operates.
  5 There is an agreement or a decision that when father becomes sixty he will retire. The normal fixed plan will operate at the right, future time.

● All these sentences at (a) show that the future events are part of a programme which exists at the present moment of speaking. Very often we use this form for speaking of future events. e.g. when we assume that what has always happened in the past and happens now will also happen in the future see 2(a) and 3(a) as part of a repeated regular routine when we have certain knowledge that according to a programme an event or action must be repeated at a future time. The programme exists now.

Present Continuous as a future tense

● The sentences at (b) clearly show that there is an arrangement for the future. The sentences also show that these arrangements are not part of the usual routine but are exceptions from it. In 1(b) we see that the speaker's arrangement is for his own children only, and that it is for one occasion only. It is not a permanent, but a temporary arrangement for this once only, an interruption of routine.

2 The 10 a.m. Saturday train is leaving ten minutes later than usual. Again there is an exception from normal routine for a temporary period.

3 Peter's future seems to be exceptional. By joining the Navy he is not conforming to his family's custom. Again we see an exception from normal routine.

4 We see that Smith usually takes the manager's place. However both Smith and the manager will be absent at the same time next summer so Mr Brown is acting as manager. This is exceptional.

5 Father is retiring not in fulfilment of a pre-arranged plan or agreement but because he is getting old. He probably never intended to retire at any time. His action is not a normal routine one.

When we have present knowledge of an arrangement for the future we use the Present Continuous to express it when ((a) the arrangement is for a short temporary period or for one occasion only after which normal routine is resumed, and ((b) when the arrangement is an exception from normal routine, fixed programme or custom.

exercise 154

Express the future programme using the *Simple Present* or *Present Continuous* as required.

1 The S.S. Blue Star (arrive) on Monday according to plan.
2 The examinations (take place) next month as announced.
3 The office (close) an hour later than usual tomorrow.
4 We (have) breakfast very early tomorrow so that we can leave home before seven.
5 He usually works at the station but next month he (work) at the docks for a few days each week.
6 I'm sorry I can't accept your invitation. I (have) lunch with some business people next Wednesday.
7 We always go to Paris on holiday. Next year I (go) to Spain for a change.
8 Saturday is his day off, usually. However, he (play) in the finals of a tennis tournament next Friday so the firm (give) him both days off.
9 My Uncle John from Zigazag (visit) us soon. He hasn't been home for thirty years.
10 As a result of the bad weather, aeroplanes (not take off) tonight.
11 Uncle John says in his letter that he (bring) me a pet monkey.
12 If all goes well we (reach) Oxford at noon. Some of us (take) sandwiches in case the car breaks down.
13 Mary usually goes shopping on Saturdays. Next week she (go) on Thursday instead because she (visit) her mother for the weekend.
14 Most students (take) the examination in two years' time but this girl (take) it next year.
15 According to law my younger brother (join) the army next year.
16 Peter usually goes home for the holidays but this year his family (come) to visit him.
17 Grandfather doesn't feel very well so he (stay) in bed tomorrow.
18 John's employers (pay) salaries before the end of this month so that the employees will have some money for Christmas.

Shall and *will*

● These two auxiliary verbs are used in two different ways to indicate two different aspects of the future.

● First we have the form which expresses *the desire, promise or determination of the speaker*. In this form we use *will* with the first persons singular and plural and *shall* with the second and third persons singular and plural. This form of the future may be called the *Desired Future*. Consider the following sentences:

  1 *I will learn English however difficult it is at first.*
  2 *You shall have a new bicycle if you do well at school.*
  3 *That man is a traitor to his country and he shall die.*
  4 *I promise you that you shall pay no more taxes.*
  5 *The police shall know of this man's criminal act.*

● All of the above sentences show that *the speaker expresses desire, determination or a promise for the future*. Sentence **1** shows that the speaker has made up his mind, that he is determined to learn the English language eventually. In **2** a father or mother is making a promise to a child. In **3** a patriot expresses determination regarding the future fate of a traitor. In **4** a demagogue makes promises to voters. In **5** an angry citizen is determined to bring a criminal to justice. The future, so far, is in the hands of the speakers themselves and they express their intentions for the future.

● Now the future, generally speaking, is not for us to arrange. A great many happenings will occur and we mortal men and women must accept them when they come. We cannot change the future and we cannot avoid it. To express this sense in the future we use the auxiliary verbs *shall* and *will* again but this time we use *shall* for the first persons, singular and plural, and *will* for the second and third persons, singular and plural. This form may be called the *Inevitable or Automatic Future*, since personal desire, promise or determination cannot play any part in it. Let us examine some examples.

1 *I shall be twenty-two on my next birthday.*
2 *You will see Brumas, the Polar bear, when you go to the zoo.*
3 *John will be nineteen next month so he will go into the army very soon. He will serve for two years.*
4 *The sun will rise and set tomorrow and every day.*
5 *We shall be tipsy if we drink any more wine.*
6 *They will meet Mary and Peter at the dance if they go.*

● These sentences all refer to events which the subject of the verb cannot avoid. It is sure that the future happening will take place. In **1** the speaker cannot avoid his twenty-second birthday (unless he dies in the meantime). In **2** you are sure to see Brumas. In **3** John will inevitably become old enough for the army. It is beyond the power of the speaker to prevent this or influence the matter in any way. **4** is absolutely beyond human influence. In **5** the result of drinking more wine is unavoidable. In **6** Peter and Mary will be at the dance. In the ordinary normal course of events you will see them. These forms are clearly contrasted in *I shall drown, you will not save me* (simple statement of an inevitable event, implying that you will not be able to save me), and the suicidal *I will drown, you shall not save me*, (expressing an unchangeable determination).

exercise 155, exercise 156

Express the agreement, desire, promise, determination or decision of the speaker by using *shall* and *will*.

1   I . . . help you tomorrow.
2   You . . . have the reddest apple on the tree!
3   She . . . wear silks and satins and be the prince's bride.
4   We . . . never leave our friends who need us.
5   They . . . receive the freedom of the city!
6   Mary . . . come to my wedding. I . . . invite her at once.
7   You . . . not enter my house again. Keep out!
8   The two brothers . . . never be separated again!
9   I . . . pay my account at the end of the month.
10 The guilty man . . . remain in prison for six months.

Express the Inevitable or Automatic Future by using *shall* and *will*.

1   I . . . need some food before tomorrow.
2   You . . . be old enough for the navy soon.
3   He . . . feel cold without an overcoat in December.
4   We . . . all grow old, sooner or later.
5   It . . . cost a lot of money to live in such a fine hotel.
6   You . . . understand English much better in twelve months' time.
7   The boys' voices . . . break eventually. They . . . become baritones or tenors.
8   People say that the world . . . grow cold in 20,000,000 years.
9   A fine summer . . . guarantee a good harvest.
10 A fish out of water . . . die very quickly.

exercise 157   exercise 158

State the verbs in brackets with *going to* to show the
intention of the subject.

1   Mary says she (give) me a book for Christmas.
2   John's brother (not take) his examination this year.
3   Miss Smith (sing) after dinner.
4   The government (build) a new hospital near here.
5   I (live) in a warm climate when I retire.
6   They (get married) in the spring.
7   The Browns (sell) their house at the end of the year.
8   He told me he (send) you a cheque for twenty pounds.
9   She's twenty minutes late! I'm (not wait) here any longer.
10 . . . (talk) all night? Put the light out and go to sleep!

State the verbs in brackets with *will/shall* to show the
intention of the speaker.

1   He (obey) my orders or take the consequences.
2   I promise that I (work) hard in future.
3   We (do) everything in our power to help her.
4   You (have) a fair day's wage for a fair day's work.
5   Our children (go) to a good school when they are old
    enough.
6   Mr Smith (receive) an increase in salary next month.
7   You (not leave) this room until I give you permission.
8   Mary (go) to the seaside for a month, her father says.
9   We (be) good, we promise you.
10 You (pay) for your impudence, young man!

exercise 159

State the verbs in brackets to show (a) the speaker's intention or (b) the subject's intention appropriately.

1 Father (buy) a new car this year.
2 He (offer) the old one to Peter for fifty pounds.
3 Peter told me that he (not pay) so much for that old wreck.
4 Mr Brown (propose) a toast to the ladies.
5 I (not refuse) to drink to that toast.
6 The band (play) a waltz in a few minutes.
7 That's good. Peter (ask) Mary to dance with him.
8 Are you (do) any work today? Come on, roll your sleeves up.
9 Peter's uncle (take) him to the zoo tomorrow.
10 The boys (have) a whole day's holiday on Friday.

will (insist and persist)

● *Will* sometimes indicates that a person is considered stubborn, insistent or wilful. Consider the following sentences. Notice that *will* is strongly emphasised and that since it is not being used to indicate futurity it may appear in conditional clauses (see p. 311ff).

> 1 *John is soaked to the skin! He will go out without a coat, no matter what the weather looks like.*
> 2 *Mary is getting very fat again. Well, what do you expect? She will eat chocolate and sweets.*
> 3 *If you will play with fire, you must expect to burn your fingers.*

● The above examples all refer to situations of stubbornness, or unreasonable persistence. The doers of these things are flying in the face of common sense.

NOTE: *Will* is used for all persons. *Shall* is not used in this sense. *Will* is always pronounced with emphasis when used in this way and the short forms (*I'll, you'll*, etc.) are not used.

shall and *will* (offers of service)

● *Shall* is always used in questions in which the speaker intends to offer help or service:

> *Shall I make you a cup of tea?*
> *Shall we do the washing up after dinner?*

Will is often used in asking for help or service:

> *Will you fetch some more coffee please?*
> *Will you take that old lady across the street, please?*

Will is also used when offers of help and service are accepted:

> *Shall we post these letters for you?*
> *Yes, if you will (be so kind).*

Conditions without *shall* and *will*

● In conditional clauses the *shall* and *will* constructions are not used: Instead, we use the corresponding Present tense forms of the verbs:

> *If I see Peter I shall give him your address.*
> *Unless you apologise, John will never forgive you.*

● The same rule is followed in time clauses introduced by temporal conditioners

> *when, whenever, as soon as, until, by the time, before, after.*

Future Continuous

shall be and *will be*

● When we think of a special moment in the future and wish to express what we know will be in progress at that moment, we use *shall be* and *will be* with the Present Participle of the main verb. Perhaps we shall find some examples useful.

1 *At eleven o'clock tomorrow I shall be travelling to Madrid.*
2 *At this time on Friday Peter will be having lunch with Mary.*
3 *John will be reading the book over the weekend.*
4 *When I arrive back in England the roses will be blooming.*
5 *They will be watching television tomorrow evening.*

● In **1** the journey begins before 11 a.m. Eleven o'clock is a particular point of time during the journey. In **2** no reference is made to the commencement of lunch nor to the end of lunch. Just as, in the present time, I can say

I am having lunch now (at this present temporary moment,)

so can I say of the future time

They will be having lunch (then).

At the present moment I say *I am travelling now* and of the future moment *I shall be travelling then.*

exercise 160

**Put in the correct Future Form. Indicate extreme
probability or near certainty in the speaker's mind.**

NOTE: *Shall/ will be —ing.*

1   I envy you John! This time next week you . . . sunbathing at
    Palermo.
2   At three o'clock tomorrow I . . . (cross) the Atlantic.
3   Please don't telephone between two and four o'clock. I . . .
    (teach) then.
4   We can't meet before Saturday as I (work) overtime until
    then.
5   Father is late tonight! He . . . (travel) by a later train,
    probably.
6   Yes, he . . . (work) late at the office, no doubt.
7   Come at one o'clock. I (wait) for you in my office.
8   As soon as he arrives conduct him to the library. A good
    fire . . . (burn) there soon.
9   Please don't disturb me. I . . . (write) in the study till
    bed-time.
10 If you need my help, please call me; I . . . (watch) television
    in the lounge.

Assumption

● We use the Future Continuous to express what we suppose to be very probable in the future.

● Sometimes we know a person's character, habits and peculiarities so well that we can say with almost perfect certainty what he or she *will be doing* at any given time in the future. Events and happenings can be so well known to us that we can predict the most probable future action.

● The following examples help to illustrate these points.

1 *Tomorrow is Sunday so Mary will be going to church after breakfast.*

2 *Robert's leg is better now so he will be playing football on Saturday as usual.*

3 *My wife's mother will be coming for Easter.*

● Each of the three speakers gives his own opinion of future events which seem very probable in view of the facts and information in his possession.

● Sometimes an ironic, sarcastic or humourous note is expressed by using the *shall be, will be* forms of the verb.

1 *Grandma's rheumatism is much better. She'll be dancing the polka before long.*

2 *What! Forty pounds for bed and breakfast! You'll be serving golden eggs in a week or two.*

exercise 161

State the verbs in brackets, using the *shall be/will be* forms.

1 It's my wife's birthday next Friday. We (give) a party as usual.
2 She (send) out her invitations at the last minute again, I suppose.
3 I'm afraid I shan't be able to come as I (visit) my parents in the country.
4 Tomorrow is Sunday. I take it that we (go) to church in the morning.
5 Mary (not come) with us unless she feels much better.
6 It's no use calling on Saturday afternoon. Tom (get ready) to go to the match.
7 You must change for dinner. Everybody (wear) evening dress, I'm sure.
8 . . . we (have) that awful dance band again this year? It gets worse every year.
9 The kettle (boil) in a minute or two. Do stay and have a cup of tea.
10 I'm sorry, my husband isn't home yet but he (arrive) at any moment now.
11 Peter's examinations are next month. Naturally he (study) hard till then.
12 Are we to understand that we (not see) him for a whole month?
13 Not exactly, but he (spend) most of his evenings with his books.
14 If all goes well, the firm (do) much more business this time next year.
15 What . . . you (do) in five year's time?
16 How can anybody know for sure what (happen) to him in the future?
17 The holiday season (come) round again soon, won't it?
18 Yes, I think I (stay) at home this year. Business isn't very good.

Future Perfect

- An event can happen or an action can take place at any
  time between now (the time of speaking) and then (a point
  in the future). We must consider then three points of time:

  A. the moment of speaking.
  C. the moment when the action will take place or the
  event will occur, and
  B. the time in the future between **A** and **C**.

  The following examples and explanations make the
  question clear.

  1 *I shall have finished my work by nine o'clock.*
  2 *Mary will have come back from Paris before we leave.*
  3 *The boys will have eaten all the cake by the time we get
  home.*
  4 *The telegram will have reached New York before your
  plane lands.*

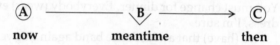

now   **meantime**   **then**

- Let **A** represent the present moment of speaking and **C**
  represent the future times which are underlined in the
  sentences. Then **B** represents a time which is future if we
  relate it to **A**. When we compare **B** with **C** however we see
  that **B** is not so far into the future as **C**. The action at **B**
  occurs and is complete before the future time which **C**
  represents. The outcome, result, consequence or
  development of the action at **B** will be effective at future
  time **C**.

- In **1** Before nine o'clock I shall finish my work. As a result I
  shall be free to go to the theatre, have a glass of beer with
  my friends, go to bed early or do anything else I choose to
  do at nine o'clock.

  The previous future **B** affects the later future **C**. In **2**
  since Mary will be here, we may see her before we leave,
  we can leave the children with her, or she can help us pack
  our luggage.

  Again the previous future event at **B** affects the future
  time at **C**. In **3** there will be no cake for us; the boys will be
  sick or they won't be hungry.

Again the event at **B** will affect the future at **C**. In **4** the people in New York will know you are coming, they will come to the aerodrome, a hotel room will be ready. Again, the previous future action or event at **B** has an effect on the future time **C**.

● When an action or event happens in the meantime, that is between now and a stated future time and particularly, though not necessarily, when that action affects the given future time or event, then we use the **Anterior Future Form** which people usually call the **Future Perfect Tense**.

exercise 162

Insert the correct Future Perfect form.

1 The magistrates will give their decision tomorrow. They (hear) the evidence by then.
2 The firm will be more prosperous by next summer. We (begin) work on an important contract in the meantime.
3 You will find the key under the doormat. I (leave) it there on my way to work.
4 He gets a pension in 1998. He (work) for us for thirty years then.
5 We hope to go to England next year. We (learn) quite a lot of English before then, of course.
6 By the time we come back, we (visit) most places of interest in London.
7 We can call on the manager about two o'clock. He (have) lunch by that time.
8 I'm sorry I can't see you at seven tomorrow evening. I (not finish) work then.
9 Mary will return my book next week. She (have) time to read it carefully, I hope.
10 What shall I be doing in ten years from now? I (marry) but I don't know whether I (settle) down.

Future Perfect Continuous

- We may want to reckon the total length of time during which an action has been repeated or carried on continuously since some previous moment up to a moment in the future. Note carefully that the previous moment may occur before, at, or after the moment of speaking. The action may or may not stop at the future time to which we refer. Some examples will make my meaning clear.

    1 *By June of next year I shall have been teaching for ten years.*
    2 *Joanna will have been living in England for five years by the summer.*
    3 *The battalion will have been fighting for ninety-six hours at dawn.*
    4 *By lunch time I shall have been walking for four hours.*

- The phrases underlined indicate *the future moment which completes the period of time* (ten years, five years, ninety-six hours, four hours) *which will have passed since the commencement of the action.* There is no indication that the action itself will stop. It may stop, but generally speaking we feel that the action will go on after the future moment.

- The person speaking these sentences may do so before the action begins, when it begins or during the course of the action. In **4** for example the speaker is perhaps still in bed in the morning. He is probably making plans for a walk before lunch. He is speaking of the action. In **1**, **2** and **3** the speaker says the sentence during the time of the action, that is the action has already begun and some time has elapsed before the speaker's remarks are made.

exercise 163

Supply the Future Perfect or Future Perfect Continuous to complete these sentences appropriately.

1 By the time Peter is forty he (teach) for fifteen years.
2 John (finish) work by six o'clock.
3 We shall be free about nine o'clock. We (have) dinner by then.
4 In 1995 we (live) here for twenty-five years.
5 By noon tomorrow we (travel) more than a thousand miles.
6 If you don't hurry up the shops (close) before you get there.
7 Peter can't see you at ten o'clock. He (go) to bed earlier than that.
8 At Easter I (write) this book for three years.
9 By next Sunday we (be) on holiday for three weeks.
10 That's right! You (stay) at the hotel since the first of the month.
11 . . . the doctor (arrive) before the ambulance is ready to leave?
12 Our guests are staying until eleven o'clock. The rain (stop) by then.
13 I can't write a criticism of the book tomorrow. I (not read) it all.
14 . . . you (complete) your report in time for the committee meeting on Friday?
15 If you (not do) it by then, we (call) a meeting for nothing.
16 This little seed (grow) into a fine tree by the baby's twenty-first birthday.
17 When the time comes for me to retire I (rise) to a high position in the firm.
18 . . . the children (write) their letters in time for the last post?
19 Mr Brown can't attend the meeting. He (not come) back from Italy then.
20 Mrs Black (not bake) her cake yet, becuse she wants to have it fresh for the party.

exercise 164

Insert the Future Perfect Continuous.

1   The directors are going to give him a gold watch on his birthday. He (work) for forty years in the same office, on that day.

2   At the end of this year we (live) in this house for twenty-five years.

3   Next Christmas we shall celebrate our silver wedding. We (celebrate) our wedding anniversary every year for twenty-five years.

4   On the final examination day I (study) English for about six years.

5   By this time tomorrow Mary (travel) for more than eight hours.

6   When she arrives in Karachi she (travel) for eight days.

7   Poor girl. She (read) the same old newspaper over and over again.

8   Mary will be very tired when her husband gets home. She (shop) and (cook) all day.

9   He won't mind doing the washing up although he, too, (work) all day long.

10 When the bell rings I (teach) for exactly one hour.

Conditional Forms

Probability

- There are two kinds of condition. There is the condition that we ourselves or someone else can fulfil and there is the condition the fulfilment of which is impossible or at least highly improbable. Let us now consider the first of these kinds.

- There are two parts to the sentence one of which states what the condition is and the other states a perfectly reasonable consequence of observing that condition. The following sentences will help to clarify the point:

Condition	Consequence
1 If you finish work early,	we shall go to the theatre.
2 If Mary writes today, then	John will receive the letter tomorrow.

Consequence	Condition
3 They will go to the Zoo tomorrow	if it doesn't rain.
4 Peter will telephone this evening	if he remembers.

- There is nothing imaginary about these sentences. The conditions do not ask anybody to do anything impossible. Notice that the conditional part of the sentence can apply to the present as in number 2 or to the future as in the other sentences. Remember that after *if* (used to introduce a condition) the present forms of the verb are used to express the future.

Improbability

- We use a second type of conditional when we wish to state conditions which cannot be fulfilled. The conditions are not met and so the consequences are unrealised. Consider the following sentences:

   1 *If I were rich, I would buy a fine house.*
   2 *If I earned fifty pounds a day, perhaps I could afford to have a holiday.*
   3 *If sugar cane grew in England, we would make rum here.*

- The conditions are underlined. Let us examine them one by one. *If I were rich* implies that I am not rich, therefore the fine house is just a dream. *If I earned fifty pounds a day* says this cynic. Clearly he means us to understand that he does not earn fifty pounds a day, therefore there will be no holiday. Sugar cane obviously does not and cannot grow in England so we do not and shall not make rum here.

- Each of these conditions implies a negative parenthesis which is not usually spoken, although it may be. The full significance of these three sentences is:

   1 *If I were rich* (but I am not rich) *I would buy a fine house* (but as I am not rich I shall not buy one).

   2 *If I earned fifty pounds a day* (but I do not) *perhaps I could afford to go on holiday* (however, I cannot afford to go on holiday)

   3 *If sugar cane grew in England* (but it does not grow here) *we could make rum.* (However, as it does not grow here we cannot make rum).

- Do not confuse this form of the verb with the Past form. An examination of the negative phrases in parentheses above will show you quite clearly that the speaker is talking about now (present) and then (future). There is no mention of the past at all. The *if* phrase can be used to refer to the present or to some time in the future. (The same form of the verb is used in both the Simple Past and in the Unrealised Conditional constructions).

exercise 165

Insert the correct form of the verbs in brackets so that the sentences express real conditions and consequences.

1   If I (see) John, I'll tell him your news.
2   He (be) very pleased if it (be) really true.
3   If you (go) to town on Monday, you (meet) my brother, Tom.
4   If you (need) help, my father (help) you.
5   We (have) a picnic lunch if the day (be) fine.
6   If you (ask) a policeman, he (tell) you the way.
7   I (finish) the job tomorrow if I (can).
8   I (not require) an umbrella if it (not rain).
9   If she (think) it over carefully, she (form) a clear opinion.
10 If they (catch) the bus now, they (arrive) at half past nine.
11 He (find) the answers if he (look) at the back of the book.
12 If you (want) me to, I (come) for a walk with you.
13 If he (write) to her, she (answer) at once.
14 If you (wait) a few moments, the waiter (bring) your coffee.
15 He (lose) weight if he (stop) eating too much.
16 If she (be) patient, I (try) to explain.
17 I (wear) a purple tie but only if I (must).
18 If we (leave) at once, we (catch) the early train.
19 If he (do) that again, his father (punish) him.
20 If she (drink) this medicine, she (feel) much better.

● NOTE: The conditional word *unless* means *except if* and is often negative in sense.

> *We shan't buy the house unless it has four bedrooms.*
> = except if it has four bedrooms or if it does not have four bedrooms.
> *You can't come into this room unless you have permission.*
> = except if you have permission.

Except if is a very inelegant expression. *Unless* always sounds and reads better.

exercise 166

Form the verbs in brackets so that the sentences express
(a) real conditions with reasonable consequences, and
(b) unrealised conditions with improbable consequences.

1 If I (know), I (tell) you.
2 If she (want) to talk to me, she (ring up).
3 Her health (improve) if she (sleep) longer.
4 If he (have) enough money, he (buy) a larger house.
5 She (feel) lonely if Peter (go) out every evening.
6 We (be) pleased to see you if you (arrive).
7 If we (can) come on Sunday, we (come).
8 I (understand) Mr Brown if he (speak) slowly.
9 We (not go) by ship unless there (be) no other way.
10 If you (not give) him good meals, he (not be able) to work hard.
11 Peter (join) us later if he (can) find time.
12 I (not speak) to him unless he (speak) to me first.
13 You (make) a fortune if you (take) my advice.
14 It is more likely that I (lose) my money if I (listen) to you.
15 If it (be) necessary, we (do) it.
16 If I (think) that about him, I (say) so.
17 He (write) much better if he (use) a good pen.
18 We (not wear) an overcoat unless it (be) cold.
19 If he (promise) to behave in future, his mother (forgive) him.
20 It (not seem) nearly such a long way if she (walk) fast.

Unfulfilled conditions

● It is true that we cannot always predict the future with accuracy. However, we know very well what happened in the past, why it happened and very often we even know what, if it had happened at the right time, would have changed events completely. The fact that it did not happen makes it unreal.

> 1 *If you had posted the letter, mother would have received it last Monday.* (but you did not post it and she did not receive it).
>
> 2 *If they had sent for a doctor, perhaps the patient would not have died.* (but they did not send for a doctor and the patient died).

In these examples the *if* clause and the clause which mentions the consequences of the *if* clause both refer to actions which are past.

● When we introduce a suitable time adverb into the consequence clause it may express a past condition with a present effect. We then use the Present Conditional for the consequence only.

> 1 *If I had saved my money, I would not be poor now.*
>
> 2 *If he had not received a cheque from his uncle, he would be in difficulty now.*
>
> 3 *If he hadn't driven the car dangerously, he wouldn't be facing the magistrates next Monday.*
>
> 4 *If John had left Hong Kong on the earlier ship, he would be arriving tomorrow.*

● Notice that in **3** and **4** we use the form *would be* with the present participle (*—ing*). This frequently happens when the present or future event would be an unusual occurrence, not part of a person's normal routine. If the consequence expressed a normal regular routine event we should use the form *would arrive*. These sentences will demonstrate the point:

> (a) *If your son had passed the entrance examination last May, he would enter the university next term.* (according to regulations and routine)
>
> (b) *If I hadn't chosen to learn English, I wouldn't be reading this book.* (at this moment or temporary period)

exercise 167

Restate these unreal Present Conditional sentences in the unreal Past.

1 If she tried, she could do better.
2 He would do more work if he were able.
3 I should live better if I earned more money.
4 If I knew the answer, I should tell you.
5 He wouldn't come unless you invited him.
6 We shouldn't remember it if it weren't so strange.
7 If I had time, I would help you.
8 Peter would come if you wanted him to.
9 He wouldn't know my address unless someone gave it to him.
10 If I wrote more often, you would receive more letters.
11 They wouldn't sell the house unless they had to.
12 They would prefer to keep it if they could.
13 I would buy it myself if I had the money.
14 If they offered it to me for nothing, I wouldn't take it.
15 You wouldn't refuse it unless you knew something about it.
16 I should break a promise if I answered your question.
17 If you swore to keep it a secret, I would tell you.
18 Mary wouldn't work so hard unless it were necessary.
19 We should be very ill if we drank that dirty water.
20 If we didn't wear warm clothing, we should be cold.

exercise 168

Restate the verbs in brackets to give the sentences the most suitable conditional form. Say which kind of condition each sentence expresses.

1 If it (rain), I shan't go out.
2 You would learn more if you (study) sometimes.
3 If he (ask) me, I would have told him the answer.
4 You would have done well if you (take) Peter's advice.
5 He wouldn't phone me here unless it (be) urgent.
6 She'll catch cold if her feet (get) wet in this weather.
7 If an egg (cost) twopence, how many you (buy) for a pound?
8 Peter (stay) the night there if he (miss) the last train.
9 Unless you apologise at once, I never (speak) to you again.
10 I'm sorry. I shouldn't have done it if I (not be) upset.
11 I should arrive there too late unless I (catch) the earlier train.
12 John will manage to save a little money if he (do) without luxuries.
13 If Peter (need) help, will you go to his assistance?
14 If he (need) help, I would gladly give it.
15 She wouldn't have bought it unless she (like) it.
16 If I (pay) for it, I should have demanded a receipt.
17 If we (have) nothing to do, life would be monotonous.
18 Unless he (receive) some money soon, he will be bankrupt.
19 She would never have known Peter if Mary (not introduce) him.
20 If you (smoke) less, you would feel better.

Doubt and Improbability

● The conditional is used to express doubt and improbability in the mind of the speaker. Consider the following.

    1 _If George worked hard_, he would make more money.
    2 _If they loved each other_, they wouldn't quarrel so much.

Each of the _if_ clauses underlined indicates that the speaker has doubts. He thinks that the statement (George works hard, they love each other, etc.), is improbable or doubtful. The sentences apply to the present or to the future.

Tentative suggestions and opinions

● Sometimes when giving advice or making suggestions the speaker does not wish to appear too forthright. He gives his opinion with some reserve. He does not say:

    You will make a thousand pounds if you follow my advice

unless he is very sure of himself and his full responsibility. More usually one hears something like this:

    If you invested your money in this way, (I think) you would make a good profit.

Let us look at some examples.

    1 _If Peter asked Mary_, I'm sure she would marry him.
    2 _If you paid cash within ten days_, you would get a discount.
    3 _If John smoked less_, his cough would get better.
    4 _If you walked to Trafalgar Square_, you would get fit.

At first sight these examples look very much like _doubt and improbability_ sentences and indeed, when spoken in a certain tone of voice, they are. However, here they simply give the speaker's opinion. In the _if_ phrase there is no suggestion of doubt and improbability; Peter hasn't asked Mary so far, but the speaker does not intend to suggest that he never will ask her. In the other sentences the speaker does not suggest that 2 you will not pay cash, 3 John will not smoke less or 4 that you will not walk to Trafalgar Square. He states his opinion with some reserve and perhaps even hesitation.

Wishes

- Wishes are usually imaginative rather than practical and for that reason cannot be fulfilled. We usually wish for something we want, but have not, or for circumstances that cannot exist. Wishes usually then take the same form as the second conditional as the following will show:

    I wish I were a millionaire.
    If only I had a car.
    If you could only help me!

- NOTE:

    (a) *I wish you a happy birthday.*
    (b) *We wish you long life and happiness.*
    (c) *My father wishes me to become a doctor.*

    These sentences are not impossible or improbable. The speaker or, in (c), the speaker's father announce their hope and desire. There is no suggestion of doubt or improbability.

if I should and *should I*

- *Should* is used with all persons, singular and plural, to indicate extreme doubt or improbability.

    If I should ever make a fortune, I shall give you half of it.
    If John should sell his house, he will offer it to me first.
    Should I forget to phone, my secretary will remind me.
    Should we want to change our jobs, we can easily do it.

- These forms are used generally to admit the possibility (of my making a fortune) and at the same time to deny the probability of the proposition. *If I should* is conversational while the *should I* form is used in careful speaking and writing. Be careful not to confuse *Should I? =* Ought I? with this inverted affirmative form. The negative forms are *if I shouldn't* and *should he not*, etc.

exercise 169

Restate the following sentences 1 by using *if I should* constructions and 2 *should I* constructions.

1   If I live to be a hundred, I shall never understand Picasso.
2   If you see Peter tomorrow, will you ask him to phone?
3   If we hear of a good house going cheap, we'll let you know.
4   If you need anything, please ring the bell.
5   If she wins the lottery, she might buy a large car.
6   If Peter wants to, he can stay here overnight.
7   If we run out of food, we shan't worry. There's a café quite near.
8   You'll be late if the car breaks down.
9   It will be annoying if the singer catches a cold at the last moment.
10 You can always turn the radio off if the programme bores you.
11 If Mr Brown doesn't come to work tomorrow, Mr Black will do his work.
12 I can just catch the train, if it is a few minutes late.
13 Please correct my spelling if I make a mistake.
14 What shall we do if the man refuses to tell us his name?
15 There isn't much you can do if he doesn't want to answer.
16 Ask me to explain the lesson again if you don't understand it.
17 If she has time, she might look in for a few minutes tonight.
18 If he gives you his word, he will keep it.
19 Dr Brown told me to call him if I feel giddy.
20 If you feel hungry during the night, get some food from the kitchen.

Should/would prefer to

● Consider the following sentences:

1 *I should prefer to go by car (if it were possible).*
2 *He would prefer to have gone by car (if it had been possible).*
3 *We should have preferred to go by car (if it had been possible).*
4 *They would have preferred to have gone by car (if it had been possible).*

● **1** clearly indicates present preference for going by car either now or in the future. **2** shows that he didn't go by car (perhaps he went by train) and that his present opinion is that going by car would have been better. **3** is much commoner than **2** and indicates our preference then on a past occasion. **4** is a rather clumsy though very common way of expressing **3**.

● The construction **3** often conveys exactly the same meaning as **2** but when it is necessary to emphasise present preference **2** is used while **3** emphasises past preference. The construction **4** is included here so that students might recognise it. It is very often heard and written in spite of its awkwardness. Notice that when the main verb is one of those which is usually followed by an —*ing* form the infinitives are replaced by —*ing* forms:

1 *I should dislike <u>travelling</u> at Christmas.*
2 *She would regret <u>having</u> hurt your feelings.*
3 *They would have appreciated <u>hearing</u> the orchestra.*
4 *We should have liked <u>having lived</u> in the country during our childhood.*

NOTE: Again **4** is common although awkward and **3** is really much the better way:

We should have liked living in the country during our childhood.

The Passive

Construction

- The Passive form of the verb is constructed by taking the desired part of the verb *be* and adding the past participle of the principal verb. Thus the active infinitive of a verb is, for example, *to sell* or *to buy* and the passive infinitive of these is *to be sold* and *to be bought*. In the same way *It sells* (Active) becomes *It is sold* (Passive) and the form *It is selling* becomes *It is being sold*.

Impersonal Passive

- Often when we use the Passive forms it is quite unnecessary, and undesirable, to mention the names or identities of the persons who carry out the action of the verb.

  Whisky is made in Scotland

- In this example the addition of the agent is unnecessary, since it gives us no information over and above what is conveyed in the sentence without the agent.

- When we speak of public opinion or wish to convey the prevailing impression we frequently use the Passive Voice.

    1 *It is said* that there is a ghost in the old castle.
    2 *It is thought* that we shall be able to prevent cancer soon.

In these examples note carefully that we do not mention the name or identity of the persons who

    1 say,
    2 think

We wish to imply that the community, as a whole, holds these opinions. We could convey the same meaning by using the active voice constructions:

    1 *They say there is a ghost* . . . .
    2 *They think we shall* . . . .

In some languages this idea is expressed by using the third person singular impersonal of the active verb.

exercise 170

Restate the Active constructions as Impersonal Passive ones. Remember to suppress the active subject.

1 Somebody called the fire brigade.
2 Nobody opened the door. (negative verb)
3 People often prefer coffee for breakfast.
4 Somebody opened the door early this morning.
5 Somebody checks their names in the book on my desk.
6 Somebody will wake you at seven o'clock.
7 One wears a top hat at a wedding, sometimes.
8 They all expected the Prime Minister at three o'clock.
9 Nobody reads my poems nowadays. (negative verb)
10 People make mistakes sometimes.
11 The public demands immediate action.
12 Somebody has broken Mary's new vase.
13 One eats rice with chopsticks in the east.
14 We serve the soup before the fish at dinner.
15 A man supports his family as well as possible.
16 The public reads many newspapers and magazines.
17 People use trains and buses to travel to work.
18 Everybody drinks tea in England.
19 One never mentions certain matters, except in private.
20 Somebody will meet us at the station.

Passive voice with indirect object

- Consider the following sentences:

	Subject	Active verb	I.O.	D.O.
1	Peter	sent	Mary	a dozen roses
2	Grandmother	told	the children	a story
3	They	will give	her	a silver teapot

- Some verbs very often or nearly always have a direct and indirect object, e.g. *give, send, tell,* etc. The passive voice construction can be made by using either object of the active as the new subject of the passive verb. Thus, these sentences can each have two Passive forms; the chosen subject is the focus of interest i.e. **1**(a) roses, **1**(b) Mary.

  1 (a) *A dozen roses were sent to Mary.* or
    (b) *Mary was sent a dozen roses.*
  2 (a) *A story was told to the children.* or
    (b) *The children were told a story.*
  3 (a) *A silver teapot will be given her.* or
    (b) *She will be given a silver teapot.*

- In modern English there is no grammatical distinction between (a) and (b) sentences.

- NOTE: The verb agrees in number with its subject. (*A dozen roses were sent/Mary was sent.*)

exercise 171

Restate the following Active sentences twice using (a) the
direct object and (b) the indirect object as the new
subjects in the Passive. Suppress the agent.

1 His firm has given Mr Brown a gold watch.
2 She brings me a cup of tea at eleven o'clock.
3 We shall send a letter to John.
4 The doctor asked Mary a great many questions.
5 The Minister granted me an interview.
6 Somebody has told the police a lie.
7 They teach the students English literature.
8 A soldier handed a telegram to the general.
9 His employers allowed Mr Black three days to finish the
   job.
10 The king granted the criminal a free pardon.

Passive with preposition

● We have already seen that the Passive forms are used impersonally and with indirect objects. The latter are usually the objects of a preposition. Consider the active sentences that follow:

	Subject	Verb	Object
1	Nobody	spoke to	me
2	Somebody	is asking for	Peter on the phone
3	They	always refer to	Alexander the Great as a fine general

● These sentences are active statements and the subjects of the verbs are vague. The verbs are prepositional that is to say, they require the particle or preposition to complete their meaning. *Ask Peter*, for example, is not at all the same thing as *Ask for Peter*.

● Such English sentences are very often rendered in the Passive, when the prepositional verb is transitive. However improbable and ungrammatical this usage may seem to students of classical grammar, it is perfectly normal, common English, in speech and writing. The Passive forms of the sentences above are:

    1 *I was not spoken to.*
    2 *Peter is being asked for on the phone.*
    3 *Alexander the Great is always referred to as a fine general.*

exercise 172

Restate the following Active phrasal verbs in the Passive.
Mention the agent only where necessary.

1 Everybody was talking about the extraordinary weather.
2 We are looking for new business premises.
3 The government paid for my education.
4 Creditors took over the family business.
5 They make up a football team among their classmates.
6 An old servant looks after the house.
7 Uncle John will speak for my brother at his interview.
8 People usually tie up a parcel with string.
9 The landlord himself waited on us at dinner.
10 You must write down everything I say.
11 They have put off their wedding for six months.
12 Did the captain of the ship send out an S.O.S.?
13 Nobody referred to Peter's mistake again.
14 One doesn't speak of private affairs in company.
15 Somebody has rubbed out the date on this exercise.
16 Someone is asking for Mr White on the telephone.
17 A waiter poured out coffee and gave it to us.
18 People generally tear up old letters, after a while.
19 The police are looking into these suspicious circumstances.
20 That firm breaks up old ships for scrap metal.

NOTE: The particle is an essential element of the phrasal
verb and must not be omitted in the Passive construction.

exercise 173

State the following Active sentences in the Impersonal Passive. Remember that the vague, impersonal active subject is not included in the Passive construction.

1 People say the world's natural resources are running out.
2 They think we shall be able to find alternative sources of energy.
3 We now know that man can return from the moon.
4 Public opinion considers this project too expensive.
5 Everybody can hear the news at nine o'clock.
6 Anybody can buy aspirin without a doctor's prescription.
7 People do not eat sweets in class.
8 People celebrate special days like birthdays and wedding days by having parties.
9 They give parties on New Year's Day in Scotland.
10 Somebody informed the police of the accident.
11 The public reads very many newspapers here.
12 In Germany people drink beer.
13 People in Switzerland speak more than one language.
14 The commanders ordered an attack at dawn.
15 The men on Clydeside build fine ships.
16 We buy eggs by the dozen.
17 They sell coal by the ton.
18 An assistant in this shop speaks English.
19 Somebody shaves Mr Smith every day.
20 Nobody needs help, so I shall go home now.

exercise 174

Restate these Active phrasal verbs in the Passive. Mention the agent only where necessary.

1 The ministry has asked for an explanation.
2 Someone will call for the parcel in the afternoon.
3 The army will call him up next summer.
4 We have looked for the ring everywhere. Nobody has found the thief yet. He has covered up his tracks.
5 The government is sending out another expedition to the South Pole.
6 People have always looked up to men of honour.
7 They have always looked down on cheats and liars.
8 Someone has broken into the bank.
9 The police have taken the matter up. They are looking into it now.
10 The parents look after the children very well.
11 They are bringing the children up very carefully.
12 The clerk was taking down every word I said.
13 He wrote it out in longhand later.
14 They shut him up in prison for six months.
15 They took him in with their lies.

Reported or
Indirect Speech

- The actual words that come from a person's mouth and go straight to the ears of those who listen to him are called Direct Speech. Consider:

  > Peter said, 'I will see John tomorrow.'
  > 'It is my birthday,' said Mary.

  The words between quotation marks are the actual words exactly as Peter and Mary spoke them. Now, when I tell another person what Peter and Mary said to me I do not use direct speech, since their words are carried to my companion, indirectly through me. I do not quote Peter or Mary but make a report of their original words. Consider:

  (a) *Peter said he would see John next day.*
  (b) *Mary said that it was her birthday.*

  In each sentence there is a report of the direct words that were spoken by Peter and Mary at a time before my present *indirect report* of these words. When we wish to report speech we make use of certain verbs to introduce the reported part of our sentence:

  > 'We always have dinner at seven o'clock,' she told me.
  > <u>She told me</u> that <u>they always had dinner at seven o'clock.</u>

- *Told* is the introducing verb in this reported sentence. Useful introducing verbs are:

  tell, say, declare, announce, state, affirm, confirm, advise, order, command, ask, enquire, want to know, answer, reply, report, remark, observe and so on,

  according to the sense of the report.

- Look again at the sentence underlined above. The first part underlined is *the introduction* and the second part underlined is the *the report*. Notice that the introduction is joined to the report by the connective *that*. The connective *that* is very often dropped from the reported sentence in conversation:

  > She told me they always had dinner at seven.

  Let us now go on to see how to convert direct speech sentences into indirect speech reports.

Present Tense

● The Present tense forms are:
   1 Simple Present.
   2 Present Continuous.
   3 Present Perfect.
   4 Present Perfect Continuous.

exercise 175

(a) Convert these direct sentences into indirect speech
using the phrases

  she tells me . . .
  he informs us . . .
  she reminds him . . . etc.,

(b) Use appropriate past forms of reporting verbs to make
suitable introductions. Notice examples 1, 2, 16, 17, 18
and 19 in which a pronoun is necessary to complete the
introduction.

NOTE: When the reporting verb is in a Present Tense do
not change the tenses of the verbs in Direct Speech to
convert them into Reported Speech.

1 'Peter is going into the army soon.' His father informs . . . .
2 'We usually have roast beef on Sundays.' Chris is
   saying . . . .
3 'There have been too many road accidents lately.' The
   report states . . . .
4 'Something must be done.' The evening newspaper
   says . . . .
5 'I don't know Peter Brown from Adam.' John declares . . . .

exercise 175 (contd.)

6 'They haven't been to the seaside for five years.' Robin explains . . . .

7 'I don't earn enough to feed a mouse.' Peter complains . . . .

8 'An important person has died.' The headlines say . . . .

9 'A rose by any other name would smell as sweet.' The poet declares . . . .

10 'I have never heard such nonsense in all my life,' says the gardener . . . .

11 'You are quite right in what you say.' Peter agrees . . . .

12 'Mr Nonsuch is going to be the next Prime Minister.' Everybody says . . . .

13 'I will do everything I can to help them.' She has promised . . . .

14 'We can't afford a long holiday.' John and Mary regret . . . .

15 'That is the man I saw at the scene of the crime.' The witness affirms . . . .

16 'There is to be a film at school today.' My son informs . . . .

17 'You must pay more attention to your lessons.' Your teacher tells me . . . .

18 'I must have a little more pocket money.' His son sometimes tells him . . . .

19 'You ought to have your hair cut.' My father often reminds me . . . .

20 'You can't go out until you have finished.' Our teacher says . . . .

● When the introducing verb is in either the Simple Past or Past Continuous the present verb forms in the direct speech assume their corresponding past forms in the report. That is to say Simple Present becomes Simple Past. Present Continuous becomes Past Continuous; Present Perfect becomes Past Perfect; Present Perfect Continuous becomes Past Perfect Continuous.

1 (a) *'The London train leaves in five minutes,'* the stationmaster informed us.
  (b) *The stationmaster informed us that the London train left in five minutes.*
2 (a) *'Father is waiting in the garden,'* Mary told me.
  (b) *Mary told me that Father was waiting in the garden.*
3 (a) *'No, I have never visited Mr Brown,'* I replied.
  (b) *I replied that I had never visited Mr Brown.*
4 (a) *'Peter has been working very hard for some time,'* the manager said.
  (b) *The manager said that Peter had been working very hard for some time.*

● In these examples both the introducing verb and the report are in past forms of the verb, although the report may still refer to the present time:

I saw John this afternoon. He told me that he was working (is working) in a bank now.

Generally speaking, when the report refers to the future or present time we do not change the tenses of the verbs from Direct to Reported Speech:

1 *Mary told me she will come next week.*
2 *Peter said he is very busy today.*

exercise 176

Report these sentences using the past form introductory verb given. Notice where objective pronouns are needed to complete the introduction and where there is a change of personal number when the direct speech pronoun is reported, e.g. *I* sometimes becomes *he* and so on.

1 'I can't come out.' I told . . . .
2 'She is trying to find a job.' He informed . . . .
3 'We aren't going to the theatre.' They let me know . . . .
4 'I think it is a very silly idea.' She protested . . . .
5 'They haven't any children.' John's brother said . . . .
6 'I am bringing the books back.' He stated . . . .
7 'I buy everything I need there.' She declared . . . .
8 'When he drinks iced water, it hurts his stomach.' His mother said . . . .
9 'I often write to my friends in Canada.' Peter remarked
   . . . .
10 'They send me a beautiful Christmas card each year.' He added . . . .
11 'We haven't been to the pictures for ages.' I remarked . . . .
12 'They aren't working very hard.' The manager observed . . . .
13 'We are just having a cup of tea.' Mary said . . . .
14 'We are just finishing it, in fact.' She added . . . .
15 'Most English people have a cup of tea about eleven.' He agreed . . . .
16 'Some of them drink coffee instead of tea.' He remarked . . . .
17 'There is no accounting for taste.' I said . . . .
18 'I'm afraid he has broken his arm.' The doctor confirmed . . . .
19 'He doesn't need to stay in bed for long.' The doctor thought . . . .
20 'I can't remember where John has gone to.' I said . . . .

Present Perfect Continuous

> *'The last bus leaves at midnight.'*
> *'The boys are writing letters upstairs.'*
> *'John has almost finished work for today.'*
> *'We have been reading some of Shakespeare's plays.'*

● The four sentences above give one example of each of the present verb forms. When the introducing verb is also a present form there is usually *no change* in the form of the verbs in the report.

> *John tells me that the last bus leaves at midnight.*
> *Their mother has informed us that the boys are upstairs writing letters.*
> *The manager is saying that John has almost finished work for today.*
> *The headmaster confirms that the students have been reading some of Shakespeare's plays.*

Notice that the introducing verb and the report both refer to the present time in one or other of its forms.

● We have already seen that when the introducing verb is in a past form the verbs in the report change from present to corresponding past forms. However, although these verbs take the past forms they do not necessarily refer to actions or states which are past and finished. The past verb forms in reported speech often refer to the present time. Consider the following:

> *'I'm going on holiday today,' said Mary.*

Report:

> (a) *Mary said she was going on holiday today.*
> (b) *Mary said she is going on holiday today.*

● The report (a) is grammatically correct with its reported
  verb in the past form although it refers to this present day.
  The report (b) is also correctly written and is often used,
  especially in conversation, when the action or state in the
  direct form is still present at the time of reporting. When
  we report eternal truth, unchanging routine, laws of
  nature and similar unvarying actions and states, we very
  often leave them in their direct speech Simple Present
  forms (except for changes from 1st to 3rd person, etc). The
  following examples will help you.

  1 *'Thirty six inches <u>make</u> one yard,' she informed him.*
     (a) *He learned that thirty-six inches <u>make</u> one yard.*
     (b) *He learned that thirty-six inches <u>made</u> one yard.*
  2 *'The earth <u>travels</u> round the sun once a year,' he wrote.*
     (a) *He wrote that the earth <u>travels</u> round the sun once a
         year.*
     (b) *He wrote that the earth <u>travelled</u> round the sun once a
         year.*
  3 *'We always <u>catch</u> the eight-thirty train,' they told him.*
     (a) *They told him that they always <u>catch</u> the eight-thirty
         train.*
     (b) *They told him that they always <u>caught</u> the eight-thirty
         train.*

● The reports in (a) unmistakably refer to actions which
  happened when the words were spoken, still continue to
  happen now when we report and will, presumably, go on
  happening in the future. In (b) the reports are made quite
  correctly and in numbers **1** and **2** no real confusion of
  meaning can arise. In number **3** however, you have an
  example that shows how the same report may refer either
  to a present routine, or to an action or routine that took
  place and finished in the past. The present verb form as in
  (a) is preferred when we wish to make it quite clear that
  our reports concern present routines, habits, customs and
  so on.

exercise 177

Report the following sentences by using a past form of the reporting verb. Give both forms of the report wherever possible.

> *'My name is Robert.' He said his name was Robert* (grammatically correct present and past form in reported speech), and
> *He said his name is Robert* (logically correct form if he is still alive to bear his name).

Use a variety of reporting verbs.

1 'Paper is made from wood,' he informed us.
2 'Dogs have a very acute sense of smell,' we were told.
3 'John is three years older than his sister,' his mother said.
4 'I always take milk in coffee,' Mary remarked.
5 'She always has three lumps of sugar, too,' added her husband.
6 'Napoleon is the master of Europe,' the messenger reported.
7 'Queen Anne is dead,' the letter said.
8 'I never eat between meals,' she informed me.
9 'You speak with a Scots accent,' he remarked.
10 'Australia exports a great deal of wool,' the newspaper said.
11 'I am giving him a watch for his birthday,' his mother said.
12 'His favourite pastime is reading,' his sister told me.
13 'She never gets up before eleven,' her son told us.
14 'We seldom go to bed before midnight,' they remarked.
15 'Most people catch a cold at least once a year,' the doctor said.
16 'You can't make an omelette without breaking eggs,' she observed.
17 'The milkman hasn't come yet,' she announced.
18 'I can't drink tea without milk in it,' her husband replied.

Imperative and Infinitive

● When the direct speech form of the verb is imperative we report it by using the infinitive:

    'Come on Monday,' he said.

  This we report as:

    He asked me to come on Monday.

● The imperative is generally used for giving orders or for making requests or demands. It follows that the reporting verb conveys the sense of command, request or invitation,

    e.g. *order, command, tell, ask, request, invite, demand, instruct* and verbs of similar meaning very often introduce the imperative report.

● The infinitive presents no difficulty as it is reported in the same infinitive form:

    'John is going to buy a car,' said Peter,

  is reported as:

    Peter said that John was (is) going to buy a car.

exercise 178

Report the following imperative and infinitive direct speech sentences. Use a variety of reporting verbs.

1 'Go away,' he ordered.
2 'Don't interrupt me,' I said to them (I told them . . .)
3 'Children, be quiet,' mother said.
4 'Put your hands up,' ordered the robber.
5 'Please help me,' the old lady begged.
6 'Mind your heads,' she warned us.
7 'Write it again,' my teacher told me.
8 'Don't smoke in this room, please,' the old lady requested us.
9 'Do your coat up, it's cold outside,' she advised me.
10 'Don't work too hard for a few months,' the doctor ordered her.
11 'Sit down, please,' she requested.
12 'Come to my birthday party,' he invited.
13 'Take some bicarbonate of soda,' they advised her.
14 'Put the green powder in the water first,' he instructed them.
15 'Stir it with a wooden spoon,' she told me.
16 'Don't sit on the wet grass,' said Peter.
17 'Give me a large steak and chips,' the customer ordered the waiter.
18 'Bring your brother with you,' he invited.
19 'Don't go out without your keys,' she reminded me.
20 'Finish this exercise now,' our teacher said.

Future

- In direct speech we express the future in several ways. For example, we use two of the present forms of the verb:

    'The ship leaves next Friday night,' the agent informed me.
    'They are going to the theatre tomorrow evening.' John replied.

    When we report future events which are still in the future at the present moment at which we are making the report, we often leave the verb in its direct speech present form, at least, in conversational English. Also, when *shall* and *will* auxiliary forms express an action or state which is still future at the present moment we often report them without any change in the time form of the direct speech verbs, again conversationally.

    'I'm coming tomorrow.'   He told me he is coming tomorrow.
    'We are leaving next Saturday.'   She said they are leaving next Saturday.
    'He will come back on Monday.'   He told me he'll come back on Monday.
    'She won't be at home tomorrow.'   He informed me that she won't be at home tomorrow.

- Strict grammar demands that the present time verb forms change to their corresponding past time forms and that *shall* and *will* auxiliary forms become *should* and *would* in all reports of the future.

- We must always do this when there is even the slightest doubt or improbability concerning the future event, whenever the truth or accuracy of the information in the report is questioned. The direct speech forms cannot remain unaltered in such circumstances.

    'I shall repay the money next Christmas,' the thief promised.
    The thief promised that he would repay the money next Christmas. (However, we cannot be sure that he will.)

    'I'll close the front door when I leave,' said John.
    John said that he would close the front door when he left (Perhaps we ought to remind him before he goes).

● In each of these examples the reporters have some doubt concerning the realisation of the future event.

● NOTE: The direct speech *shall* becomes either *will* or *would* in reported speech although many people retain *shall* or *should* when the first person (direct) becomes third person (reported).

● In the same way *will* sometimes becomes *shall*. Students must be careful to observe the difference between the automatic future (*shall, will, will*) and the desired future (*will, shall, shall*) and use the corresponding auxiliary forms accordingly.

exercise 179

Assume that the direct speech events are still in the future, and report the following sentences, preserving the time form of the direct speech verbs when possible, or changing the verb forms where necessary. Try reporting each sentence in more than one way, that is to say, make your report by the first person to the third, by the third to the first, and so on.

I told them ⎫
You told us ⎬ *that the sun rises at quarter past six tomorrow.*
He told you ⎭

1 'The sun rises at quarter past six tomorrow,' he instructed them.
2 'My brother is leaving for South America next week,' she informed me.

3 'He will be on the ship for a fortnight,' she added.
4 'You shall have a new book next Friday,' he promised.
5 'We shall arrive on the afternoon train,' they wrote in their letter.
6 'I will meet you at seven o'clock tonight,' she promised.
7 'I shan't be able to come on Mondays any more,' he told us.
8 'It doesn't matter, we shall be pleased to see you at any time, we replied.
9 'We break up for the holidays on 30 June,' our teacher told us.
10 'We shan't have any lessons for six whole weeks,' the boys shouted.
11 'I will help you with the washing up,' John said.
12 'You will be in London this time next year,' he reminded them.
13 'We are leaving for London early in the new year,' he remarked.
14 'We shall be speaking fluently when we come back,' they told him.
15 'She's going to play the piano for us,' our host announced.
16 'I wonder whether she will play some Chopin,' said John.
17 'She will if you ask her to,' our host replied.
18 'He's having lunch with me one day next week,' said Robert.
19 'We shall have a long talk about old times,' he added.
20 'She shall have anything she wants, within reason,' her husband promised.

Future in the Past

- In the past, words were spoken which referred to a future time. When we consider these words we see that not only the time at which those words were spoken is past but the future time to which they referred has also, now, passed.

  'I shall be master of Europe before next summer,' declared Napoleon.

  Clearly, anything that concerned Napoleon during *his* future, while he was living, must be in the past when we look at it now.

- To report verbs that expressed the future when they were first spoken and indicate the reporter's point of view we use the future in the past form of the verb. Thus, the report of the sentence above reads:

  Napoleon declared that he would be master of Europe before the following summer.

  Notice that *shall* and *will* future forms become *should* and *would* future in the past forms. Pay close attention to the type of future tense and the person of the verb when making reports.

- The present time verb forms that often express the future take their corresponding *past forms* to express the future in the past. Thus:

  'The Tsar of Russia is coming to London next month,' the newspapers reported.
  They said that the Tsar of Russia was coming to London the following month.

- To report the past time accurately, it is necessary to adjust certain time expressions and other words that may refer to future or present time in direct speech, so that they now refer to past time in reported speech. All the expressions which begin with *this* and *these* (this week, this afternoon, etc.) to indicate present time are changed to *that* and *those* (that afternoon, at that time etc.).

  > *Today* becomes *that day, tomorrow* becomes *the next day* or *the following day*,
  > *next week, month, year* become *the following week, month, year*.
  > *Now* becomes *then* or *at that time, at that moment*, according to the sense of the report.

- Adverbs and expressions of past time in the direct speech also need adjustment when we report them:

  > *yesterday* becomes *the previous day* while
  > *last week, month, year, Friday, Tuesday*, etc. become *the previous week, the previous Friday*, etc.

- NOTE: *Ago* is not used when we report the past. We use *earlier, previously*, and sometimes *before* + *—ing* or *before* + *finite verb construction:*

  > *'I saw him three days before leaving'* or *'I saw him three days before I left.'*

exercise 180

Convert the following future form sentences into
Reported Speech. Use a variety of reporting verbs, and
make all necessary changes.

1 'We shall meet next Tuesday.'
2 'She will be coming tomorrow.'
3 'Mary will be preparing dinner soon.'
4 'You won't know the result of the test till next week.'
5 'I shall try to be early in future.'
6 'The headmaster will be coming in shortly.'
7 'You won't set the Thames on fire!'
8 'He shall not come here again!'
9 'We will be good children.'
10 'They will never succeed if they never try!'
11 'It will be raining hard tonight.'
12 'There will be plenty of time for a walk before dinner.'
13 'John will be travelling to Australia next week.'
14 'Mary will always remember this day.'
15 'I shan't forget it for a long time, either.'
16 'He isn't sure whether he'll be able to come.'
17 'We shall be expecting you at the end of the month.'
18 'We shall be having dinner about seven.'
19 'I shall arrive about half past six.'
20 'That's fine. We shall have time for a chat.'

exercise 181

Turn the following into Reported speech. Remember to use a variety of introducing verbs so as to avoid monotonous repetition.

1 'I often see Peter in the evenings,' she said.
2 'We sometimes play bridge with Tom and Mary,' they replied.
3 'I am going out with Lisa tomorrow,' John wrote.
4 'We are having dinner with the Browns,' they answered.
5 'I haven't spoken to Peter for ages,' she confirmed.
6 'I know that he is married to Catherine,' she said.
7 'We never find time to write to John,' they declared.
8 'We often see you as you go by our house,' they told us.
9 'I miss Mary very much,' John agreed.
10 'I've bought a wonderful present for Peter,' Mary announced.
11 'We've known the Smiths for years,' they exclaimed.
12 'We've never met Lord Luddy,' they stated.
13 'I recognise her,' said Mr Brown.
14 'I know her by her happy smile,' he added.
15 'We are driving my mother to the station,' said Mary.
16 'We are seeing her off on the 10 o'clock train,' added John.
17 'I'm discussing business with Peter,' John explained.
18 'I am quite sure that he's wrong,' she said.
19 'We don't often have father at home for lunch,' mother remarked.
20 'I work with John in town,' she confirmed.

exercise 182, exercise 183

Rewrite the following direct speech sentences in reported
forms. Use a variety of introducing verbs.

1 'You haven't told me about your holiday,' John said.
2 'I'm just going to show you some snapshots of me,' she
   answered.
3 'You're looking at me very strangely,' she whispered.
4 'You remind me of someone I know,' he replied.
5 'I remember your saying that,' Mary confirmed.
6 'You're taking us to the cinema,' the family announced.
7 'I want you to marry me,' he insisted.
8 'You are telling me a lot of nonsense!' she answered.
9 'I'm asking you to believe me, just the same,' he repeated.
10 'You didn't need to help us much this time,' the students
   observed.

Report the following sentences. Use a variety of reporting
verbs.

1 'I am sending a present for him.' Your brother told me . . . .
2 'We promise to help him as much as we can.' He also said
   that . . . .
3 'I don't know them very well.' You stated . . . .
4 'We never see her now.' You complained . . . .
5 'They don't write to us any more.' You informed him . . . .
6 'We haven't seen him since Christmas!' You remarked . . . .
7 'He hasn't spoken to me for a week.' She wanted to know
   why . . . .
8 'She hasn't visited us since the spring.' You reminded
   him . . . .
9 'We don't want to see him again.' You declared . . . .
10 'I can't stand the sight of him.' You added . . . .
11 'She gets on my nerves, too.' He concluded by saying . . . .
12 'He doesn't like us very much. (I'm afraid).' They told
   you . . . .
13 'They haven't told us the truth.' We admitted . . . .
14 'We can't trust them to keep a secret.' Mary told us . . . .

Reported questions

See also 'Connectives' page 58.

● When we report questions we do not use the interrogative forms and structures. The reported form of the question must be made as though it were a positive statement:

'Where are you going?' she asked him. = She asked him where he was going.
'What time will the train leave?' she enquired. = She enquired what time the train would leave.
'Whom did you meet at the party?' he wanted to know. = He wanted to know whom I had met at the party.

● We do not use question marks either in front of or at the end of reported questions.

Whether and *If*

● Consider the following direct speech questions:

1 *'Are you coming to the party?'*
2 *'Has the postman brought anything for me?'*
3 *'Will you do me a favour, please?'*
4 *'Did Mary phone last night?'*

Answers to such questions must indicate 'Yes' or 'No' in some way:

1 *'Yes, I am.'* or *'No, I am not.'*
2 *'Yes, he has.'* or *'Not today, I'm afraid.'*
3 *'Of course, I will.'* or *'I'm sorry, I can't.'*
4 *'Yes, I think so.'* or *'No, she must have forgotten.'*

- We report such questions by using the linking word
  whether
     1 *She asked me whether I was coming to the party.*
     2 *He enquired whether the postman had brought anything
        for him.*
     3 *He wanted to know whether I would do him a favour.*
     4 *He asked me whether Mary had phoned the previous
        evening.*

- *If* is informally used instead of *whether* but it is better to
  avoid *if* whenever there is a possibility of confusing it with
  its conditional sense:
     'I was asked if I was free' might mean *'I was invited, on
     occasions when I wasn't busy'.*

  If we put a comma after asked (and not everybody would)
  then this is certainly what the sentence means. Of course
  whether cannot replace *if* in a conditional clause.

- NOTE: *Ask* may be followed by a noun or pronoun.
     They asked (us) whether we should come by train.

  The pronoun object is not strictly necessary with *ask* when
  its omission does not lead to confusion but

  $$\text{They asked} \left\{ \begin{array}{c} \text{Father} \\ \text{him} \end{array} \right\} \text{whether} \left\{ \begin{array}{c} \text{Mary} \\ \text{she} \end{array} \right\} \text{would come.}$$

  Enquire, want to know, wish do not take noun or pronoun
  objects before *whether.*

  $$\left. \begin{array}{l} \textit{They enquired.} \\ \textit{They wished to know} \\ \textit{They wanted to know} \end{array} \right\} \textit{whether you had arrived.}$$

exercise 184

Report these questions using the introductions given.
Both Present Perfect and Simple Past are reported by Past
Perfect.

1 'Where has John left his bicycle?' I asked.
2 'When did David buy his new car?' Peter wanted to know.
3 'Where shall we meet on Saturday?' John asked Mary.
4 'What have you bought for Mary's birthday?' I asked
   mother.
5 'Whom did you see at the cinema last night?' she wanted
   to know.
6 'Whose book has Betty borrowed?' Father enquired.
7 'Why haven't you written to us for such a long time?' they
   asked Mary.
8 'Which of the two boys is the elder son?' the lawyer
   enquired.
9 'When will you pay back the money father lent you?' asked
   Peter.
10 'What are you going to prepare for dinner?' he asked the
    cook.
11 'Whose telephone number are you looking up?' my
    secretary asked.
12 'Which of these films have you seen?' my friend enquired.
13 'Why don't you get up earlier in the mornings?' the
    manager wanted to know.
14 'How much should we pay for a month in Spain?' they
    wondered.
15 'Whose money is that on the table?' Peter wanted to know.

exercise 185

Report these questions using the introduction given.

1 'Do you know where she lives?' John asked.
2 'Does this bus go along Market Street?' the lady wanted to know.
3 'Did you remember to phone the Browns?' I asked.
4 'Is it wrong to write surprise with a 'z'?' Mary enquired.
5 'Are these the new plans for the Town Hall?' he enquired.
6 'Am I to stand here all day waiting for something to happen?' he wanted to know.
7 'Was the money paid to you without delay?' he asked.
8 'Were you going to meet John for lunch?' mother asked.
9 'Will you be free on the nineteenth?' I asked my dentist.
10 'Shall we be able to have a holiday this summer?' we wondered.
11 'Should you drink so much coffee as you do?' she asked.
12 'Would you mind sitting on the other chair, please?' the barber asked.
13 'Ought we to offer our help to these unfortunate people?' we wanted to know.
14 'Need we say anything more about this disgusting affair?' he enquired.
15 'Must a policeman always wear uniform?' little Peter asked.
16 'Used your secretary to work with Metals Ltd?' Mr Brown asked me.
17 'Did the doctor give you any medicine?' Mary asked her husband.
18 'Can one tractor do as much work as ten horses?' the farmer wanted to know.
19 'May I come swimming with you, next time?' I asked.
20 'Do your friends all live in the country in summer?' he asked me.

Common irregular verbs

The simple present, simple past and past participle of common irregular verbs are shown below:

arise, arose, arisen
awake, awoke, awoken, (awakened)

be, was, been
bear, bore, borne
beat, beat, beaten
become, became, become
begin, began, begun
bend, bent, bent
bet, bet, (betted) bet, (betted)
bid, bid, bid
bid, bade, bidden
bind, bound, bound
bite, bit, bitten
bleed, bled, bled
blow, blew, blown
break, broke, broken
breed, bred, bred
bring, brought, brought
broadcast, broadcast, broadcast
build, built, built
burn, burnt, (burned) burnt, (burned)
burst, burst, burst
buy, bought, bought

cast, cast, cast
catch, caught, caught
choose, chose, chosen
cling, clung, clung
come, came, come
cost, cost, cost
creep, crept, crept
cut, cut, cut

deal, dealt, dealt
dig, dug, dug
do, did, done
draw, drew, drawn
dream, dreamt, (dreamed), dreamt (dreamed)
drink, drank, drunk
drive, drove, driven

eat, ate, eaten

fall, fell, fallen
feed, fed, fed
feel, felt, felt
fight, fought, fought
find, found, found
flee, fled, fled
fly, flew, flown
forbid, forbade, forbidden
forecast, forecast, forecast
forget, forgot, forgotten
forgive, forgave, forgiven
freeze, froze, frozen

get, got, got
give, gave, given
go, went, gone
grind, ground, ground
grow, grew, grown

hang, hung, (hanged) hung, (hanged)
have, had, had
hear, heard, heard
hit, hit, hit
hold, held, held
hurt, hurt, hurt

keep, kept, kept
kneel, knelt, knelt
knit, knitted, (knit) knitted, (knit)
know, knew, known

lay, laid, laid
lead, led, led
lean, leant, (leaned) leant, (leaned)
learn, learnt, (learned) learnt, (learned)
leap, leapt, (leaped) leapt, (leaped)
leave, left, left
lend, lent, lent
let, let, let
lie (down), lay (down), lain (down)
light, lit, (lighted) lit, (lighted)
lose, lost, lost

make, made, made
mean, meant, meant
meet, met, met
mistake, mistook, mistaken
misunderstand, misunderstood,
  misunderstood
mow, mowed, mown

pay, paid, paid
put, put, put

read, read, read
rid, rid, (ridded) rid, (ridded)
ride, rode, ridden
ring, rang, rung
rise, rose, risen
run, ran, run

saw, sawed, sawn
say, said, said
see, saw, seen
sell, sold, sold
send, sent, sent
set, set, set
sew, sewed, sewn, (sewed)
shake, shook, shaken
shed, shed, shed
shine, shone, shone
shoot, shot, shot
show, showed, shown, (showed)
shrink, shrank, shrunk
shut, shut, shut
sing, sang, sung
sink, sank, sunk
sit, sat, sat
sleep, slept, slept
slide, slid, slid
slit, slit, slit
smell, smelt, (smelled) smelt, (smelled)
sow, sowed, sown, (sowed)
speak, spoke, spoken
spell, spelt, (spelled) spelt, (spelled)
spend, spent, spent
spill, spilt, (spilled) spilt, (spilled)
spin, span, (spun) spun
spit, spat, spat
split, split, split
spoil, spoilt, (spoiled) spoilt, (spoiled)
spread, spread, spread
spring, sprang, sprung

stand, stood, stood
steal, stole, stolen
stick, stuck, stuck
sting, stung, stung
stink, stank, stunk
strike, struck, struck
strive, strove, striven
swear, swore, sworn
sweep, swept, swept
swell, swelled, swollen, (swelled)
swim, swam, swum
swing, swung, swung

take, took, taken
teach, taught, taught
tear, tore, torn
tell, told, told
think, thought, thought
throw, threw, thrown
thrust, thrust, thrust
tread, trod, trodden

upset, upset, upset

wake, woke, woke, (woken)
wear, wore, worn
weave, wove, woven
wed, wed, (wedded) wed, (wedded)
weep, wept, wept

win, won, won
wind, wound, wound
wring, wrung, wrung
write, wrote, written

KEY

Exercise 1 Countable(+) Uncountable(−)

1 Potatoes (+)   vegetables (+)
2 Dogs (+)   cats (+)
3 Horses (+)   tails (+)
4 Boys (+)   games (+)
5 Diamonds (+)   stones (+)
6 Girls (+)   chocolate (−)
7 Sugar (−)   cups (+)
8 Slices (+)   bread (−)   pieces (+)
    cheese (−)   sandwiches (+)
9 Omelettes (+)   eggs (+)
10 Books (+)   paper (−)
11 Paper (−)   wood (−)
12 Letters (+)   sheets (+)   paper (−)
13 Cowboys (+)   America (−)
14 Milk (−)   cows (+)
15 Cows (+)   farms (+)   grass (−)
16 Soldiers (+)   officers (+)
17 Lines (+)   rulers (+)
18 Tea (−)   cups (+)
19 Dogs (+)   friends (+)   man (−)
20 Englishmen (+)   bacon (−)
    eggs (+)   breakfast (−)

Exercise 3

1 I have an apple and an orange in my bag.
2 A policeman is sometimes a very tall fellow.
3 A mother looks after little children.
4 A house often has a pretty garden.
5 A schoolboy likes a holiday.
6 We write with a pen and a pencil.
7 A river runs into the sea.
8 We need a pen and ink to write a letter.
9 A table is an article of furniture.
10 A child is a son or a daughter.
11 A week is a period of seven days.
12 A cat catches a mouse.
13 A dog chases a cat.
14 An apple grows on a tree.
15 A man in a white coat is a doctor.
16 We can go to America on a ship or an aeroplane.
17 A boy and a girl go to the same school.
18 A horse and a donkey both work hard.
19 An onion and a potato make a good salad.
20 A cherry tree and a plum tree are beautiful
    in spring.

Exercise 2

1	A	a	
2	a		
3	a	a	
4	an	a	
5	An	a	
6	an		
7	a	a	
8	an		
9	A	a	
10	a	a	
11	a	a	
12	a	a	a
13	a	an	
14	A	a	a
15	A	a	
16	a	a	
17	A	a	a
18	A	a	
19	a	a	
20	A	a	a

Exercise 4

1	...	...	
2	the	the	
3	...	...	
4	...	...	
5	The		
6	...		
7	The		
8	...	...	
9	the	the	
10	The	the	
11	The	the	the
12	...		
13	...		
14	The	the	
15	the		
16	...	...	
17	...		
18	...		
19	...		
20	...	...	

Exercise 5

1 The ... ...
2 The the the
3 The ...
4 ... the
5 ... the
6 The the ...
7 The ...
8 the the the
9 ... ...
10 the ... ...
11 The ...
12 The ...
13 ... the
14 ... ...
15 ... the
16 ... ...
17 ... ...
18 ... ...
19 ... ...
20 ... the ...

Exercise 6

1 the the the
2 ... the
3 the the
4 The the
5 the ...
6 ... ... the
7 the the
8 the ...
9 ... the
10 The the
11 ... ...
12 The ...
13 The ... ...
14 the the
15 the the
16 the the
17 the the
18 the ...
19 the ...
20 the the the

Exercise 7

1 this / that
2 these / those
3 that
4 these / those
5 this / that
6 that / this
7 that
8 that
9 this / that
10 this / that
11 these / those
12 this / that
13 these / those
14 this / that
15 this / that
16 that
17 these / those
18 this / that
19 this / that
20 that / this

Exercise 8

1 This that
2 these
3 This
4 Those
5 These those
6 this that
7 these those
8 this that
9 That this
10 those that
11 those that
12 that those
13 This that
14 these this
   (or those that)
15 this those
16 these those
17 those that
18 this that
   (or that this)
19 this those
20 these those

Exercise 9

1 one
2 one
3 one ones
4 ones one
5 ones ones
6 ones one
7 ones ones
8 one ones
9 ones ones
10 ones ones
11 one one
12 one one
13 ones one
14 one ones
15 ones ones
16 ones one
17 ones ones
18 ones one one
19 ones ones one
20 one one

Exercise 10

1 any some
2 some any
3 anywhere
   somewhere
4 anybody
   somebody
5 any
   something
6 any some
7 any some
8 any some
9 some any
10 some anybody
11 some any
12 some any
13 any any
14 any any
15 some any
16 any some
17 something
   anything
18 anywhere
   some

19	anything
	something
20	some any
21	anybody some
22	anywhere
	someone
23	somebody
	anybody
24	some any
25	anything some

Exercise 11

1	any
2	some
3	anywhere
4	anybody
5	any
6	anything
7	some any
8	any
9	some
	some / any
10	sometimes

Exercise 12

1	some
2	any
3	any
4	some
5	somebody
6	some / any
7	anybody
8	anywhere /
	somewhere
9	some / any
10	any
11	some
12	something
13	anybody
14	anything
15	some
16	Anyone
17	some
18	anything anything
19	some
20	something / anything

Exercise 13

1	No-one.	I didn't see anyone.
	(Nobody.)	(I didn't see anybody.)
2	Nowhere.	I'm not going anywhere.
3	None.	I didn't have any.
4	Nothing.	There's nothing in it.
5	Nothing.	I'm not reading anything.
6	Nobody.	Nobody gave me permission.
		(No-one gave me permission.)
7	Nowhere.	You can't find one anywhere.
8	None.	I haven't written any.
9	Nothing.	I won't give you anything.
10	None.	I haven't spent any.
11	Nowhere.	You can't get one anywhere.
12	Nobody.	No-one told me.
	(No-one).	(Nobody told me.)
13	None.	None of us is over sixty.
14	Nobody.	There's no-one on the
	(No-one).	telephone.
15	Nowhere.	We're not going anywhere.
16	None.	Don't put any milk in my tea.
17	Nothing.	I don't expect anything will
		happen.
18	Nowhere.	I didn't put it anywhere.
19	None.	I never shave.
20	None.	I haven't put any salt in the
		soup.

Exercise 14

1	Nobody	14	nowhere
2	Nowhere	15	nobody
3	None		(no-one)
4	Nothing	16	nobody
5	nothing	17	nowhere
6	Nobody	18	Nothing
	(No-one)	19	none
7	nowhere	20	Nobody
8	none	21	nowhere
9	None	22	None
10	nobody	23	nothing
	(no-one)	24	nobody
11	nothing	25	nothing
	nobody (no-one)		
12	None		
13	nothing		

Exercise 15

1 a great deal of
   (a lot of)
2 much
3 many
4 much (a lot of,
   a great deal of)
5 a lot of   much
6 much
7 much
8 Many   (a lot of)
9 a lot of
   (a great deal of)
10 much

Exercise 16

The asterisk * indicates where omission of the articles may also occur with a resulting change in sense.

1 a little   a few*
2 a little   a few
3 a little*   a few*
4 a little   few
5 a little   a few
6 few   little
7 A few*   a little
8 a little   a few
9 Few   little
10 A little   a few
11 Few   little
12 A few*   a little*
13 a little   few
14 a little*   a few*
15 a little   a few
16 Few   little
17 a little   few
18 a little   a few
19 a little   a few
20 Few   a little

Exercise 17

1 no
2 no
3 does not
4 no
5 no
6 no
7 does not
8 no
9 no
10 no
11 no
12 do not
13 does not
14 no
15 no
16 no
17 does not
18 do not
19 no
20 not eat

Exercise 19

neither . . . nor
(each time)

Exercise 18

1 I haven't any money today.
2 She hadn't any time for play.
3 They don't do any homework.
4 There isn't any sugar in my tea.
5 We don't buy any potatoes.
6 There isn't any space behind our house.
7 She doesn't tell any lies.
8 I'm not going anywhere.
9 We don't eat any meat on Fridays.
10 My brother doesn't speak any English.
11 Peter doesn't bring any sandwiches with him.
12 Mary doesn't take any sugar in her coffee.
13 There aren't any buses in Redhill Street.
14 I don't need any help, thank you.
15 There aren't any trains after midnight.
16 Mr Brown doesn't read any periodicals.
17 I can't find my glasses anywhere.
18 They don't talk to anyone during lessons.
19 I don't eat anything between meals.
20 There aren't any more of these exercises.

Exercise 20

1 speak neither Spanish nor French
2 can neither read nor write
3 was neither exciting nor
     interesting
4 speaks neither quietly nor clearly
5 speaks neither kindly nor politely
6 is neither fierce nor disobedient
7 I neither dance nor sing
8 works neither hard nor fast
9 came neither early nor late
10 feels neither unhappy nor lonely

Exercise 24

1 Never have I . . .
2 Rarely has the world . . .
3 Hardly ever do we hear . . .
4 Scarcely had the king . . .
5 Seldom did the people see . . .

Exercise 21

either. . . or
(each time)

Exercise 22

1 Neither
2 neither
3 Either
4 Neither
5 Neither
6 Either
7 Neither
8 neither
9 either
10 Neither
11 either
12 either
13 Neither
14 Neither
15 either
     neither
16 Either
17 Neither
18 either
19 Either
20 either
     neither

Exercise 23

1 so am
2 neither
3 Neither can
4 Neither do
5 Neither does
6 So does
7 Neither have
8 neither did
9 So did
10 so do
11 so do
12 So does
13 So has
14 Neither will
15 So ought
     (So should)
16 Neither
     ought
     (should)
17 neither
     ought
     (should)
18 neither
     does it
19 Neither does
20 So do

Exercise 25

1 doesn't he? Yes, he does.
2 aren't we? Yes, we are.
3 doesn't she? Yes, she does.
4 do you? No, I don't.
5 do we? No, we don't.
6 isn't it? Yes, it is.
7 doesn't she? Yes, she does.
8 have they? No, they haven't.
9 mustn't we? Yes we must.
10 can't you? Yes, I can.
11 does she? No, she doesn't.
12 does she? No, she doesn't
13 have we? No, we haven't.
14 is he? No, he isn't.
15 isn't he? Yes, he is.
16 can't I? Yes, you can.
17 musn't they? Yes, they must.
18 don't we? Yes, we do.
19 doesn't he? Yes, he does.
20 isn't he? Yes, he is.

Exercise 26

1 do we?
  . . . we don't.
2 isn't it?
3 has he?
4 hasn't it?
5 does she?
6 have you?
7 mustn't we?
8 can you?
9 oughtn't they?
10 has he?
11 does it?
12 aren't you?
13 does she?
14 don't they?
15 haven't you?
16 do they?
17 have we?
18 hasn't it?
19 are you?
20 oughtn't he?

Exercise 27

1 will you?
2 shan't I?
3 could she?
4 did she?
5 shall we?
6 haven't you?
7 hasn't he?
8 didn't you?
9 do you?
10 will you?
11 can't you?
12 will you?
13 mustn't you?
14 shan't I?
15 won't they?
16 will it?
17 couldn't they?
18 will you? (will you!)
19 had he?
20 will you? (will you!)

Exercise 28

1 would you?
2 is he?
3 were you?
4 shan't I?
5 will he?
6 mustn't they?
7 had he?
8 shouldn't I?
9 hadn't we?
10 weren't we?
11 won't you?
12 had you?
13 wouldn't you?
14 shouldn't we?
15 weren't they?
16 weren't they?
17 aren't we?
18 don't they?
19 won't they?
20 haven't they?

Exercise 29

1 They   him
2 them
3 We
4 He   them   us
5 She   him
6 He   her
7 We   her
8 It   him
9 He   him
10 They   it
11 They   he
12 She   it
13 It   us
14 She   it   them
15 They   it
16 They   them
17 She   them

Exercise 30

1 The doctor has given Robert a pill.
2 John told Peter the news.
3 Please fetch your father the newspaper.
4 The waiter offered the guests chicken and fried potatoes.
5 Will you bring me back a pot of jam, please?
6 My father wrote me a long letter . . .
7 We shall send your parents a telegram at once.
8 Some students give their English lessons a lot of time.
9 I'll fetch you a cushion to sit on.
10 A baker makes us bread to eat.
11 If you know, tell me the answer, please.
12 These large pipes bring the town its water.
13 John's father gives each of his children fifty pence pocket money.
14 When . . . please bring me your report.
15 The girls are sending their teacher some flowers on her birthday.
16 Those ships bring us our food . . .

17 We must give the lesson all our attention.
18 Our teacher tells the class historical stories.
19 My wife is making our youngest daughter a new dress.
20 The gentleman offered the porter a tip.

Exercise 31

1 himself
2 himself
3 herself
4 themselves
5 yourself
   (yourselves)
6 ourselves
7 herself
8 himself
9 myself
10 himself
11 herself
12 themselves
13 themselves
14 yourself
   (yourselves)
15 himself
16 herself
17 yourself
   (yourselves)

Exercise 32

1 myself
2 herself
3 itself
4 himself
5 myself

Exercise 33

1 each other
2 himself
3 myself
4 one another
5 one another
6 one another
7 each other
8 themselves
9 each other
10 each other

Exercise 34

1 one another
2 each other
3 each other
4 one another
5 each other
6 themselves
7 each other
8 each other
9 one another
10 yourselves
   yourselves

Exercise 35

One word or short form answers required here
(other answers are possible).

1 ... (girl's name)
2 a ... (name of job or profession)
3 ... (name)
4 I do *or* mother does
5 ... (student's own name)
6 Shakespeare did
7 *Hamlet, Twelfth Night, Henry IV etc*
8 It's the first of January *etc*
9 ... (teacher's name)
10 Persians
11 Bridegrooms do
12 That's ... (man's name)
13 (He's) a ... (name of job or profession)
14 a ... (name of job or profession)
15 Nobody does
16 Nothing *or* I said '...'
17 I do *or* she does
18 Nothing (*or* whatever you know)
19 Dr ... (name of doctor)
20 The U.S.S.S. Nimetz.

Exercise 36

(other answers are possible here)

1 Who's that?
2 What does he do?
3 Why are you studying medicine?
4 What does Carol do for a living?
5 Why do Massimo and Carla always cook Italian food?
6 What language do you speak in class?
7 What's the date today?
8 Mary and Anna have interesting jobs, don't they?
9 Which is Mr Brown and which is Mr Green?
10 Who's that beautiful girl I saw you with last night?
11 What are you doing at university?
12 What's that?
13 How do you know?
14 Why do rafts float?
15 Are you allowed to paint the classroom wall?

Exercise 37

Which: nos. 1, 2, 4, 6, 8, 10, 11, 12, 14, 15, 16, 18
What: nos. 3, 5, 7, 17, 19
Who: nos. 9, 13, 20

Exercise 38

Whose: nos. 1, 4, 6, 8, 9, 11, 13, 14, 16
Who(m): nos. 2, 3, 5, 7, 10, 12, 15

Exercise 39

1 What at / for
2 What at
3 What to
4 Which in
5 What at
6 Which for
7 Who for
8 What for
9 Whose at / in
10 Which on
11 Which in
12 Who with
13 Which in
    (whose in)
14 Who to
15 What for
16 Which for
17 What
18 Whose for
19 Where from
20 Whose on / at

Exercise 40

Free answer

Exercise 41

that:
that or who:
Whose:
  nos. 1, 2, 4, 5, 6, 7, 10
  nos. 3, 8, 9, 11, 15, 17, 18, 19, 20
  nos. 12, 16

Exercise 42

1 Omit all relatives in this exercise
2 Change 'whom' and 'which' to 'that' throughout the exercise

Exercise 43

Prepositions:

1 letters to
2 works in
3 paid for
4 you to
5 attention to
6 prices for
7 went to
8 things in
9 quotes from
10 information from
11 situation through
12 business with
13 advice to
14 refers to
15 in common with
16 suffered from
17 worked for
18 grateful for
19 work for
20 no use for

Exercise 44

who: nos. **6, 12, 19, 20**
whom: nos. **1, 2, 3, 7, 16**
whose: nos. **5, 11, 17, 18**
which: nos. **4, 8, 9, 10, 13, 14, 15**

Exercise 45

1 The cat, which
2 On Tuesday, which was
3 Mary, who studies
4 George, who had forgotten
5 Chocolate, of which
6 The weather, which we expected
7 John's brother, who studied
8 Mrs Smith, who lives
9 The Queen, whom I have
10 Mr Black, whom we respect
11 Tea, which is
12 The Bible, which is published
13 Peter's father, whom we have
14 Our dog, which is usually
15 The postman, who is
16 Mary's birthday, which I had
17 In February, which is
18 Jane, who went to
19 Mrs Green, whom you met
20 John's birthday, which was on a

Nos. **1, 3, 4, 7, 8, 12, 13, 14, 15, 18, 19, 20** may all produce two versions readily.

Exercise 46

1 who I was at school with
2 who we are governed by
3 which I am grateful for
4 who I am very fond of
5 who we complained to
6 which we read the latest reports in
7 whose party we are invited to
8 which I have nothing against
9 whose table they dined at
10 which she used to be afraid of
11 who I told the news to
12 who we expect politeness from
13 whose cottage we spent the night i
14 which . . . pay no attention to
15 whose son I am engaged to
16 which salaries are based on
17 which I owe my excellent health to
18 which we don't believe in
19 who you have your music lesson from
20 which he got the credit for

Exercise 47

1 adj. pron.
2 adj. pron.
3 adj. pron.
4 adj. adj. pron.
5 adj. pron.
6 adj. pron.
7 adj. pron.
8 adj. pron.
9 adj. pron.
10 pron.
11 adj. pron.
12 pron. pron. pron.
13 adj. pron.
14 adj. pron. pron.
15 adj. pron.
16 pron. pron.
17 adj. pron.
18 adj. pron.
19 adj. adj. (my your)
    pron. pron. (mine, yours)
20 adj. pron.

Exercise 48

1 a friend of mine.
2 a cousin of mine.
3 an old school friend of mine.
4 old pupils of his.
5 an old comrade of mine.
6 Some friends of ours . . .
7 an old jacket of mine.
8 a book of yours.
9 two books of mine.
10 friends of theirs.

1   some compatriots of mine.
2   shipmates of his.
3   relatives of theirs.
4   that old car of yours.
5   that old bone-shaker of yours.
6   that brother of mine . . .
7   a pencil of mine.
8   some photographs of hers.
9   some of that wonderful coffee of hers.
0   A friend of yours is a friend of mine.

Exercise 49

s': nos. **3, 14, 16, 17**;
's: all the others

Exercise 50

1   boy's father
2   wife's brother
3   friend's car
4   friend's employers
5   . . .
6   driver's seat
7   . . .
8   Engineers' College
9   a two month
      holiday
10 John's sister
11 Chopin's music
12 . . .
13 musician's playing
14 month's salary
15 a three minute
      walk
16 The dog's teeth
17 grandfather's farm
18 . . .
19 The king's palace
20 . . .

Exercise 51

1   mother and father's friends
2   Pasteur's and Fleming's discoveries
3   of Peter's
4   of John's
5   Edison's and Marconi's inventions
6   Smith and Black's offices
7   Uncle David and Aunt Margaret's house
8   Mr and Mrs Brown's (The Browns') family
9   Picasso's paintings
10 Margaret and Robert's duet
11 Mary's and Margaret's weddings
12 of Mr Brown's
13 of my father's
14 of the children's pets
15 gentlemen's morning newspapers
16 Epstein's statues
17 Socrates' arguments
18 mother-in-law's house
19 cat's whisker
20 That old man's name

Exercise 52

There is: nos. **1, 3, 5, 6, 8, 9, 10, 11, 12, 13, 14, 19**
There are: nos. **2, 4, 7, 15, 16, 17, 18, 20**

Exercise 53

There was: nos. **1, 12, 14, 15**
There were: nos. **2, 9, 10, 11, 13**
There is: nos. **3, 8**
There are: nos. **4, 5, 6, 7**

Exercise 54

1 Here it is
2 Here you are
3 There you are.
4 Yes, here you are.
5 There he / she is, over there.
6 There you are
7 There they are
8 Here you are
9 There he is
10 There it is
11 there he is
12 Here you are
13 here you are
14 here he is
15 here you are
16 there it is

Exercise 55

It was: nos. 1, 4, 5, 15, 19, 20
It is: nos. 2, 3, 6, 7, 8, 9, 10, 11, (12), 13, (14), 16, 17, 18
It has been: nos. 12, 14

Exercise 56

1 subj.
2 obj.
3 obj. (subj.)
4 obj.
5 subj.
6 obj.
7 obj.
8 subj.
9 obj.
10 obj.
11 obj. (subj.)
12 subj.
13 obj.
14 subj.
15 obj.
16 obj.
17 obj. (subj.)
18 subj.
19 obj.
20 subj. (obj.)

The alternatives in brackets are often heard.

Exercise 58

1 a February is shorter than March.
  b March is longer than February.
2 a Winter is colder than summer.
  b Summer is warmer than winter.
3 a John's father is older than his mother.
  b John's mother is younger than his father.
4 a Paris is nearer to London than Berlin is.
  b Berlin is farther from London than Paris is.
5 a Lemons are more bitter / sharper / more sour / than oranges.
  b Oranges are sweeter than lemons.
6 a Cream cake is cheaper than fruit cake.
  b Fruit cake is more expensive than cream cake.
7 a Peter eats less than John does.
  b John eats more than Peter does.
8 a Dogs swim more slowly than otters. (or slower than otters)
  b Otters swim faster than dogs.
9 a Mary's books look older than Jane's.
  b Jane's books look newer than Mary's.
10 a Robert buys fewer apples than I do.
   b I buy more apples than Robert does.

Exercise 57

... as ... as:
  is possible in all cases
... so ... as:
  is possible for nos 1, 3 and 5

Exercise 59

1 the hardest stone . . .
2 the sweetest smell of . . .
3 best of all . . .
4 the youngest captain in . . .
5 . . . the coldest capital . . .
6 . . . the most determined tennis player.
7 . . . the most important sport.
8 . . . the most important bee.
9 . . . the most powerful man.
10 . . . the most expensive ring . . .

Exercise 60

1 as . . . as
2 more careful
3 as . . . as
4 the most beautiful
5 the most tiring
6 worse
7 farthest (furthest)
8 more dangerous
9 better English than
10 less business than
11 more
12 tastiest
13 eldest
14 younger
15 more

Exercise 61

1 The sick need
2 The lazy
3 The deaf
4 The wounded went
5 The young   the old.
6 The rich   the poor.
7 the dead.
8 The blind
9 The unusual often
   interests journalists
10 the good

Exercise 62

1 so
2 so
3 such
4 so
5 such
6 such
7 so
8 such a
9 so
10 such
11 so
12 such a
13 such a
14 such a
15 such a
16 such a
17 such
18 so
19 such a
20 such

Exercise 63

1 What a
2 How
3 What a
4 What
5 How
6 How
7 What a
8 What
9 what   what
10 How   What
11 What   How
12 What
13 How
14 What a   How
15 How

Exercise 64

1 already   still
2 yet   still
3 yet   still
   already
4 yet   still
5 yet   already
6 yet   still
7 yet   still
   (already   still)
8 yet   yet
9 already   still
10 yet   still
11 yet   already
12 yet   already
13 already   yet
14 already   still
   yet
15 yet   already

| 16 | yet | still |
| 17 | still | already |

Exercise 65

still: nos. **1, 4, 5, 6, 7, 8, 9, 11, 12, 13, 14, 15, 16, 17, 19, 20**
yet: nos. **2, 3, 8**
yet, still: no. **10**

Exercise 66

1 we never have
2 John generally goes
3 He always plays
4 I can scarcely see.
5 he can hardly walk.
6 Brown has just gone out.
7 I nearly missed
8 baby is almost asleep.
9 I quite agree. Peter is quite right.
10 has never been
11 Peter sometimes forgets.
12 he often forgets
13 Brown rarely meets
14 train is seldom late.
15 I hardly ever travel
16 it is usually full
17 we sometimes have to stand
18 we scarcely ever go

Exercise 67

1 Peter sometimes works
2 He always arrives
3 we often walk
4 He has never been ill in his life
5 we rarely see

6 They hardly ever leave
7 We seldom drink
8 father generally sends me
9 Have you ever ridden
10 I can just imagine
11 brother usually rings
12 Does she ever do
13 sisters often help
14 boys sometimes have
15 It never rains
16 I shall always remember
17 shall I ever learn
18 people rarely ride
19 we hardly ever see
20 had just struck

Exercise 68

1 often am
2 hardly ever does
3 never did (come)
4 occasionally could
5 seldom does
6 rarely did
7 hardly ever does
8 never shall (will)
9 occasionally had
10 always do (ask)

Exercise 69

1 it on
2 it away
3 it off
4 it up
5 them off
6 it up
7 it off
8 it off
9 them over with you
10 it out
11 them down
12 it out
13 it down
14 it over
15 it out

6   it on
7   them out
8   it off
9   them in
0   it up

Exercise 70

1   at (in)
2   beside
3   under
4   on
5   over
6   by (beside)
7   between

Exercise 71

1	from	to	
2	on	on	
3	into		
4	out of	into	
5	over (across)	from	to
6	across		
7	backward(s) and forward(s) (to and fro)		
8	through		
9	along (up down)	to	over on
0	to	on	
1	from	back	
2	through	round	
3	up	down	
4	toward(s)	forward	
5	through (along)	towards (to)	
6	into	up	
7	up	down	

8   behind
9   at
10   on
11   in
12   between
13   under
14   over
15   behind
16   in (at)   in
17   in   on
18   under
19   at (on)   in the valley below
20   at (by)   in (along)

Exercise 72

1   about
2   till
3   after
4   at
5   in
6   by
7   within
8   till (until)
9   under
10   over   by
11   until (till)
12   by
13   about
14   over
15   within
16   After
17   by (before)
18   until (till)
19   after
20   on

Exercise 73

1   of (with)
2   from
3   of
4   into
5   out of
6   into
7   into
8   up
9   up
10   up
11   up
12   into
13   into
14   in (with)   by   in
15   into
16   by   of
17   into
18   among
19   on (out of)

Exercise 74

1   to. . .from
2   on. . .off
3   through. . .into
4   out of
5   at. . .until
6   in. . .with
7   at. . .at (about)
8   with. . .round
9   on. . .by
10 at. . .in
11 between
12 for. . .by. . .in
13 off. . .over
14 behind. . .into. . .out of
15 from. . .behind. . .under. . .up
16 out of. . .on
17 out of. . .without. . .in
18 of. . .on. . .in
19 with. . .with
20 in. . .in

Exercise 75

1   over
2   under. . .of. . .without
3   below
4   in. . .of. . .of
5   out of. . .by
6   until. . .by. . .back
7   between. . .from
8   for. . .in. . .of
9   for. . .at. . .with. . .in
10 from. . .with
11 up. . .into. . .out of. . .into
12 down. . .in. . .of. . .back to
13 up / down / along. . .on. . .over. . .to
14 across. . .without. . .back
15 over / across. . .in
16 under. . .across to / through to
17 against. . .up / over. . .into
18 through. . .of
19 to. . .before / without. . .on
20 on. . .under

Exercise 76

1   round. . .in / of. . .from / out of
2   at / in. . .in
3   To. . .in
4   of. . .at
5   in. . .at. . .with
6   in. . .at / by
7   in. . .with
8   for. . .on
9   of. . .away. . .on
10 on / for. . .off to
11 at / by. . .during / in
12 round. . .to. . .for
13 to. . .in
14 at. . .into
15 on. . .in
16 under. . .off
17 with. . .on
18 of. . .(about). . .of. . .at
19 for. . .with
20 on. . .in. . .off
21 into. . .among

Exercise 77

1   with. . .on / about
2   in. . .in. . .for
3   on. . .of. . .to
4   to. . .with
5   on. . .from. . .by
6   in. . .with. . .in
7   up
8   to
9   to. . .so
10 to. . .for
11 to. . .in. . .to
12 back. . .front
13 of / from. . .in. . .for
14 out. . .to. . .in
15 for. . .of. . .of
16 to. . .on. . .before
17 to. . .of. . .by
18 with. . .up for. . .by
19 of / from. . .up
20 for. . .for

Exercise 78

1 on...to...in
2 to...out...among
3 in...about...for
4 to...in...with
5 to...by
6 from...without
7 to...in
8 to...on...of
9 to...for...with
10 towards / for...up
11 of...up
12 to...for...to
13 to...from...to
14 with...to / from
15 with...in...about
16 In...of...to
17 with...over / about...of
18 to...in...of

Exercise 79

1	in	down
2	up	
3	with	
4	for	
5	on / ahead	up
6	out	
7	after	
8	down	
9	out	
10	out	up
11	off	
12	up	
13	up	off / out
14	down	up
15	out	out
16	off	
17	up	
18	up	out

Exercise 80

1	up	
2	for	
3	after	
4	off	
5	on	
6	at	out
7	off	
8	up	
9	on / off	
10	up	off
11	up	
12	on	
13	up	
14	up	
15	up	
16	into	
17	up	
18	for	
19	up	
20	down	

Exercise 81

1 out
2 out
3 up
4 out
5 out
6 out
7 out
8 up
9 off
10 up
11 down
12 out
13 for
14 up
15 up
16 down
17 for
18 up   out
19 up
20 up

Exercise 82

1	up	out
2	in	
3	out	
4	on	
5	to	
6	down	
7	up	
8	up	
9	off	
10	for	
11	of / from	
12	on	
13	out	
14	off	
15	off	
16	up	off
17	off	
18	into	
19	for	
20	off	

Exercise 83

1	in	off
2	with	off
3	back	up
4	after	over
5	forward	back
6	to	off
7	for	across
8	for	up
9	round	out
10	into	to
11	up to	out
12	off	on
13	down	up
14	up	out
15	off	off
16	out	up
17	into	out

Exercise 84

1	down	up
2	up	after
3	out	
4	with	
5	away	
6	up	
7	out	
8	to / with	
9	to	up / in
10	up	
11	off	
12	out	
13	down	
14	up	
15	off	
16	up	
17	up	
18	down	
19	up with	
20	down on	

Exercise 85

1	out / off	
2	out	
3	off	to
4	through	
5	up	
6	out	
7	with	
8	down / through	
9	out / through	
10	out	
11	down	
12	out	
13	off	
14	up / down	
15	with	
16	down	
17	on	
18	up	
19	for	
20	off	

Exercise 86

1	out	in
2	without	
3	across	
4	on	
5	up	without
6	off	
7	out	
8	at	
9	out	
10	out	up
11	off	
12	down	
13	off	up
14	out	
15	off	
16	out / down	
17	down	
18	up	
19	down	
20	up	

Exercise 87

1	b
2	a / b
3	a / b
4	a
5	a

Exercise 89

Must: nos. 1, 3, 4, 6
8, 9, 11, 12, 13, 14
15, 16, 18, 20
Must not: nos. 2, 5,
7, 10, 17, 19

Exercise 90

Must: nos. 2, 5, 7,
10, 14, 17, 18, 20
Have / has to: nos.
3, 4, 6, 8, 11,
12, 15, 16, 19
Had to: no. 9

Exercise 91

1	had to
2	weren't to
3	wasn't to
4	had to
5	had to
6	had to
7	had to
8	had to
9	was to
10	was to. . .had to
11	were to
12	had to
13	was to
14	had to
15	was to. . .was to . . .had to
16	had to
17	were to
18	was to. . .had to
19	had to
20	had to

Exercise 92

1 You don't have to
2 She needn't / drink
3 He doesn't have to
4 He doesn't have to
5 I don't have to
6 He needn't / doesn't have to do
7 She doesn't have to
8 We don't have to / I don't need to
9 They don't have to / needn't write
10 He doesn't have to stay / needn't stay
11 She doesn't have to / doesn't need to
12 You don't have to be rude / You needn't be
13 They don't have to / don't need to
14 You needn't / don't need to / don't have to
15 He doesn't have to / doesn't need to
16 We don't have to / don't need to
17 She doesn't have to have any
    / doesn't need to have any
18 Peter doesn't have to / needn't take
19 They don't have to come / needn't come
20 She needn't stay / doesn't need to stay
    / doesn't have to stay

Exercise 93

(didn't need to =
   didn't have to,
   throughout)

1 didn't need to
2 needn't have
3 needn't have
4 didn't need to
5 needn't have
6 needn't have
   needn't have
7 didn't need to
8 needn't have
   / didn't need to
9 needn't have
10 didn't need to
11 needn't have
12 didn't need to
13 needn't have
14 didn't need to
15 didn't need to
16 needn't have
17 didn't need to
18 needn't have
19 didn't need to
20 needn't have

Exercise 94

1 must
2 must have
3 must have
4 must
5 must
6 must have
7 must have
8 must have
9 must
10 can't
11 must
12 must have
13 must have
14 can't have
15 must have
16 must have
17 must
18 must have
19 must have
20 must have

Exercise 95

1 ought to
2 must
3 must have
4 ought to / must
5 ought to
6 must
7 ought to
8 ought to
9 must
10 must
11 ought to
12 must
13 must
14 must
15 ought to
16 must
17 must
18 ought to
19 ought to
20 must

Exercise 96

ought to: nos. 1, 2,
   3, 4, 7, 8, 9, 10, 11,
   12, 13, 14, 15, 20
ought not to: nos. 5,
   6, 16, 17, 19
ought we to spend:
   (18)

Exercise 97

1 ought to
2 must
3 must
4 ought to
5 oughtn't to
6 must
7 ought to
8 must
9 ought to
10 ought to / must
11 ought to / must

Exercise 98

(ought to = should, throughout)

1 ought to
2 ought to
3 must
4 ought to
5 must
6 ought to
7 must
8 must
9 must
10 ought to
11 ought to
12 ought to
13 must
14 must
15 must
16 ought to / must
17 ought to
18 must
19 must / ought to
20 ought to

Exercise 99

(ought to have = should have, throughout)

1 ought to have
2 ought to have
3 must have
4 ought to have
5 ought to have
6 must have
7 ought to have
8 must have
9 ought to have
10 must have
11 ought to have
12 ought to have
13 ought not to have
14 must have
15 must have
16 oughtn't to have
17 can't have
18 must have
19 ought not to have
20 can't have

Exercise 100

1 should
2 must
3 must
4 must...should
5 shouldn't / mustn't
6 shall have to
7 must
8 should
9 should...should
   ...shouldn't
10 must
    should / must
11 Must...Ought
12 shall have to
13 should
14 has to
15 should
16 should...should
17 must / has to
18 should
19 have to
    ...must / have to
20 should

Exercise 101

1 were allowed to stay up late
2 could have used ... whenever she wanted to
3 were allowed to spend
4 John could have worn ... if he needed one.
5 could get up yesterday.
6 could have
7 could stay here
8 weren't allowed to / couldn't
9 could eat...wanted
10 weren't allowed to / couldn't
11 wasn't allowed to
12 weren't allowed to / couldn't
13 could have as much as I liked.
14 couldn't go
15 could come
16 could pick as many flowers as she liked
17 couldn't marry
18 could have
19 could have / was allowed to have
20 could leave / was allowed to leave

Exercise 102

able to forms for past and future throughout.
could for the past may also be used in all the
examples but in nos. **3, 4, 5, 11, 13, 14, 16, 19, 20**
able to is more applicable.

Exercise 103

1 ability
2 ability (neg.)
3 permission
4 permission (neg.)
5 permission (neg.)
6 ability (neg.)
7 ability (neg.)
8 permission
9 permission
10 ability (neg.)
11 permission
12 ability (neg.)
13 ability
14 ability
15 permission
16 permission
17 ability (neg.)
18 ability
19 permission (neg.)
   / or ability
20 permission (neg.)

Exercise 104

		(a)		was able to		(b)		will be able to ...
1	(a)	... wasn't busy ...				(b)	... won't be busy ...	
4	(a)	... was ...				(b)	... will be ...	
5	(a)	... was ready ...				(b)	... will be ...	
6	(a)	... was working ...				(b)	... will be working ...	
7	(a)	... was ...				(b)	... will be ...	
18	(a)	... lived ...				(b)	... will be living ...	

		(a)		were able to		(b)		will be able to
2	(a)	... had stopped ...				(b)	... has stopped ...	
3	(a)	... didn't break up ...				(b)	... doesn't break up ...	
8	(a)	... went ...				(b)	... go ...	
10	(a)	... had ...				(b)	... has ...	
11	(a)	... was ...				(b)	... is ...	
14	(a)	... didn't have to ...				(b)	... don't have to ...	
19	(a)	... weren't driving ...				(b)	... aren't / won't be driving	

9	(a)	. . . sold . . . . . . would be able to . . .	(b)	. . . is selling . . . . . . will be able to.

			wasn't able to			won't be able to
12	(a)	. . . was . . .		(b)	. . . will be . . .	
13	(a)	. . . had to go . . .		(b)	. . . was to go . . .	
15	(a)	. . . saw . . .		(b)	. . . will see . . .	
16	(a)	. . . had to study . . .		(b)	. . . will have to . . .	
17	(a)	. . . had just broken down . . .		(b)	. . . has just broken down . . .	

Exercise 105

Either *may* or *might* in
  nos. **6, 11, 15, 18**.
No key required.

Exercise 106

May: nos. **1, 4, 5, 6,**
  8, 10, 11, 14, 17, 20
Might: nos. **2, 3, 7,**
  9, 12, 13, 15, 16,
  18, 19

Exercise 107

1 Might. . .may
2 might / may
3 may
4 may have
5 Might
6 might
7 might have
8 might have
9 might
10 might
11 might have
12 mayn't
13 mightn't
14 Might
15 might have
16 may
17 might / may
18 may / might
19 may
20 might

Exercise 108

1 Peter has / gets his car cleaned
2 Mary has / gets her clothes made
3 I have / get my hair cut
4 The Smiths will have / get their new house built
5 George has / gets his suits pressed
6 Mrs Black has / gets her shopping sent
7 We get our shoes mended
8 They have / get their windows cleaned
9 Jane has / gets the heavy work done
10 We have / get our teeth inspected
11 The manager has / gets his letters typed
12 He has / gets them posted
13 I have / get my room cleaned
14 I always have / get my coffee brought
15 David has / gets his newspapers delivered
16 My mother has / gets her garden looked after
17 I have / get my laundry done
18 We are having / getting a new front door made
19 We are going to have / get this translated
20 They had / got a cake baked

Exercise 109

1 She had them show her
2 We had the taxi driver call
3 The manager had me copy it
4 He had me write it all
5 Will you have the doctor come
6 Mrs Brown had the maid wash
7 She had me polish all
8 Our teacher had us learn
9 Please have my secretary come
10 They had him come
11 The doctor had us keep

12 That customer had me run
13 The bank manager had the police keep
14 Sergeant Smith had the platoon double march
15 Have Miss Brown write this letter
16 A policeman had me accompany him
17 His mother had him apologise
18 Have someone mend that
19 Have the porter fetch my luggage
20 Father had John go back

11 Don't let
12 let
13 Let
14 Let
15 didn't let
16 Let
17 let
18 Let
19 doesn't let
20 lets

Exercise 110

have: nos. **4, 5, 6, 10, 12, 14, 18**
get: nos. **1, 2, 3, 7, 8, 9, 11, 13, 15, 16, 17, 19, 20**
get or *have*: nos. **4, 5, 7, 17, 19** according to sense

Exercise 111

1 getting
2 get
3 getting
4 getting
5 gets
6 got
7 get to
8 get
9 get
10 got
11 got
12 goes
13 get
14 got
15 got
16 get
17 get
18 getting
19 got
20 goes

Exercise 112

1 get
2 got
3 got
4 got
5 get
6 got
7 get
8 got
9 got
10 gets
11 get
12 get
13 get
14 get
15 get
16 got
17 get
18 is getting / gets
19 got
20 got

Exercise 113

1 Let
2 Don't let
3 Let
4 doesn't let
5 let
6 Don't let
7 Let
8 let
9 Let
10 let

Exercise 114

1 made
2 made
3 did
4 does
5 make
6 do
7 doing
8 makes
9 make
10 do
11 do
12 make
13 made
14 do
15 making
16 do
17 make
18 making
19 does
20 making

Exercise 115

1 makes
2 made
3 did
4 made
5 make
6 doing
7 make
8 make
9 makes
10 make

11 does
12 make
13 do
14 makes
15 makes
16 doing
17 do   make
18 made
19 do
20 make

Exercise 116

1 buying a hat / purchasing a hat
2 in manufacturing radio sets
3 way of thinking
4 preparing his work.
5 by agreeing to
6 after consulting with
7 in escaping at . . .
8 through overworking.
9 of living in
10 of seeing
11 with lighting and heating.
12 After seeing
13 of working
14 by speaking.
15 by smelling
16 for smoking and chatting
17 for fighting
18 flooding
19 waiting in

Exercise 117

Both infinitive and gerund:
   nos. 1, 2, 3, 4, 5, 6, 7, 8, 9, 10, 11,
   15, 16, 17
Gerund only:
   nos. 14, 19, 20
Gerund or infinitive according to
   sense required:
   nos. 13, 18
Infinitive only:
   no. 12

Exercise 118

1 his playing and singing
2 his hurting . . . insulting
3 his mistaking . . . mishearing
4 his leaving . . . giving
5 waking up . . . shouting
6 his wanting . . . laying
7 her walking . . . getting
8 his / her trying . . . breaking
9 his taking . . . writing
10 his smoking
11 telling . . . her being
12 his serving . . . allowing
13 their thinking . . . our leaving
   . . . saying
14 his whistling . . . singing.
15 it running . . . pressing.

Exercise 119

1 enough money
2 cheap enough
3 early enough
4 old enough
5 enough time
6 enough sugar
7 well enough
8 sweet enough
9 strong enough
10 enough leisure
11 hard enough
12 enough sunshine
13 brightly enough
14 enough food
15 enough bread
16 fresh enough
17 enough time
18 fast enough
19 easy enough
20 enough salt

Exercise 120

1 too large for me to carry
2 enough food to last
3 clearly enough to know him
4 too small to hold
5 enough money to live
6 too softly for him to hear
7 enough time to have
8 enough patience to do
9 too cheap to be very good
10 too sweet for Father to drink
11 too quickly for us to do anything
12 too often for us to go out
13 enough flour to make a cake
14 too dear for Peter to buy
15 strong enough to pull
16 well enough to go to
17 hot enough for me to shave with
18 enough trouble of her own to understand
19 too much work for one man
20 too young to stay out late

Exercise 121

1 they want to
2 he wants to
3 want me to
4 you want to
5 they want to
6 want me to
7 to
8 don't want to
9 want to
10 doesn't mean to
11 would like to
12 hope to
13 about to

Exercise 122

1 inf; ger.
2 inf; ger.
3 inf; inf / ger.
4 inf; ger.
5 ger / inf; ger.
6 ger; inf.
7 inf; ger.
8 inf; ger.
9 inf; ger.
10 ger; inf.
11 inf; inf.
12 inf; inf.
13 ger.
14 ger; inf.
15 ger; inf.
16 inf; ger.
17 inf; inf; ger.
18 inf; ger.

Exercise 123

1 to have learnt
2 to have been
3 to have spoken to
4 to have died
5 to have made
6 to have finished
7 to have completed
8 to have done
9 to have taken up
10 to have given
11 to have bought
12 to have lost
13 to have said
14 to have paid
15 to have left
16 to have rung
17 to have been
18 to have mastered
19 to have lived
20 to have done

Exercise 124

1 to fly
  / to have flown
2 to leave
  / to have left
3 to see
  / to have seen
4 to arrive
5 to come
  / to have come
6 to buy
7 to sit
8 to advise
9 ever to have come
10 to swim
  / to have swum
11 to cross
  / to have crossed
12 to have given
13 to have occurred
14 to solve
15 to give
16 to do

17	to survive	4	it to them	13	it for her / him
18	to live	5	it to him	14	it for him
19	to be able to /	6	it to them	15	it to him / her
20	to have been able to	7	it to them	16	it for her
		8	it for her	17	it to her
	Exercise 125	9	it for him	18	them for him
		10	it for her	19	it for her / him
1	it to him	11	it to them	20	it to her
2	it to her	12	them to them		
3	it to him				

Exercise 126

1 Does Mary take . . .? She doesn't take . . . she does not take . . .
2 Does Peter buy . . .? He doesn't buy . . . he does not buy . . .
3 Does he read . . .? He doesn't read . . . he does not read . . .
4 Does Mr B teach . . .? He doesn't teach . . . he does not teach . . .
5 Do you come . . .? I don't come . . . I do not come . . .
6 Do the boys . . . write . . .? They don't write . . . they do not write
7 Do we use . . .? We don't use . . . we do not use.
8 Does our teacher say? . . . Our teacher doesn't say . . . does not say . . .
9 Do we go . . .? We don't go . . . we do not go . . .
10 Do I drink . . .? I don't drink . . . I do not drink . . .
11 Do you go . . .? You don't go . . . You do not go . . .
12 Does Peter play? Peter doesn't play . . . Peter does not play . . .
13 Does the sun rise . . .? The sun doesn't rise . . . does not rise . . .
14 Does it shine . . .? It doesn't shine . . . It does not shine . . .
15 Does . . . know everything. He doesn't know . . . He does not know . . .
16 Do dogs like . . .? Dogs don't like . . . do not like . . .
17 Do some children like . . .? Some children don't like . . . do not like . . .
18 Does a deaf person hear well? A deaf person doesn't hear . . . does not hear . . .
19 Does it rain . . .? It doesn't rain . . . It does not rain . . .
20 Does soap cost . . .? Soap doesn't cost . . . does not cost.

Exercise 127

Yes, it does: nos. **1, 7**
Yes, they do:
  nos. **2, 6, 8**
Yes, it is: nos. **3, 10, 20**
No, it isn't: no. **4**
Yes, I am: nos. **5, 13**
No, they don't:
  nos. **9, 11, 12**
Yes, it is *or*
No, it isn't: nos. **14, 15**
Yes, she (he) is *or*
No, she (he) isn't:
  nos. **16, 17, 19**
Yes, she (he) does:
  no. **18**

Exercise 128

1 do not eat
2 do not agree
3 is visiting
4 does not (doesn't)
  see
5 goes
6 does not always see
7 goes
8 is not going
9 is trying
10 comes
11 is meeting
12 does not work
13 stays
14 has . . . does not
  need
15 is sitting

Exercise 129

1 goes
2 is shining
3 is barking
4 is sleeping
5 is having
6 travel

7 comes
8 is riding
9 shaves
10 is shaving
11 go . . . are visiting
12 am having . . . take
13 is smoking . . .
  prefers . . .
  does not buy.
14 go . . . are going
15 lives . . . is studying
16 am speaking . . .
17 expect . . . receive
  . . . is giving
18 drinks . . . takes
19 interrupts
  . . . is speaking
20 lies . . . is resting
  . . . falls

Exercise 130

1 has done
2 has made
3 have learnt
4 has added
5 have progressed
6 has discovered
7 have invented
8 have forgotten
9 has gone out
10 has never seen
11 have risen
12 has not bought
13 has gone up
14 has worn
15 have lived
16 has visited
17 has been
18 has stood
19 has been
20 have attended

Exercise 131

Yes, I have *or* No, I
  haven't: nos. **1, 3, 6, 9,
  11, 13, 15, 18, 19, 20**
Yes, she has *or* No, she
  hasn't: nos. **2, 12,
  16, 17**
Yes, he has *or* No, he
  hasn't: nos. **4, 5**
Yes, it has *or* No, it
  hasn't: nos. **7, 10**
Yes, you have *or* No,
  you haven't: no. **8**
Yes, they have: no. **14**

Exercise 132

1	for	since
2	since	for
3	for	since
4	since	for
5	since	for
6	for	since
7	since	for
8	for	since
9	since	for
10	since	for
11	for	since
12	since	for
13	for	since
14	for	since
15	for	since
16	for	since
17	since	for

Exercise 133

(a) for . . .
  + free answer,
  including time.
(b) since . . .
  + free answer,
  including time.

Exercise 134

A variety of present consequences to each
example may be produced e.g.

1 I can hand it to my teacher / Now it's perfect
   / At last I can go out / etc. and
2 I want to see him / There is no doctor in the village
   now / How can I get my prescription?

Exercise 135

A variety of previous causes may be produced
for each example e.g.

1 It has been raining / They've been washing them
   / The main water pipe has burst and
2 He has been in the rain / They've turned the
   hosepipe on him.

Exercise 137

1 smoke ... smokes ... prefer
2 has been living ...
3 is going ... is helping ...
4 have been eating ... are ... is talking
5 have gone ... has prescribed ... is giving
6 visits ... is travelling
7 has read ... knows
8 have been listening ... have not understood ... think ... speak
9 has been driving ... has never driven
10 is going ... has just put
11 has been reading ... has
12 leaves ... has been travelling
13 is it raining? ... did not bring / have not brought
14 have you been ... have been looking for
15 is sitting ... is writing ... sits
16 Have you finished? ... am still preparing
17 has been standing ... say ... want
18 knows ... has been growing ... is still trying
19 don't know ... has stopped
20 does not go ... come / are coming ... go / are going ... takes
    ... finds
21 does ... cooks ... cleans, knits ... sews ... is baking
22 Have you ever heard ...? ... Do you recognise ...? ... am
    playing

Exercise 136

1 has been playing
2 has been serving
3 have been watching
4 has been practising
5 has been living
6 have been behaving
7 has been working
8 has been sleeping
9 have been travelling
10 have been spending

23 has been doing ... is staying
24 has not had ... is working ... has been living

Exercise 138

1 (a) Did he go out early?   (b) He did not go out early.
2 (a) Did he come   (b) He did not come
3 (a) Did they give   (b) They did not give
4 (a) Did father take you   (b) Father did not take us
5 (a) Did we sit   (b) We did not sit
6 (a) Did you see   (b) You did not see
7 (a) Did they buy   (b) They didn't buy
8 (a) Did we eat   (b) We didn't eat
9 (a) Did some of the ladies drink tea? (b) Some of the ladies did not drink tea
10 (a) Did we speak to   (b) We didn't speak
11 (a) Did one of them write   (b) One of them did not write
                                          (= all the others did write . . .)
12 (a) Did she keep it   (b) She did not keep it
13 (a) Did she lose   (b) She did not lose
14 (a) Did a friend find   (b) No-one found or A friend did not
15 (a) Did you spend   (b) You did not spend
16 (a) Did the grocer forget   (b) The grocer did not forget
17 (a) Did you ring him up   (b) You did not ring him up
18 (a) Did he hurt   (b) He didn't hurt
19 (a) Did his head strike   (b) His head did not strike
20 (a) Did you cut   (b) You did not cut

Exercise 139

1 went ... was ... stayed
2 bought ... paid ... ran ... could
3 kept ... bit ... came
4 made ... tasted ... spat
5 spoke ... understood ... was
6 had ... was
7 rode ... came ... took
8 began ... said ... read ... led
9 knew ... met ... told ... wrote ... drank
10 ate ... knew

Exercise 140

1 Yesterday, I thought you were right. *or*
  I thought you were right yesterday.
  (Note difference in emphasis).
  Nos. **2, 3, 4, 5, 6, 8, 10, 11, 12, 13, 14, 15, 16, 17, 18, 20**; the past time expression may come first or last with no change in meaning, see list of irregular verbs for simple past forms.

7 The boy brought my newspaper before seven o'clock yesterday.

9 I knew Peter Smith before he got married.

19 She got a lot of information from them then.

Exercise 141

1 was ... got
2 interested ... saw
3 did ... felt
4 ate ... became
5 went ... could not
6 did not know ... look
7 saw ... screamed
8 died ... took
9 struck ... broke
10 brought ... pleased.

Exercise 142

A variety of additions may be produced for each example e.g.

1 there were no cars / T.V. sets / people couldn't travel easily / few people spoke foreign languages
2 the Napoleonic Wars ended / they began to build railways in England / gold and silver coins were still common / people were moving from the country to the towns etc.

Exercise 143

1 was staying ... met
2 was shining ... set
3 was raining ... arrived
4 was having ... came
5 was serving ... kicked
6 kicked ... was passing
7 were you living
8 were you talking to
9 was typing ... noticed
10 was carving ... was laying / carved ... laid

6 was suffering ... saw
7 saw ... was working
8 was lying ... paid
9 hurt ... was digging
10 was falling ... arrived.

Exercise 144

1 was going ... saw
2 were sitting ... rang
3 was trying ... found
4 was watching ... broke in
5 met ... was crossing

Exercise 145

1 was cleaning ... fell
2 were you speaking to ... brought
3 was asking / asked ... took
4 polished
5 was she wearing ... saw
6 Was John working ... called
7 was trying ... did not look
8 heard ... was talking
9 went ... were
10 drank ... went

11 did she want ... visited
12 knocked ... was having
13 did you spend
14 gave ... spent
15 was not feeling / did not feel
    ... consulted
16 were you living
17 were staying ... working
18 was not looking / did not look
    ... spoke
    was speaking
19 arrived ... was sleeping
20 dropped ... were passing

Exercise 146

1 had met
2 had been
3 had prepared
4 had forgotten
5 had rained
6 had not stopped
7 had not eaten
8 had saved

Exercise 147

A variety of additions may be produced from most of the
    items e.g.

2 so we didn't go into the cinema / but didn't mind seeing it
again / but liked it better the second time   *and*
3 so we lit the lamps / so we couldn't see to read / but there
was still light in the sky / so we stopped work for the day, *etc.*

Exercise 148

1 had spent ... did not know
2 had finished ... sat
3 had been ... began
4 gave ... had done
5 had thanked ... left ... went
6 told ... had seen
7 had just returned ... gave
8 had broken ... needed
9 had hoped ... felt
10 had gone ... was
11 had always lived ... did not
    understand
12 could not ... had forgotten
13 had ... had gone
14 had never been ... wanted
15 had lost ... could not buy

Exercise 149

A variety of previous causes may
    be produced for each item e.g.

1 because it had jumped so well
/ because it had had a fright
/ as it had always liked sugar   *and*
2 because she hadn't heard it well
/ because I hadn't spoken clearly
/ because she had never heard such
a name before / as she had
forgotten to write it down, *etc.*

Exercise 150

1 pressed ... started
2 had forgotten ... stopped
3 had not eaten ... felt
4 had not arrived ... went
5 misunderstood ... had not heard

6 heated ... expanded
7 gave ... had earned
8 had missed ... travelled
9 introduced ... had not met
10 sunbathed ... got
11 had not been ... seemed
12 Did he refuse ... had not written
13 did not go ... did not have
14 Did he become ... accused
15 had not had ... did not expect
16 struck ... knocked
17 Did she find out ... did someone tell   *or*
   had someone told ...?
18 woke up ... had not rung
19 put ... stopped
20 had gone cold ... warmed

Exercise 151

1 had been reading
2 had been trying
3 had been asking
4 had been raining
5 had been teaching
6 had been taking
7 had been complaining
8 had been wanting
9 had been teaching
10 had been writing
11 had been losing
12 had been burning
13 had not been taking
14 had been waiting
15 had been worrying

10 will not put up with
11 will not listen
12 will get
13 will be
14 will stay
15 will ask
16 will look
17 will not work
18 will take
19 will sit
20 will need
going to: for all
   items **3, 4, 15, 20**
going to can give
   meaningful
   sentences.

Exercise 152

1 will be
2 will drop
3 will grow
4 will not develop
5 will break
6 will buy
7 will die
8 will not sell
9 will live

Exercise 153

1 are to arrive
2 is to command
3 are to be raised
4 are to report
5 is to spend
6 are not to light
7 are not to
8 is to pay
9 are to attend
10 is to leave

Exercise 154

1 arrives
2 take place
3 is closing
4 are having
5 is working
6 am having
7 am going
8 is playing
   ... is giving
9 is visiting
10 are not taking off
11 is bringing
12 reach ... are
   taking
13 is going ... is
   visiting
14 take ... is taking
15 joins
16 is coming
17 is staying
18 are paying

Exercise 155

1 will
2 shall
3 shall
4 will
5 shall
6 shall   will
7 shall
8 shall
9 will
10 shall

Exercise 156

1 shall
2 will
3 will
4 shall
5 will
6 will
7 will   will

8 will
9 will
10 will

Exercise 157

1 is going to give
2 is not going to take
3 is going to sing
4 is going to build
5 am going to live
6 are going to get
   married
7 are going to sell
8 is going to send
9 am not going to
   wait
10 are you going to
   talk

Exercise 158

1 shall
2 will
3 shall
4 shall
5 shall
6 shall
7 shall
8 shall
9 will
10 shall

Exercise 159

1 going to
2 going to
3 not going to
4 going to
5 will not
6 going to
7 will
8 going to
9 going to
10 shall

Exercise 160

1 will be
2 shall be
3 shall be
4 shall be
5 will be
6 will be
7 shall be
8 will be
9 will be / shall be
10 shall be

Exercise 161

1 shall be giving
2 will be sending
3 shall be visiting
4 shall be going
5 won't be coming
6 will be getting
7 will be wearing
8 Shall we be having
9 will be boiling
10 will be arriving

Exercise 163

1 will have been teaching
2 will have finished
3 shall have had
4 shall have been living
5 will have travelled
6 will have closed
7 will have gone
8 shall have been writing
9 shall have been
10 will have been staying
11 will the doctor have arrived
12 will have stopped
13 will not have read
14 Will you have completed
15 If you have not . . . shall have called
16 will have grown
17 will have risen
18 Will the children have written?
19 won't have come
20 will not have baked / won't have baked

11 will be studying
12 shan't be seeing
13 will be spending
14 will be doing
15 will you be doing
16 will be happening
17 will be coming
18 shall be staying

Exercise 162

1 will have heard
2 shall have begun
3 shall have left
4 will have worked
5 shall have learnt
6 shall have visited
7 will have had
8 will not have
   finished
9 will have had
10 shall have married . . .
   shall have settled
   down.

Exercise 164

1 He will have been working
2 shall have been living
3 will have been celebrating
4 shall have been studying
5 will have been travelling
6 will have been travelling
7 will have been reading
8 will have been shopping and cooking
9 will have been working
10 shall have been teaching

Exercise 165

1	see	
2	will be	is
3	go	will meet
4	need	will help
5	shall have	is
6	ask	will tell
7	will finish	can
8	shan't require	doesn't rain
9	thinks	will form
10	catch	will arrive
11	will find	looks
12	want	will come
13	writes	will answer
14	wait	will bring
15	will lose	stops
16	is	will try
17	shall wear	must
18	leave	shall catch
19	does	will punish
20	drinks	will feel

Exercise 166

1	**(a)** know	will	**(b)** knew	would
2	**(a)** wants	will	**(b)** wanted	would
3	**(a)** will	sleeps	**(b)** would	slept
4	**(a)** has	will	**(b)** had	would
5	**(a)** will	goes	**(b)** would	went
6	**(a)** shall	arrive	**(b)** should / would	arrived
7	**(a)** can	will	**(b)** could	would
8	**(a)** shall understand	speaks	**(b)** should / would	spoke
9	**(a)** won't	is	**(b)** shouldn't / wouldn't	were / was
10	**(a)** don't give	won't be	**(b)** didn't	wouldn't
11	**(a)** will	can	**(b)** would	could
12	**(a)** shan't / won't	speaks	**(b)** wouldn't	spoke
13	**(a)** will	take	**(b)** would	took
14	**(a)** shall lose	listen	**(b)** would	listened
15	**(a)** is	shall do	**(b)** were / was	would / should
16	**(a)** think	shall say	**(b)** thought	should / would
17	**(a)** will	uses	**(b)** would	used
18	**(a)** shan't / won't	is	**(b)** wouldn't	were / was
19	**(a)** promises	will forgive	**(b)** promised	would
20	**(a)** won't seem	walks	**(b)** would not	walked

Exercise 167

1 If she had tried she could have done better
2 He would have done more work if he had been able
3 I should have lived better if I had had more money
  – and so on throughout the exercise.

Exercise 168

1 rains
2 studied
3 had asked   (unfulfilled)
4 had taken   (unfulfilled)
5 was / were
6 get
7 cost . . . could you buy
8 would have stayed . . . had missed (unfulfilled)
9 will never speak
10 had not been
11 caught
12 does
13 needs
14 needed
15 liked
16 had paid   (unfulfilled)
17 had
18 receives

19 had not introduced
20 smoked

Exercise 169

There is no other change necessary.

Exercise 170

1 The fire brigade was called
2 The door wasn't opened
3 Coffee is often preferred
4 The door was opened
5 Their names are checked
6 You will be wakened / woken
7 A top hat is worn
8 The Prime Minister was expected
9 My poems aren't read
10 Mistakes are sometimes made
11 Immediate action is demanded
12 Mary's new vase has been broken
13 Rice is eaten
14 Soup is served
15 A man's family is supported
16 Many newspapers and magazines are read
17 Buses and trains are used to travel
18 Tea is drunk
19 Certain matters are never mentioned
20 We shall be met

Exercise 171

1 (a) A gold watch has been given to
2 (a) A cup of tea is brought to me
3 (a) A letter will be sent to John.
4 (a) A great many questions were asked of Mary.
5 (a) An interview was granted me.
6 (a) A lie was told to the police.
7 (a) English literature is taught to the students.
8 (a) A telegram was handed to the general.
9 (a) Three days were allowed Mr Black to
10 (a) A free pardon was granted to the criminal.

1 (b) Mr Brown has been given a . . .
2 (b) I am brought a cup of tea . . .
3 (b) John will be sent a letter.
4 (b) Mary was asked . . .
5 (b) I was granted an interview.
6 (b) The police were told a lie.
7 (b) The students are taught . . .
8 (b) The general was handed . . .
9 (b) Mr Black was allowed . . .
10 (b) The criminal was granted . . .

Exercise 172

1. The extraordinary weather was being talked about.
2. New business premises are being looked for.
3. My education was paid for.
4. The family business was taken over (by creditors).
5. A football team is made up . . .
6. The house is looked after by . . .
7. My brother will be spoken for.
8. A parcel is usually tied up with string.
9. We were waited on.
10. Everything I say must be written down.
11. Their wedding has been put off for six months.
12. Was an S.O.S. sent out (by the captain)?
13. Peter's mistake wasn't referred to again.
14. Private affairs aren't spoken of in company.
15. The date on this exercise has been rubbed out.
16. Mr White is being asked for on the telephone.
17. Coffee was poured out and given to us.
18. Old letters are generally torn up after a while.
19. These suspicious circumstances are being looked into (by the police).
20. Old ships are broken up for scrap metal (by that firm).

Exercise 173

1. It is said
2. It is thought
3. It is now known
4. It is considered
5. The news can be heard
6. Aspirin can be bought
7. Sweets aren't eaten
8. Special days are celebrated . . .
9. Parties are given
10. The police were informed
11. Very many newspapers are read
12. Beer is drunk
13. More than one language is spoken
14. An attack at dawn was ordered
15. Fine ships are built (by the men) on Clydeside
16. Eggs are bought by the dozen
17. Coal is sold by the ton
18. English is spoken in this shop.
19. Mr Smith is shaved
20. No help is needed

Exercise 174

1. An explanation has been asked for.
2. The parcel will be called for.
3. He will be called up.
4. The ring has been looked for everywhere. The thief hasn't been found yet. His tracks have been covered up.
5. Another expedition is being sent out.
6. Men of honour have always been looked up to.
7. Cheats and liars have always been looked down on.
8. The bank has been broken into.
9. The matter has been taken up by the police. It is being looked into now.
10. The children are very well looked after.
11. They are being brought up very carefully.
12. Every word I said was being taken down.

13 It was written out in longhand
    later.
14 He was shut up in prison for
    six months.
15 He was taken in by their lies.

Exercise 175

(a) Needs only re-ordering of the
sentences thus:

1 (a) His father informs us that
        Peter is going into the
        army soon.

1 (b) His father informed us
        that Peter was going
        into the army soon.
2 (b) Chris was saying that we
        (they) usually had
3 (b) The report stated that
        there had been
4 (b) The evening newspaper
        said that something
        would have to be . . .
        done.
5 (b) John declared that he did
        not know
6 (b) Robin explained that they
        had not been
7 (b) Peter complained that he
        didn't earn
8 (b) The headlines said that . . .
        had died.
9 (b) The poet declared   that
        . . . would smell
10 (b) The gardener said that he
        had not heard . . . in all
        his life.
11 (b) Peter agreed that you
        were   (I was) quite
12 (b) Everybody said that . . .
        was going to be
13 (b) She had promised that she
        would do
14 (b) John and Mary regretted
        that they couldn't afford

15 (b) The witness affirmed that
        that was the man he
        saw
16 (b) My son informed me that
        there was to be . . .
17 (b) Your teacher told me that
        you should pay
18 (b) His son sometimes told
        him that he ought to
        have
19 (b) My father often reminded
        me that I ought
20 (b) Our teacher said that we
        couldn't

Exercise 176

1 I told them I couldn't come
   out.
2 He informed us that she was
   trying
3 They let me know that they
   weren't going
4 She protested that it was a
   very silly idea.
5 that they hadn't any children.
6 that he was bringing the
   books back.
7 that she bought everything
   she needed.
8 that when he drank iced
   water, it hurt his stomach.
9 that he often wrote
10 that they sent him
11 that we hadn't been
12 that they (we) weren't
   working
13 that they (we) were
14 that they (we) were just
15 that most . . . had
16 that some . . . drank
17 that there was
18 that he had broken
19 that he didn't need
20 that I couldn't remember

Exercise 177

nos. **1–5** both forms may be used in the reports.
6 and **7** past only.
nos. **8–16** both forms
nos. **17–18** past only.

Exercise 178

Note that *say* is not suitable as a reporting verb in this exercise. Use *tell, ask, order*, etc. instead.

Exercise 179

No key required.

Exercise 180

(Other reporting verbs are possible here)

1 We agreed that we should meet on the following Tuesday.
2 You told me that she was coming the next day.
3 He said that Mary would be preparing the dinner soon.
4 The teacher told us that we wouldn't know ... till the following week.
5 I promised that I would try to be early in future.
6 The teacher warned us that the headmaster would be coming in shortly.
7 He said that we wouldn't set the Thames on fire.
8 Mother declared that he should never come here (there) again.
9 We promised that we would be good children.
10 He said that they would never succeed if they never tried.

11 The weather report predicted that it would be raining hard that night. (tonight)
12 He thought that there would be ...
13 She said that John would be travelling to Australia the following week.
14 John declared that Mary would always remember that day ...
15 and he added that he wouldn't forget it for a long time either.
16 He wasn't sure whether he would be able to come.
17 They told us that they would be expecting us at the end of the month.
18 They said that they would be having dinner about seven.
19 She promised that she would arrive about half-past six.
20 They told her that would be fine. They would have time ...

Exercise 181

1 She said that she often saw
2 They replied that they sometimes played
3 John wrote that he was going out with Lisa the following (next) day.
4 They answered that they were having dinner with
5 She confirmed that she had not spoken to
6 that she knew he was married to Catherine.
7 that they never found time to write
8 that they often saw
9 that he missed Mary
10 that she had bought
11 that they had known

12 that they had never met
13 that he recognised
14 that he knew her
15 that they were driving
16 that they were seeing her off
17 that he was discussing
18 that she was quite sure he was
   wrong.
19 that we didn't often have
20 that she worked with

Exercise 182

1 John asked me to tell him
  about my holiday.
2 She answered that she was
  just about to show him
  some snapshots of herself.
3 She whispered that I was
  looking at her very
  strangely.
4 I replied that she reminded
  me of someone I know.
5 Mary confirmed that she
  remembered our saying
  that.
6 The family announced that I
  was taking them to the
  cinema.
7 He insisted that he wanted me
  to marry him.
8 I answered that he was telling
  her a lot of nonsense.
9 He repeated that he wanted
  me to believe him . . .
10 The students observed that I
   hadn't needed to help them
   much this time.

Exercise 183

1 was sending
2 they promised to help him as
  much as they could.
3 that you didn't know them
  very well.
4 that you never saw her any
  more.

5 that they didn't write to us
  any more.
6 that you hadn't seen him since
  Christmas
7 he hadn't spoken to her . . .
8 that she hadn't visited you
  since the spring.
9 that you didn't want to see
  him again.
10 that you couldn't stand the
   sight of him
11 that she got on his nerves too.
12 that they were afraid he didn't
   like them very much.
13 that we hadn't told them the
   truth.
14 that we couldn't trust them to
   keep a secret.

Exercise 184

1 I asked where John had left
  his bicycle
2 Peter wanted to know when
  David had bought
3 John asked Mary where they
  should meet on Saturday
4 I asked mother what she had
  bought for Mary's birthday.
5 She wanted to know whom
  we had seen at the cinema
  the other night.
6 Father enquired whose book
  Betty had borrowed.
7 They asked Mary why she
  hadn't written to them for
  such a long time.
8 The lawyer enquired which of
  the two boys was the elder
  son.
9 Peter asked when I would pay
  back the money father had
  lent me.
10 He asked the cook what she
   (he) was going to prepare
   for dinner.

11 My secretary asked whose
    telephone number I was
    looking up.
12 My friend enquired which of
    the films I had seen.
13 The manager wanted to know
    why I didn't get up earlier
    in the mornings.
14 They wondered how much
    they should pay for a month
    in Spain.
15 Peter wanted to know whose
    money that was on the
    table.

Exercise 185

1 John asked whether (if) we
   knew where she lived.
2 The lady wanted to know if
   (whether) this bus went
   along
3 I asked whether (if) you
   remembered
4 Mary enquired whether (if) it
   was wrong
5 He enquired whether (if) these
   were
6 He wanted to know whether
   (if) he was
7 He asked whether (if) the
   money had been paid
8 Mother asked whether (if) we
   were going to meet
9 I asked my dentist whether (if)
   he (she) would be
10 We wondered whether (if) we
    should be able to
11 She asked whether (if) I ought
    to drink so much
12 The barber asked whether (if)
    I would mind
13 He wanted to know whether
    (if) we ought to
14 He enquired whether (if) we
    needed to say

15 Little Peter asked whether (if
    a policeman always had to
    wear
16 Mr Brown asked me whether
    (if) my secretary used to
17 Mary ... whether (if) the
    doctor had given him
18 The farmer wanted to know
    whether (if) one tractor
    could do
19 I asked whether (if) I might
20 He asked me whether (if) my
    friends all lived in the
    country

INDEX